rommer's®

IRELAND'S BEST-LOVED DRIVING TOURS

Written by Susan Poole and Lyn Gallagher

Revised third edition published 2000
Revised second edition published in this format 1998
First published January 1992
Reprinted 1999

Edited, designed and produced by AA Publishing.

Published by AA Publishing

Published in the United States by IDG Books Worldwide, Inc.
An International Data Group Company
919 E. Hillsdale Blvd., Suite 400, Foster City, CA 94404

Find us online at www.frommers.com

ISBN 0-02-863839-5
ISSN 1520-9970

Color separation: Daylight Colour Art, Singapore

Printed and bound by:
G Canale & C. S.P.A., Torino, Italy

Opposite: *South Cross detail, Kells*

i *Arthur's Row, Ennis*

RECOMMENDED WALKS

For an interesting historic walk, try the excellent town trails in Ennis.

▶ *Take the **N85** for Lahinch. After 9 miles (14km) turn left at Inagh on to the **R460** for Milltown Malbay. After another 9 miles (14km) turn right on to the **R474** for Milltown Malbay.*

1 Milltown Malbay, Co Clare

The coastline of County Clare is better endowed with cliffs and rocky foreshore than with beaches, but there is good bathing at White (or Silver) Strand. Close by is Spanish Point, which owes its name to the unhappy fate of shipwrecked sailors from the Spanish Armada, executed by Sir Turlough O'Brien in 1588.

Milltown Malbay feels like a seaside resort, even though it is a little inland. It is an important centre for traditional music.

SPECIAL TO...

Two important summer schools take place in Co Clare: for traditional music followers, the Willie Clancy School in Milltown Malbay in July is a week of workshops, concerts and impromptu 'sessions', while the Merriman Summer School, held each August in Lisdoonvarna, is renowned for its combination of good learning and great fun.

▶ *Take the **N67** to Lahinch.*

2 Lahinch, Co Clare

The busiest resort in Clare, Lahinch earns its reputation from its splendid beach, good for bathing and popular for surfing. The name Lahinch comes from the Irish name for peninsula, as it has water on three sides. Its name today is perhaps most often associated with the championship golf course.

Across the bay lies Liscannor, birthplace of John Holland, the man who developed the submarine into a useful naval vessel in 1900. In appreciation of his achievement, the US Navy erected a commemorative stone at the small fishing harbour.

▶ *Take the **R478** for 6 miles (10km) to the Cliffs of Moher.*

The precipitous Cliffs of Moher, home to flocks of sea birds, are positively breathtaking

3 Cliffs of Moher, Co Clare

These awe-inspiring bastions of rock rise sheer from the sea to a height of nearly 670 feet (200m) and run relentlessly for 5 miles (8km). The great Irish naturalist Robert Lloyd Praeger, writing in the 1940s, suggested: 'If you want to feel very small, go out in one of the canvas curraghs on a day when a ground swell is coming in from the ocean, and get your boatman to row you along the base of those gigantic rock-walls. The rollers and their reflections from the cliffs produce a troubled sea on which your boat dances like a live thing, like a tiny cork, and the vast dark precipice above, vertical and in places overhanging, seems to soar up to the

troubled sky. It is a wonderful experience.'

Generations of visitors have not failed to be impressed by the monumental quality of these cliffs. In 1835 Sir Cornelius O'Brien MP built O'Brien's Tower as an observation point for 'strangers visiting the Magnificent Scenery of this neighbourhood' on the highest point of the cliffs and overlooking a rockstack called Breanan Mor. Today's visitor has the advantage of a Visitor Centre, which has leaflets explaining the history and geology of the area, as well as giving information about walks and bird life.

i Visitor Centre (March–October)

RECOMMENDED WALKS

The best way to appreciate the full grandeur of the Cliffs of Moher is on foot. At the Hags Head there are sea arches and a cave to be seen, while from O'Brien's Tower the view extends from Kerry to Connemara. A walking guide for the path starting at O'Brien's Tower is available from the Visitor Centre. The Burren Way stretches for 28 miles (45km) along the 'green roads' of this magical limestone landscape, passing many ruined churches and stone forts and monuments along the way.

SPECIAL TO...

'Wasdoolins' is an affectionate term for the countless traditional music lovers who visit the tiny village of Doolin, about 4 miles (6km) north of the Cliffs of Moher. From its harbour you may also take a ferry to the smallest of the Aran Islands, Inisheer.

► *Continue on the **R478**, turning left to bypass Lisdoonvarna, and follow the coastal route, **R477**, by Black Head to Ballyvaughan, 25 miles (40km).*

4 Ballyvaughan, Co Clare
Ballyvaughan is an attractive village, focused on a large harbour used for a small fishing fleet, for sailing and for boat trips to the islands. Close to the village is a cluster of holiday homes in traditional style, known as 'Rent an Irish Cottage', which is a popular feature of this area. As a centre for contemporary and traditional craftspeople, this is a good place to look for quality souvenirs.

► *Take the **N67** up Corkscrew Hill for 10 miles (16km) to Lisdoonvarna.*

FOR CHILDREN

The Burren is widely known for its potholes and caves but only experienced potholers can attempt to explore most of them. Aillwee Cave, south of Ballyvaughan, is perfect for a memorable family visit. Guided tours are informative and often amusing, and passages are safe and lit throughout. The reception building has been built to blend in with the remote and beautiful environment.

SCENIC ROUTES

The descent to Ballyvaughan, down Corkscrew Hill, provides a wonderful combination of the extraordinary Burren rock formations with the little village of Ballyvaughan, its whitewashed cottages and harbour and the wide expanse of Galway Bay beyond. Kinvarra and Finavarra Head are to the right, Gleninagh Mountain and Black Head to the left.

The wild and treeless Burren landscape is eerily beautiful

ly a botanist's paradise, but the grey shimmering contours of this strange and lonely landscape will leave an impression on all who see it.

FOR HISTORY BUFFS

From the little roads which cross the Burren north of Kilfenora much of archaeological interest can be found within a very small area. There are stone forts at Caherconnell and Caherballykinvarga. An ancient monastic site stands at Noughaval. At Poulawack is a cairn, thought to be Bronze Age, and there is a portal dolmen at Poulnabrone. In Gleninsheen wedge tomb a sheet-gold ribbed gorget, or crescent-shaped collar, dating from the 8th century BC, was found. Of the finest quality and workmanship, it was recognised as a national treasure and is held in the National Museum in Dublin.

5 Lisdoonvarna, Co Clare
Lisdoonvarna has long been synonymous with the art of 'matchmaking', and festivals are held to persuade traditionally reluctant bachelor farmers to the altar. The town has a great reputation for fun and good company, which is at its height in September when the harvest is gathered in. It also has Ireland's only active spa. The Spa Centre has a Pump House and a variety of health and recreational facilities.

▶ *Take the **R476** for 5 miles (8km) to Kilfenora.*

6 Kilfenora and the Burren, Co Clare
You will already have passed through part of the Burren, but here at Kilfenora, the Burren Centre puts this unique landscape and its plants into context. May is the best time to see the wild rock garden of flowers that covers the Burren, crowding together in crevices or covering the limestone outcrops in profusion. It is not only the abundance of the plants that makes the Burren so special, as bright blue gentians blossom in the shallow turf and mountain avens, clear white with golden centres, tumble across the limestone terraces. The Burren also harbours a profusion of rare varieties. Species normally found only in the Arctic or at high altitude, such as the alpine saxifrage, appear in the Burren, but so does the dense-flowered orchid, which is a Mediterranean plant. Twenty-two varieties of orchid grow here, favouring a unique ecosystem created by a combination of factors, including fast drainage into the limestone, mild, moist weather conditions, the absence of grasses and the control of hazel scrub by goats. The Burren is certainly a botanist's paradise, but the grey shimmering contours of this strange and lonely landscape will leave an impression on all who see it.

▶ *Take the Corofin road, **R476**, for 4 miles (6km), then turn left on to the **R480** for Ballyvaughan. Turn right and follow the **N67** to Kinvarra.*

7 Kinvarra, Co Galway
Kinvarra is a fishing village in Galway Bay, and the hill above gives splendid views of these much-loved Irish waters. Dunguaire Castle – the 7th-century seat of the King of Connacht, Guaire Aidhneach, a man of celebrated hospitality – stands on a promontory in Kinvarra Bay. The 17th-century tower house and bawn that now stands here was built by his descendants, the O'Heynes.

South of Kinvarra, near Gort, is Thoor Ballylee, where Yeats lived and which came to be symbolic to the poet. You can climb the 'narrow winding stair', and see an audio-visual presentation on Yeats's life and times. Yeats often visited Coole Park, home of Lady Gregory, co-founder of the Abbey Theatre

The house-painter's art – an appropriate mural for this shop in Kinvarra

in Dublin. The house, where many of the figures involved in the literary renaissance met, was demolished in 1941, but the beautiful woods of which Yeats wrote are in state care.

▶ *Turn right for Gort. After 4 miles (6km) bear left, and go through Tirneevin to Gort. Take the* ***N18*** *for Ennis and after 6 miles (10km) follow the* ***R462*** *for Tulla. Half a mile (1km) further on, turn right on to the* ***R352*** *for Ennis, and then after 2 miles (3km) turn left for Quin.*

8 Quin, Co Clare
A Franciscan friary, of which altars and tombs, a graceful tower and cloister remain, was built by the MacNamaras in the 15th century, on the site of a 13th-century castle. It also incorporates the buildings of a large Anglo-Norman castle. Close by, Knappogue Castle is typical of hundreds of medieval castles that are scattered throughout Clare, many of them, like the 1467 tower house at Quin, the preserve of the MacNamara family. The present castle has Georgian and Regency extensions. Set in pretty gardens, and at the heart of a well-planted demesne, it combines the atmosphere of sturdy stronghold and comfortable home.

Craggaunowen is close to Quin, too. An enterprising historical project has been built up around Craggaunowen Castle, a 16th-century tower house which has been completely restored and displays replicas of furniture and tools of the period. The project lifts the lid off many of the skills of the past, including the construction of wattle-and-daub buildings, and weaving and cooking techniques. There is a reconstruction of a *crannóg*, or defensive lake dwelling, used by the Celts in the 6th and 7th century. Another replica is that of the boat St Brendan the Navigator is said to have used for his legendary transatlantic voyage in the 6th century. In 1977 Tim Severin sailed the Atlantic in this replica, proving that St Brendan's could have discovered America centuries before Columbus's landfall.

▶ *Take the Limerick road* ***R469****, turning right after 4 miles (6km) on to the* ***R462****. After 6 miles (10km) turn right on to the* ***N18*** *for Bunratty and Ennis.*

SPECIAL TO...

Medieval banquets have become a very popular ingredient of many holidays in the Shannonside region. In the atmospheric surroundings of Bunratty, Knappogue or Dunguaire, medieval feasts or banquets are served with pageantry, costume, music and rhyme, with the emphasis on plenty of fun. The history of the castle dictates the mood and content of each of the entertainments.

9 Bunratty, Co Clare
One of Ireland's most popular tourist destinations, Bunratty's completely restored Norman-Irish keep sits four-square by the main road, its stout defences, including three 'murder holes' over the main door, defying entry. In fact, this is the most inviting of castles and, fur-

nished with Lord Gort's magnificent medieval collection, it gives a colourful insight into the life of a 15th-century keep. In the grounds is Bunratty Folk Park, which re-creates 19th-century life, both in the small cottages and houses of the region, and in a village street. The scenes are enlivened with traditional crafts in action – bread-making, candle-making, thatching, milling and basketweaving. Ballycasey Craft Workshops for contemporary craftsmen and women are close by.

Towards Limerick is Cratloe, where a mighty oak forest once supplied the timbers for Westminster Hall in London and the Grianan in Ulster. The woods here are still important. Cratloe Woods House, a good example of the Irish longhouse dating from the 17th century, is the family home of descendants of the O'Briens.

i Folk Park

▶ *Take the **N18** for 14 miles (23km) back to Ennis.*

Bunratty Castle combines history with entertainment

BACK TO NATURE

Ireland's rarest and shyest wild animal, the beautiful pine marten, is now plentiful only in County Clare, its numbers drastically reduced in the last century because of demand for its coat. A night hunter, it can occasionally be seen in the headlights of cars. A favoured haunt is Dromore Nature Reserve, 6 miles (10km) north of Ennis, a habitat of semi-natural woodland, and wetland that includes lake and marsh.

TOUR
2

River Shannon Rambles

2 DAYS • 112 MILES • 179KM The Celts were the first to recognise Limerick's strategic position when they built an earthen fort at the lowest ford of the River Shannon. In the 18th century the city developed its present form, and, after a period of decline in the 20th century, renovation has restored much of that style. King John's Castle and its excellent visitor centre tops the list of attractions. St Mary's Cathedral, founded in the late 12th century by the King of Munster, is filled with fine antiquities. There are splendid panoramic views from its bell tower. (See also Tour 3.)

ITINERARY	
LIMERICK	▶ **Askeaton (17m-27km)**
ASKEATON	▶ **Foynes (7m-11km)**
FOYNES	▶ **Glin (8m-13km)**
GLIN	▶ **Tarbert (4m-6km)**
TARBERT	▶ **Ballybunion (17m-27km)**
BALLYBUNION	▶ **Listowel (10m-16km)**
LISTOWEL	▶ **Abbeyfeale (11m-18km)**
ABBEYFEALE	▶ **Newcastle West (13m-21km)**
NEWCASTLE WEST	▶ **Rathkeale (8m-13km)**
RATHKEALE	▶ **Adare (7m-11km)**
ADARE	▶ **Limerick (10m-16km)**

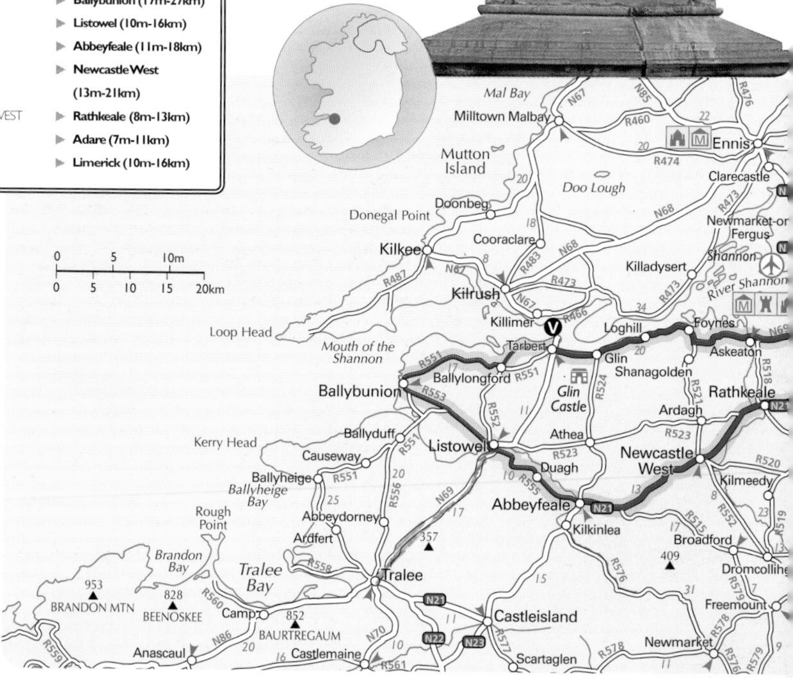

In military use from 1200 to 1922, King John's Castle gives a magnificent insight into Limerick's eventful history

[i] *Arthur's Quay, Limerick*

▶ *Take the **N69** west for 17 miles (27km) to Askeaton.*

FOR HISTORY BUFFS

Limerick's history comes to life in King John's Castle. Built in the 13th century as an instrument of royal authority and a military stronghold, it has been converted into an international visitors' centre. The centre presents an audio-visual overview of Limerick's long history, and contains historical exhibits and archaelogical remains covering a time span of some 800 years.

The excavation of archaeological treasures beneath the castle floor has provided added fascination for visitors since the dig began in 1990.

BACK TO NATURE

About 11 miles (18km) west of Limerick on the N69, turn south for 2 miles (3km) on a signposted, unclassified road to reach Currahchase National Park. This was the estate of poet Aubrey de Vere (1814-1922). The grounds contain fine landscaped gardens and an arboretum with exotic plants, as well as the tombstone that marks his pet cemetery. A nature trail leads through the estate, one of the finest in Ireland, past native Irish trees and plants, and the picnic area is an ideal spot for lunching in the open.

Askeaton, Co Limerick

A Middle Ages stronghold of the Desmond clan, Askeaton sits on the River Deel. Alive with echoes of the past, ruined Desmond Castle inhabits a rocky islet in the river, right in the village centre. Its last defending Earl of Desmond fled to the Kerry Hills when the castle and the town fell to British troops in 1580. The impressive Great Banqueting Hall measures 90 feet by 30 feet (28m by 9m) with windows set back to allow for the provision of window seats and vaulted rooms underneath. At the south end there is a small chapel.

On the east bank of the river, cloisters enclosed by black marble pointed arches and supported by cylindrical columns are relics of a 15th-century Franciscan friary.

BACK TO NATURE

The southern banks of the Shannon estuary between Askeaton and Aughinish are the most important areas of the water system for wildfowl and waders. Look for curlews, bar-tailed godwits, wigeon, teal and scaup, which are best in autumn and winter.

*Follow the **N69** to Foynes.*

2 Foynes, Co Limerick
The most scenic portion of the coastal drive along the Shannon begins in this small seaport, though these days, its waters play host to luxury yachts as well as commercial ships. The first steamship to depart its docks was a blockade runner providing uniforms made in Limerick for Confederate forces during the American Civil War. During the late 1930s and 1940s, Foynes was the home port for a transatlantic sea plane service, and the award-winning Flying Boat Museum presents an audio-visual show along with mementoes of those pioneering days in the world of air travel.

*Continue west on the **N69** for another 8 miles (13km) to Glin.*

SCENIC ROUTES

The coast road (N69) from Foynes to Tarbet along the southern banks of the Shannon is one of the most enticing riverside drives in Ireland, with sweeping views of the river estuary. Adjacent to the village of Foynes, there is a lay-by with a picnic site, scenic viewpoints of the Shannon, and forest walks. Rather different views are found at Barna Gap, a little over 7 miles (11km) southwest of Newcastle West on the N21. From roads crossing the ridge there are dramatic panoramic vistas of the great plain that runs eastward to the Galtee mountains, and viewing platforms are provided at the Gap. To the north and west, there are great high moors and young forests.

3 Glin, Co Limerick
The Fitzgeralds, powerful Earls of Desmond, dominated this village, and ruins of their Castle of Glin still overlook the Shannon estuary. It was fiercely defended in 1600 but fell to the English forces after two days of intense fighting.

Glin Castle is a mixture of 18th-century and Victorian Gothic architecture

The Desmond holdings here have passed without interruption for more than seven centuries to the present Knight of Glin, whose home, Glin Castle (not to be confused with the Castle of Glin), contains a fine collection of Irish paintings, furniture and decorative arts. The Castle, pleasure grounds and walled garden are open to the public.

About 1 mile (1.5km) west of the village, look for the Gothic-style Glin Castle Gate Lodge, a pleasant tea-room and craft shop, where cast-offs from the castle are often scattered among craft items.

The castellated building overlooking Glin pier is Hamilton's Tower, a 19th-century folly built by one Dr Hamilton to give employment to Irish famine victims.

*Continue west on the **N69** for about 4 miles (6km) to Tarbert.*

4 Tarbert, Co Kerry
A car ferry across the Shannon to Killimer in County Clare departs from the wooded headland that juts into the river's estuary at this quiet little village, a real timesaver for travellers who want to avoid Limerick traffic.

*Take the unclassified coastal road to Ballylongford, then the **R551** to Ballybunion.*

FOR CHILDREN

The attractive beaches at the lively resort of Ballybunion will send the children splashing into the Atlantic waves. Surfing is a popular sport here, along with swimming. In addition, there are fascinating caves in the seaside cliffs to be explored at low tide with extreme caution and in the company of adults. In the town itself, there are several amusement parks with rides, swings and slides, as well as computer game arcades.

5 **Ballybunion,** Co Kerry

The ruins of Ballybunion Castle stand on Castle Green in this popular Atlantic coast resort town. It is the fine beach, however, that draws visitors, as well as the network of souterrains (subterranean passages) near Castle Green, and invigorating clifftop walks.

Just north of the town are the remains of a promontory fort overlooking Doon Cove. The 18-hole golf course is an attraction for amateurs and professionals alike.

► *Continue southeast via the* ***R553*** *to Listowel.*

Castle ruins point skyward above Ballybunion's beach

RECOMMENDED WALKS

Magnificent seascapes add to the exhilaration of cliff-top walks from Ballybunion to Doon Point north of the strand. To the south is the lovely Doon Cove.

The ancient fortress from which Newcastle West takes its name stands on the wide main square

6 Listowel, Co Kerry
The castle in this bustling market town was the last to hold out against Elizabethan forces in the Desmond rebellion. When it finally fell in 1600, the entire garrison was put to the sword. Two fine Gothic-style churches dominate the town square, and the old Protestant church has been converted into an centre. Take a look at a wonderful bit of plaster fantasy, the 'Maid of Erin' figure on the Central Bar that sits on one corner of the square. A local craftsman, Pat McAuliffe, and his son created this monument and other works around the town and in Abbeyfeale.

It was from a window of the Listowel Arms Hotel on the square that Charles Stewart Parnell, campaigner for Home Rule, made one of his last public appearances just three weeks before his death in 1891. Fans of the noted playwright John B Keane should head for his pub in William Street, where he is often to be found mingling with the locals, or engaged in the storytelling for which he is famous. Lord Kitchener, of Khartoum fame, was born 4 miles (6km) northwest of town at Gunsborough in 1850.

i *St John's Church*

SPECIAL TO...

Listowel is host to hordes of aspiring writers, poets and playwrights during its Writers' Week, held annually in late May or early June. The town has spawned such noted authors as John B Keane, Bryan MacMahon, George Fitzmaurice and Maurice Walsh, and the week of workshops, lectures and theatre productions is a must for budding writers.

▶ *Take the* ***R555*** *southeast to Abbeyfeale.*

7 Abbeyfeale, Co Limerick
In the foothills of the Mullaghareirk Mountains, this little market town grew from the Cistercian abbey founded here in 1188. The only traces of the abbey have since been incorporated into the Catholic church building, The town square has a statue of Father William Casey, parish priest and leader of the tenant farmers' fight against landlordism in the mid- and late 1800s.

Abbeyfeale pubs are often the venue for traditional music, song and dance.

▶ *Take the* ***N21*** *northeast to Newcastle West.*

8 Newcastle West, Co Limerick
Adjacent to the town square of this bustling market town are the ruins of a Knights Templar castle dating from 1184. Burned in 1642, its two 15th-century halls, peel tower, keep, bastion and curtain wall have survived. While the Great Hall is largely in ruins, the Desmond Banqueting Hall is almost perfectly preserved, complete right down to a vaulted basement, and now serves as a cultural centre for recitals, concerts, lectures and exhibitions.

You can see Irish Dresden porcelain being made at the

factory and showroom in Dromcolliher, some 9 miles (15km) southeast of town via the R522.

▶ *Follow the **N21** northeast for 8 miles (13km) to Rathkeale.*

9 Rathkeale, Co Limerick
The poet Edmund Spenser and Sir Walter Raleigh first met in Rathkeale at Castle Matrix, built in 1440 and named after an ancient Celtic sanctuary that once occupied this site. The castle has furnishings authentic to its era and an outstanding library with many rare books. There is also a unique collection of documents dealing with the so-called 'Wild Geese', Irish chieftains and soldiers who fled the country to fight with European armies in the 17th and 18th centuries.

▶ *Continue northeast via the N21 to Adare.*

FOR HISTORY BUFFS

The Palatine Visitor Centre houses papers and artefacts relating to the 18th-century Calvinist refugees from the Rhine Palatinate. Many of their names, such as Bovenizer and Fitzell, are still used in the area.

10 Adare, Co Limerick
With its neat thatched cottages and broad main street, Adare is likely to come closer to the romantic image of the 'quaint little Irish village' than any other in the country, although its appearance is decidedly English. Credit for its beauty must go to the third Earl of Dunraven, who had a passion for early Irish architecture and local improvements.

The ancestral home of the Dunravens, Adare Manor, stands at the northern edge of town and is now a luxury hotel. In the heart of the hotel's golf course are the ruins of a castle on the banks of the River Maigue, a Franciscan friary dating back to 1464 and the 15th-century Desmond family chapel (check with the golf club before visiting).

In the village itself, remains of a 14th-century Augustinian friary sit near the fine 14-arch bridge across the River Maigue. Its choir was taken over as a Church of Ireland parish church in 1875 by the Earl of Dunraven. Its refectory became a school, and the cloisters were put to use as a mausoleum.

i *Heritage Centre*

▶ *Take the **N21**, then turn left on to the **N20** back to Limerick.*

SPECIAL TO...

The five-line, often bawdy verse known as the 'limerick', is said to have originated from a row between 18th-century poets who lived at Croom, near the River Maigue.

One of the delightful cottages that have made Adare one of Ireland's prettiest villages

Ancient Castles & Lake Odyssey

Limerick is a large and lively city with a long history of momentous events. (See also Tour 2). The Limerick Museum in St John's Square tells the story from the Stone Age onwards, and the famous Hunt Museum, in Rutland Street, holds more than 1,000 Irish antiquities and examples of medieval art.

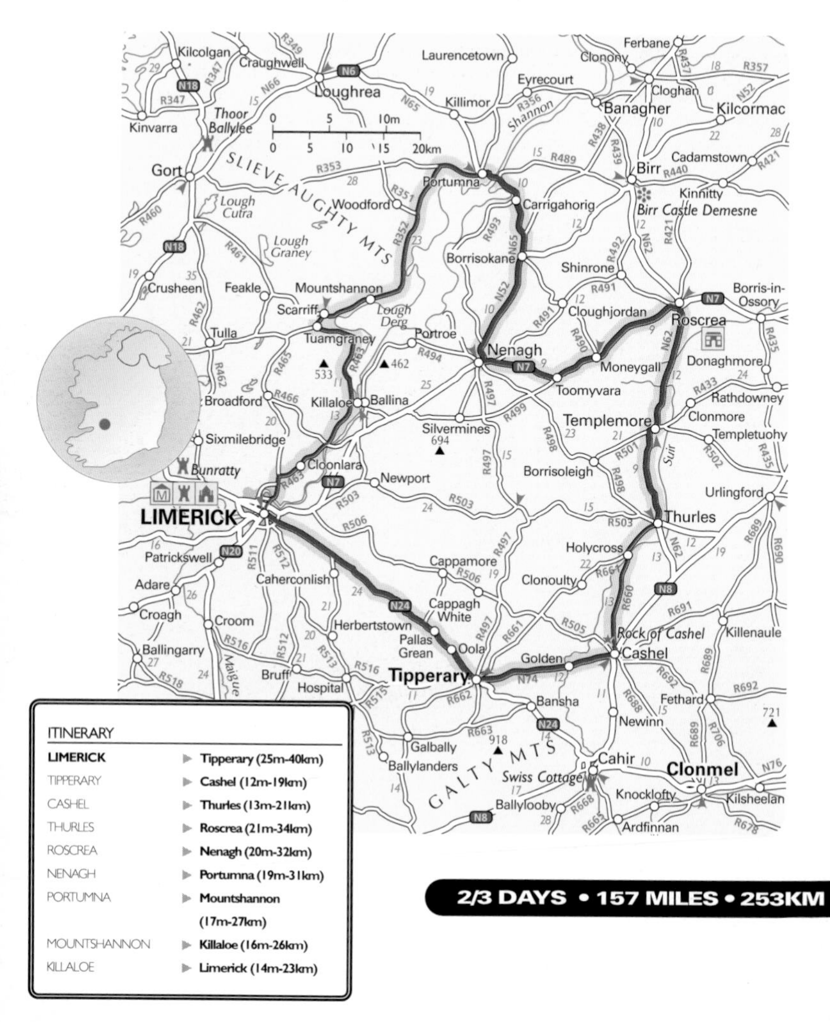

ITINERARY	
LIMERICK	► Tipperary (25m-40km)
TIPPERARY	► Cashel (12m-19km)
CASHEL	► Thurles (13m-21km)
THURLES	► Roscrea (21m-34km)
ROSCREA	► Nenagh (20m-32km)
NENAGH	► Portumna (19m-31km)
PORTUMNA	► Mountshannon (17m-27km)
MOUNTSHANNON	► Killaloe (16m-26km)
KILLALOE	► Limerick (14m-23km)

2/3 DAYS • 157 MILES • 253KM

[i] *Arthur's Quay, Limerick*

FOR HISTORY BUFFS

Eleven miles (17.5km) northwest of Limerick via the N18 west, then north on the R462 to Sixmilebridge, is the Craggaunowen Project, a fascinating historical complex. There is a superb example of a 16th-century fortified house, and the adjacent lake holds a reconstructed crannog, a prehistoric dwelling built on an artificial island. Housed in a glass structure near by, the tiny leather boat *St Brendan* is an exact replica of the vessel in which the saint crossed the Atlantic in AD700 and was used by Tim Severin and his modern-day crew to retrace the legendary voyage.

▶ *Take the **N24** southeast for 25 miles (40km) to Tipperary.*

1 Tipperary, Co Tipperary

In the heart of Ireland's fertile Golden Vale, Tipperary town is an important dairy farming centre. It figured prominently in the 19th-century Land League campaigns to legalise land ownership for Irish tenants, and today is a thriving market town, and an excellent base for hill walking in the nearby Slievenamuck and Galtee mountains. The major point of interest in town is St Michael's Church, Gothic in design and noteworthy for its fine lancet windows and west door.

About 8 miles (13km) north of town via the R497 and R505, the well-preserved circular keep of Ballysheeda Castle stands on a hillside 1 mile (1.5km) north of Annacarty village. South of Tipperary, via the R664, is the Glen of Aherlow, one of Ireland's most scenic places.

[i] *James Street*

▶ *Follow the **N74** to Cashel.*

SPECIAL TO...

The GPA Bolton Library, in the grounds of St John's Cathedral in Cashel, has a very fine collection of rare books, including two leaves from Caxton's press of 1486, and examples of early Irish printing.

2 Cashel, Co Tipperary

Ecclesiastical ruins on the Rock of Cashel dominate the town of Cashel (see Tour 10), but also of interest are the Cashel Folk Village, and the ruins of the Dominican friary, which was rebuilt in 1480 after destruction by fire, both in Chapel Lane. Be sure to see the lovely 13th-century east window. The Bishop's Palace, set in enclosed grounds in Main Street, was built for Protestant archbishops

Bru Boru Heritage Centre is an imaginative presentation of Irish crafts and culture

and is a splendid example of 18th-century architecture. It is now a hotel. Bru Boru, at the foot of the Rock, is a heritage and cultural centre which showcases Irish music and dance.

i *Main Street*

▶ *Take the **R660** north for 13 miles (21km) to Thurles.*

3 Thurles, Co Tipperary
It was in the Hayes Hotel in this old Anglo-Norman town that the Gaelic Athletic Association was founded in 1884. Bridge Castle, at the western end of the Suir river bridge, and Black Castle, near the town square, are remnants of Butler clan castles. In the 19th-century Catholic cathedral the lavish use of marble, especially in the altars, gives a special beauty to the interior.

St Mary's church is now home to the Thurles Famine Museum.

Holycross Abbey, a 12th-century Cistercian centre, is set on the east bank of the Suir, 4 miles (6km) southwest of Thurles. Long abandoned and roofless, it has been restored as the active parish church.

FOR HISTORY BUFFS

Two rectangular keeps, remnants of the castles built by the powerful Butlers in Thurles, are reminders of the town's turbulent past. In the 10th century, the Irish and Norse fought fierce battles here, and when Strongbow's Anglo-Norman troops attacked in 1174, the Irish initially repelled them, but were unable to prevent their building a castle to control traffic on the River Suir.

▶ *Take the **N62** north for 21 miles (34km) to Roscrea.*

4 Roscrea, Co Tipperary
This pleasant market town is a good base for climbing and hill walking in the nearby Devil's Bit and Slieve Bloom mountains. Its most outstanding attraction is the Roscrea Heritage Centre in an annexe to Damer House, a town house dating from the early 18th century, set within the walls of an 11th-century Norman castle and narrowly saved from demolition in the mid-1970s. There are panoramic views from the top of the gate tower, and, inside, the magnificently carved staircase is stunning. The house is lavishly decorated and furnished and holds interesting mementoes of life in the town through the ages. Available from the Heritage Centre is a booklet detailing a self-guided walking tour that incorporates the ruins of St Cronan's Church and Round Tower, and a High Cross, all of which date back to the 12th century.

The stately River Suir lends an air of tranquility to the centre of historic Thurles

At Monaincha, 2 miles (3km) southwest of town, are the remains of a 12th-century church with 16th-century additions and an elegant High Cross from a former monastery.

▶ *Take the **N7** southwest for 20 miles (32km) to Nenagh.*

5 Nenagh, Co Tipperary
Originally a Norman settlement, Nenagh served as a mid-19th-century garrison town, and finally evolved into a prosperous market town with many traditional shopfronts. One of the town's major features is the circular keep of Nenagh Castle, a mostly 1860 structure incorporating portions of a larger castle built in the early 1200s. The 100-foot-high (30m), 53-foot-wide (16m) keep, with walls up to 20 feet (6m) thick, formed part of the curtain wall of the earlier castle. Winding stairs set into the thickness of the wall lead to the roof. Nenagh's Heritage Centre is located near the castle in the old Governor's House and county gaol. There is a marvellous 'Lifestyles in Northwest Tipperary' exhibition, as well as visiting art and photographic exhibits. Nenagh Friary, in Abbey Street, was founded in about 1250 and features a 13th-century church.

Six miles (10km) northwest of Nenagh, via the R494, then the R495, Dromineer, on Lough Derg, is a lively centre for fishing, sailing and water sports.

i *Connolly Street*

SCENIC ROUTES

Six miles (10km) south of Nenagh, via the R500, look for the signposted turnoff for Step viewing point, near Silvermines village, at the foot of the Silvermines Mountains. The drive up to the viewing point is very scenic, and it culminates in panoramic views – the perfect place for a picnic.

The massive keep of Nenagh Castle is mostly Victorian

▶ *Head northwards on the* ***N52****, then turn left on to the* ***N65*** *ad continue for 19 miles (31km) to reach Portumna.*

FOR CHILDREN

Lough Derg is a natural paradise for children. Its many islands and tiny inlets invite exploration, fishing is excellent, and watersports are a favourite pastime for locals and visitors alike.
The best places for access and facilities on the lough are Dromineer, Portumna, Mountshannon and Killaloe.

6 Portumna, Co Galway
This small lakeside town at the northern end of Lough Derg is a popular centre for fishing the lake and the River Shannon, as well as a major base for cruisers. The impressive ruins of Portumna Castle stand in its demesne, laid out as an attractive forest park, on the edge of town. Built in 1609 by the Earl of Clanricarde, it was destroyed by fire in 1826, but has been restored and is open to the public. Of special interest are the Renaissance doorway with gunholes on one side, the Jacobean gables, the square towers at each corner and the lovely formal gardens.

About 7 miles (11km) south of Portumna via the N65 and the R493, the village of Terryglass, on the shores of Lough Derg, has a lovely old stone church and the ruins of a 13th-century castle. There are boats for hire and facilities for lakeside picnics.

BACK TO NATURE

Portumna Forest Park is a marvellous 1,000-acre (405-hectare) wildlife sanctuary that counts red and fallow deer among its many animal and feathered inhabitants. There is an observation tower beside the lake, and several other viewing stands, a nature trail and picnic area.

▶ *Turn south on the* ***R352*** *to follow the shores of Lough Derg to Mountshannon.*

FOR CHILDREN

At the little town of Mountshannon children can embark on an island adventure – hire a boat at the pier to visit the mysterious holy island of Iniscealtra.

7 Mountshannon, Co Clare
The River Shannon, in the course of its 230-mile (370km) rambles, forms several lakes, of which Lough Derg is the largest, stretching some 25 miles (40km) in length and sprinkled with numerous islands and islets. The drive down its western shore is delightful, with the lake in view much of the way and never more than a short detour to the east. At the little town of Mountshannon, hire a boat at the pier to visit the Holy Island of Iniscealtra and its remains of an early Christian settlement, including no less than five churches and a round tower.

SPECIAL TO...

Lough Derg, a fisherman's dream and a magnet to cruisers on the Shannon river system, is one of Ireland's most beautiful lakes, its scenic splendour astonishingly undiminished by the hydroelectric scheme it powers. Wooded islands that dot the lake have drawn monastics over the centuries, and from June to mid-August, participants from all over Ireland engage in three-day pilgrimages to Station Island, a gruelling test of physical endurance since only one meal of bread and black tea is permitted each day.

▶ *Continue southwest on the **R352** to Tuamgraney, then turn southeast on to the **R463** to reach Killaloe.*

SCENIC ROUTES

The drive from Mountshannon to Killaloe follows the shores of Lough Derg, providing splendid views of the lake and its many islands.

8 Killaloe, Co Clare
This charming little village stands at a fording point of the River Shannon at the lower end of Lough Derg. The churchyard of St Anne's is said to be the ancient site of Kincora, the palace of Irish King Brian Boru and his O'Brien descendants. In the church grounds, St Molua's Oratory, estimated to be 1,000 to 1,200 years old, reposes in safety after being rescued when its Friar's Island home was threatened by submersion in a hydroelectric development. The 12th-century Church of Ireland St Flannan's Cathedral is noteworthy for its ornately carved Irish Romanesque doorway, It has an Ogham (ancient Celtic writing) stone that also has runic writings and a crude crucifix possibly formed by a Viking convert. There are traces of a ringfort on the southeastern side of Crag or Cragliath hill.

Killaloe has been declared a heritage town, and its Heritage Centre tells a fascinating story.

The Shannon remains an important feature of the town, and fishing, boating and water sports are the main preoccupations.

i *Killaloe Heritage Centre*

▶ *Follow the **R463** southwest to return to Limerick.*

RECOMMENDED WALKS

In Killaloe, climb the sharp incline of Main Street to St Molua's Oratory, then on to Aillebaun, the ancient site of Brian Boru's Kincora, for panoramic views. Proceed along the path once followed by pilgrims to Tober Murrough and the Pier Head.

Killaloe village has an important ecclesiastical hertiage

Beehive Huts & Coastal Splendours

Known for its Rose of Tralee Festival in late August, Tralee is an important business centre and the principal gateway for the Dingle. Its many attractions include historic streets, fine churches, the 'Kerry the Kingdom' Museum (including a 'time travel experience', and the National Folk Theatre, Siamsa Tire.

2/3 DAYS • 97 MILES • 156KM

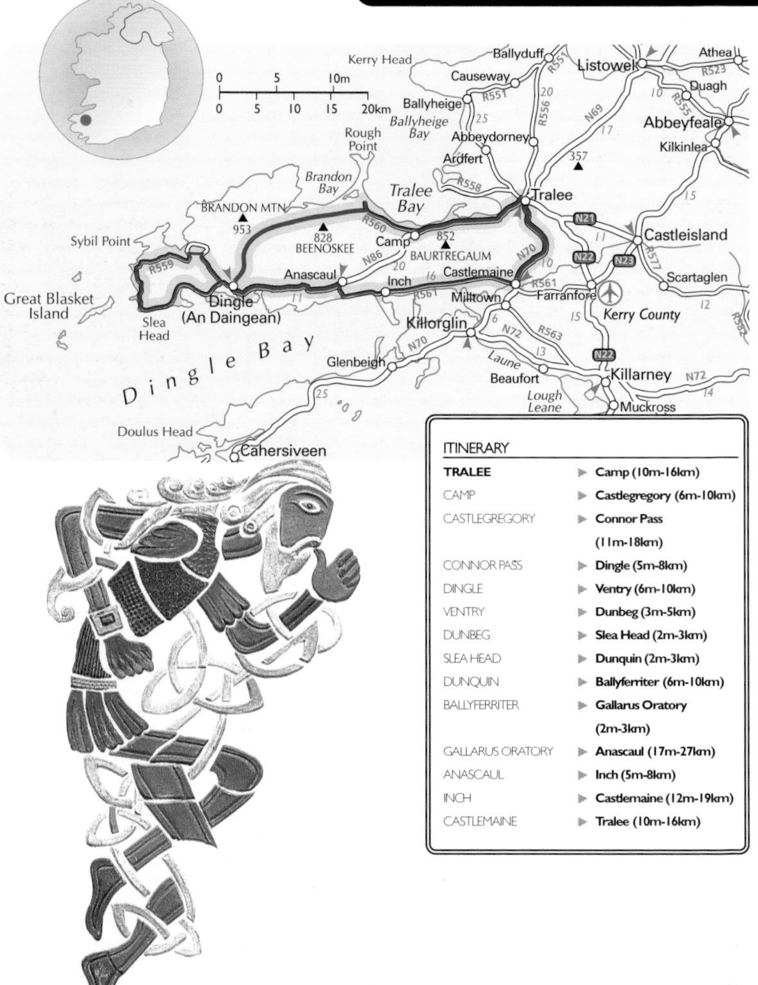

ITINERARY	
TRALEE	▶ **Camp (10m-16km)**
CAMP	▶ **Castlegregory (6m-10km)**
CASTLEGREGORY	▶ **Connor Pass (11m-18km)**
CONNOR PASS	▶ **Dingle (5m-8km)**
DINGLE	▶ **Ventry (6m-10km)**
VENTRY	▶ **Dunbeg (3m-5km)**
DUNBEG	▶ **Slea Head (2m-3km)**
SLEA HEAD	▶ **Dunquin (2m-3km)**
DUNQUIN	▶ **Ballyferriter (6m-10km)**
BALLYFERRITER	▶ **Gallarus Oratory (2m-3km)**
GALLARUS ORATORY	▶ **Anascaul (17m-27km)**
ANASCAUL	▶ **Inch (5m-8km)**
INCH	▶ **Castlemaine (12m-19km)**
CASTLEMAINE	▶ **Tralee (10m-16km)**

[i] *Ashe Hall, Denny Street, Tralee*

FOR CHILDREN

Children seem to be born with a love of trains, and a great attraction is the narrow-gauge Tralee/Blennerville railway that runs along part of the long-abandoned Tralee/Dingle line on a 5-mile (8km) round-trip. At Blennerville is a restored windmill, while at the Tralee end, adjacent to the platform, is the Aquadome, a palace of water-based fun.

► *Take the **N86** west, with the Slieve Mish mountains on your left, to the village of Camp.*

FOR HISTORY BUFFS

Five-and-a-half miles (9km) northwest of Tralee via the Ballyheigue road (R551) is imposing Ardfert Cathedral, which dates from the 13th century. A niche in the building holds the 13th- or 14th-century effigy of a bishop unearthed here in 1830, and there is an ogham stone in the graveyard. The tiny village of Fenit, 8 miles (13km) west of Tralee via the R558, is thought to be the birthplace of St Brendan the Navigator (AD484-577), who may or may not have reached the shores of America long before Christopher Columbus.

1 Camp, Co Kerry

In the village, turn off the main road west towards the mountains to reach James Ashe's pub, the epitome of everyone's image of what an old-time Irish pub should be – smoke-darkened wood, low ceilings, a peat fire glowing on the hearth, and the Ashe family carrying on a tradition of generations.

► *Go back for a ½ mile (1km) before turning left on to the **R560** west to Castlegregory.*

2 Castlegregory, Co Kerry

There are fine beaches at Castlegregory, which sits at the

The dramatically beautiful Slieve Mish Mountains

BACK TO NATURE

Tucked away in the mountains near Castlegregory, Gleann Ti An Easaigh/Glenteenassig Forest Park is a feast for the naturalist. It lies a little over 13 miles (22km) west of Tralee on the R560 to Castlegregory. Watch for signposting at Aughacasla and turn left into the mountains for 3 miles (5km). Alive with rushing streams and tiny lakes, the park is the habitat of many species of wildlife, as well as a refuge for a wide variety of birds. Mountain walks yield panoramic views of Tralee Bay and the western tip of the peninsula, with a perfectly positioned picnic site.

neck of a spit of land dividing Tralee and Brandon bays, with more along the drive from Camp. Birdwatchers will want to turn left just before reaching the town to visit Lough Gill bird sanctuary, which has attracted such exotic species as the Bewick's swan from Siberia.

▶ *Turn back east on the* ***R560****, then right on to the unclassified road signposted 'Dingle, Connor Pass'.*

3 Connor Pass, Co Kerry
Climbing between the Brandon and central Dingle groups of mountains, this drive passes through some of Ireland's most spectacular scenery. On a fine day, there are vast panoramas of mountains, sea, lakes and valleys – on a not-so-fine day, mist and clouds can turn the narrow, winding road into a real driving challenge. Just past the village of Stradbally, you cross the deep Glennahoo Valley and begin the climb to the 1,500-foot (460m) summit of the Connor Pass, with spectacular views of valleys strewn with boulders and, about a mile from the summit, tiny Pedlar's Lake. The road upwards winds along the base of great cliffs. From the lay-by at the summit, there is a fine view of Dingle Bay and Dingle town to the south, with several small lakes in the deep valley to the left; the north aspect takes in the wide sweeping bays of Brandon and Tralee.

▶ *Continue southwest for 5 miles (8km), descending to Dingle town.*

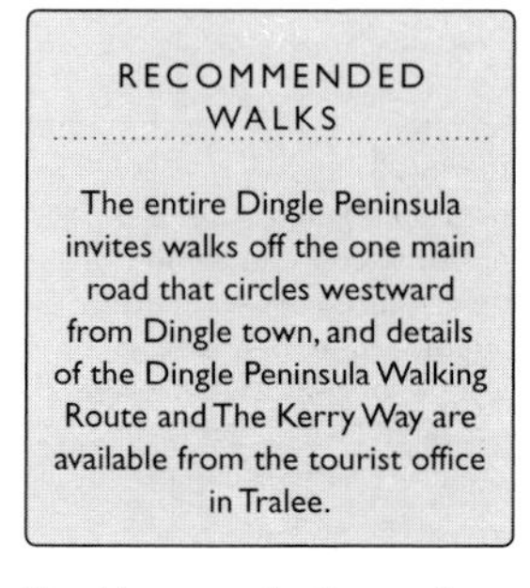
RECOMMENDED WALKS

The entire Dingle Peninsula invites walks off the one main road that circles westward from Dingle town, and details of the Dingle Peninsula Walking Route and The Kerry Way are available from the tourist office in Tralee.

The drive across the Connor Pass, in either direction, offers some of the most magnificent mountain views in Ireland

4 **Dingle,** Co Kerry

County Kerry's chief port in the old days of Spanish trading, and a walled town in the Elizabethan era, Dingle town today is a busy little market, fishing and tourism centre with a boat-building industry right on the harbour. Dingle is in the heart of a Gaeltacht district in which Irish is the everyday language, but, of course, everyone can speak English too.

Dingle is a centre for specialised tours, including riding, cycling and archaeological interests. The town itself is ideal walking territory, its highlights being in a compact area of tiny streets that climb upward from the seafront. In addition to its sightseeing attractions, the town has several excellent Irish goods shops, and there are boat rides out into the bay to see Dingle's resident dolphin (see For Children).

On the western edge of town, the Ceardlann Craft Village is a cluster of small cottages housing shops and workshops that sell handcrafted leather goods, handmade Uilleann pipes, knitted goods, and the work of a cabinetmaker and weavers.

One of the town's most impressive collections of Irish-interest publications and records can be found in the front shop section of An Café Liteartha in Dykegate Lane. For traditional music and song that stems from a long-time family tradition, look for the red-and-white pub on Bridge Street with the Irish name UaFlaibeartaig, which translates to O'Flaherty's. It is a warm, informal setting, as traditional as the music itself, its walls sporting the sort of haphazard collection of pictures, posters and other assorted items that have accumulated over the years, typical of many country pubs in Ireland. There is also music on summer nights at the O Gairbhi Pub in Strand Street, and at Benner's Hotel in Main Street.

i *The Pier*

Wonderful unspoilt beaches are dotted all around the Dingle peninsula

FOR CHILDREN

What could be more fun for the younger ones than a boat ride out into Dingle Bay to watch Dingle's friendly Dolphin, Fungi, playfully following the boats that leave from the town quays to ferry visitors out to his watery home, cavorting with scuba divers, and sometimes taking a flying leap over a small boat.

▶ *Drive due west on the* ***R559*** *for 6 miles (10km) through the village of Milltown to Ventry.*

5 **Ventry,** Co Kerry

According to legend – and a 15th-century manuscript now in the Bodleian Library at Oxford, in England – Ventry beach was the scene of a fierce battle when the King of the World, Daire Doon, attempted to invade and conquer Ireland. He and his vassal monarchs, however, suffered a massive defeat at the hands of the King of Ireland, Fionn MacCumhaill, and his loyal Fianna band. The village nestles at the head of Ventry Harbour, with the slopes of Mount Eagle and Croagh Marhin as a backdrop. The black, beetle-like boats you see upturned on the beach are currachs, the traditional canvas-covered vessels painted with tar that have been used by fishermen in these waters for centuries.

Sheehy's Pottery, on the outskirts of the village specialises in ceramic Celtic murals and plaques illustrating

D403

old Celtic myths. It also serves light meals of excellent home-cooked food.

[i] *Village Centre*

SCENIC ROUTES

The drive along the R559 from Ventry to Slea Head has a wide diversity of scenic pleasures, at times hugging the sides of sheer cliffs high above Dingle Bay, other stretches passing through stony fields reaching up sloping mountains.

▶ *Continue southwest on the **R559** to Dunbeg.*

6 Dunbeg, Co Kerry
A relic of the Iron Age, Dunbeg Fort perches on a high promontory above Dingle Bay, its landward side surrounded by earthen trenches, and its 22-foot (7m) thick wall riddled with an elaborate souterrain (inner passage). Originally, there was an inner enclosure, also with a souterrain, and a skilfully built inner house. Time has taken its toll on this strong defensive structure, and some of its stones long ago tumbled into the sea.

▶ *Cross the **R559** to the Fahan archaeological grouping.*

7 Fahan, Co Kerry
In farmyards on the southern slopes of Mount Eagle, across from Dunbeg, unmortared beehive cells, or clochans (huts), are reminders of the prehistoric people who made their homes here and, quite possibly, built the promontory fort. It is a revelation to stoop down and enter one of these unique structures that are as watertight today as when they were built.

▶ *Continue west on the **R559** for 2 miles (3km) to Slea Head.*

Working and pleasure boats bob together in the sheltered waters of Ventry harbour

The beehive huts at Fahan are a remarkable and evocative relic of prehistoric times

FOR HISTORY BUFFS

About 3 miles (5km) above the main road (R559) at Fahan, an ancient road is lined with stone huts and other remains of ages past. The stone beehive huts, souterrains, standing and inscribed stones, earthen ringforts, two sculptured crosses and two fortified headlands constitute Ireland's largest collection of antiquities.

8 Slea Head, Co Kerry
At the very tip of the Dingle Peninsula are the high cliffs of Slea Head – the westernmost mainland point in Europe. It is from here that you get the most sweeping view of sheltered coves below and the Blasket Islands across the water, sometimes called 'the last parish before America'.

The Great Blasket, the largest of these seven offshore islands, was for many years home to a hardy band of islanders who inhabited the one small village. In 1953, when a living wage could no longer be wrested from fishing, its tiny population was moved to the mainland and given government grants for small farm holdings on the peninsula. A day trip to the islands is an experience of sheer tranquillity and scenic beauty that is unequalled anywhere else in Ireland.

The Blasket Centre, on the mainland at Dunquin, highlights the extraordinary literary contribution of island writers Tomás O Crohan, Maurice O'Sullivan and Peig Sayers.

▶ *Turn north, still on the **R559**, for 2 miles (3km) heading for Dunquin.*

9 Dunquin, Co Kerry
Dunquin Pottery, on the road between Slea Head and Dunquin, is one of the many excellent potteries on the Dingle Peninsula. Its speciality is hand-thrown, ovenproof stoneware in shades of sand, browns and blues.

Boats from Dunquin harbour make intermittent trips out to the Blasket Islands (see Slea Head) during summer months, and arrangements can often be made with individual boatmen when there is no sailing scheduled.

▶ *Follow the **R559** north, then east to Ballyferriter.*

10 Ballyferriter, Co Kerry
The Ballyferriter Heritage Centre, with its interesting

'Treasures of the Dingle Peninsula' exhibition, occupies the old schoolhouse in the centre of the village.

The West Kerry Co-op office, just off Main Street, issues an excellent illustrated guidebook to the Dingle Peninsula, with great detail on its many antiquities. The Co-op began in 1968 in an effort to stem the out-going tide of young people who could not be supported by the large areas of untillable ground, and to perpetuate the unique culture and heritage of the Gaelic-speaking region. The Co-op imported a special deep-ploughing machine to break up the layer of iron ore that lay just beneath the surface and turn it into productive acres. Vast areas have been reclaimed, and the Co-op's remit has widened to include upgrading tourist facilities, and administering the Gaelic summer-school programme, in which students of all ages lodge with local families to learn their language.

Louis Mulcahy, a potter of international repute, has a pottery studio on the outskirts of town, turning out many unique items with special glazes. Giant jugs and vases, unusual lamp bases and beautiful wall plaques supplement the more practical dinner services and cookware.

Two miles (3km) southwest of Ballyferriter, turn north on to an unclassified, signposted road to reach the site of the 16th-century fortress Dún an Oir, the so-called 'Golden Fort', built within an ancient promontory fort at Smerwick. The harbour here was the disembarkation point for an expedition of Spanish and Irish, along with their families and other retinue, who arrived in September of 1580 and constructed a fort to support the cause of the Catholic Irish against the Protestant English. It was bombarded from land and sea by English forces until eventually the fort capitulated, but over 600 were slaughtered – men, women and children – once they were disarmed. Poet Edmund Spenser (most famous for *The Faerie Queene*), and possibly Sir Walter Raleigh were participants in the battle, which came to be known as the 'Massacre of Smerwick Harbour'. There is an excellent safe beach here.

FOR CHILDREN

In the grounds of Ostan Granville, the Ballyferriter Butterfly Farm is a great attraction for children. There are native and tropical butterflies, all flying free amidst butterfly-friendly plants, and other creatures to be seen include reptiles, spiders, amphibeans and stick insects.

▶ *Follow the* ***R559*** *northeast for 2 miles (3km) and turn right at the signpost to Gallarus Oratory.*

11 Gallarus Oratory, Co Kerry

This marvellous example of early Irish architecture is perhaps the most impressive of the peninsula's antiquities. Built in an inverted boat shape, it has remained completely watertight for more than 1,000 years, its unmortared stones perfectly fitted. At the crossroads just above Gallarus, turn left for Kilmalkedar, a 12th-century ruined church a short distance away. In the church is the famous Alphabet Stone, a standing pillar carved with both Roman and Ogham characters. The east window of this medieval church is known locally as 'the Eye of the Needle' through which one must squeeze to achieve salvation.

▶ *Proceed via an unclassified road to Ballynana, turning southeast on to the* ***R559*** *to Milltown and Dingle, then drive east for 10 miles (16km) on the* ***N86*** *to Anascaul.*

On Dingle's western extremity, Dunquin (and its sheep) looks out across Blasket Sound

12 Anascaul, Co Kerry
Look for the South Pole Inn as you enter the village. It is named for the former proprietor, Tom Crean, a member of the Scott Antarctic expedition. Beautiful Anascaul Lake is well worth a short detour.

▶ *Heading south, then east on the **R561**, pass through Red Cliff to reach Inch.*

RECOMMENDED WALKS

On the Dingle road west of Anascaul, park the car for a short, easy walk north along a signposted road that leads to lovely Anascaul Lake set in a boulder-strewn hollow. Hardy walkers with two or three hours to spare can continue around the lake and strike out across the hills of the Beenoskee Mountains to Stradbally and Castlegregory.

13 Inch, Co Kerry
The wide, 4-mile-long (6km) sandy beach on this spit at the head of Castlemaine Harbour is one of the best bathing beaches on the peninsula. The high dunes backing the beach have yielded archaeological evidence of ancient dwelling sites, including kitchen middens. In summer, there is sometimes horseback riding across the firm sand and through the gentle surf. From the cliffside drive, west of the village, views out over the Iveragh Peninsula across the water are nothing short of spectacular.

SCENIC ROUTES

The drive from Anascaul to Castlemaine through Red Cliff and Aughils via the R561 follows a narrow, winding road with fantastic views south across Castlemaine Bay and north to the open sea and Dingle harbour. Stop to admire the view from one of the tiny lay-bys along the way – it is extremely dangerous to stop the car and block the road.

▶ *Continue east along the **R561** for 12 miles (19km) to the little town of Castlemaine.*

14 Castlemaine, Co Kerry
In the town, immediately after turning left on to the Tralee road (N70), turn left again and look for the unclassified road signposted 'viewing park' less than a mile (1.5km) further on. There is a viewpoint about 2½ miles (4km) along this road, with splendid views of Castlemaine Harbour and beyond the Laune Valley to Killarney. A second viewpoint, a a little further on, looks north to Tralee Bay, Tralee town, and the Stack's Mountains.

▶ *Reach the **N70** and drive north to return to Tralee.*

SPECIAL TO...

The Rose of Tralee International Festival, which is in full swing for six days and nights in late August, is a fierce, but entertaining competition to see which of the beauties of Irish lineage from around the world best fits the time-honoured description from the famous song '...lovely and fair as the rose of the summer.' This gathering is much more fun than other beauty contests, which are usually taken very seriously indeed. The Rose of Tralee is a festival of light-hearted fun and frolic that includes parades, pipe bands, street entertainment and inter-festival singing competitions for the Folk Festival of Ireland, and the whole thing culminates at the end of the week in the crowning of the Rose.

TOUR

5

Killarney & The Ring of Kerry

ITINERARY

KILLARNEY	▶ **Killorglin (13m-21km)**
KILLORGLIN	▶ **Glenbeigh (8m-13km)**
GLENBEIGH	▶ **Cahersiveen (17m-27km)**
CAHERSIVEEN	▶ **Waterville (10m-16km)**
WATERVILLE	▶ **Sneem (22m-35km)**
SNEEM	▶ **Kenmare (17m-27km)**
KENMARE	▶ **Moll's Gap (6m-10km)**
MOLL'S GAP	▶ **Ladies' View (3m-5km)**
LADIES' VIEW	▶ **Killarney (11m-18km)**

2 DAYS • 107 MILES • 172KM

An abundance of natural beauty has drawn visitors to Killarney and its lakes for centuries. The scenic network of Lough Leane, Muckross Lake and Upper Lake, in a broad valley west of Killarney, is the single most powerful magnet for visitors. Kilarney was once a quiet little market town, but today, its narrow, congested streets can make for nerve-racking driving – it is, however, a perfect town to explore on foot.

The charming and peaceful town of Killorglin comes to life in August for its famous fair

[i] *Beech Road, Killarney*

▶ *Take the* **N72** *northwest for 13 miles (21km) to Killorglin.*

RECOMMENDED WALKS

Just around the road from the Cathedral in Killarney, the wooded walks of Knockreer estate offer a welcome retreat from congested town streets. A short walk brings you to Knockreer House, with occasional exhibits of the flora, fauna and wildlife of the area. A longer walk takes you to the ruins of Ross Castle (about 1½ miles (2.5km) from the town centre) on a long peninsula out on to the Lower Lake. Built in the 14th century, it was a prominent fortification during the Cromwellian wars in the 17th century. You can hire a boat here, which is undoubtedly the best way to see the lakes.

RECOMMENDED WALKS

An exhilarating walk is that over Gap of Dunloe, for which you should allow a minimum of three hours.
The Kerry Way, a splendid walk of approximately 134 miles (214km), has been laid out for dedicated walkers. It begins at Killarney National Park and extends around the Iveragh Peninsula. The tourist office in Killarney has full details.

FOR HISTORY BUFFS

In ancient times, the Hill of Aghadoe just outside Killarney was the seat of the Celtic Archdruid. *The Annals of Innisfallen*, a chronicle of Irish history from the 11th to the 13th century, was recorded by dedicated monks on one of the Lower Lake's 30 islands.

1 Killorglin, Co Kerry
Perched on hills above the River Laune, Killorglin is an ideal starting point for the Ring of Kerry drive, a 112-mile (180km) scenic drive with an ever-changing panorama of mountains, lakes, cliffs, sandy beaches and craggy offshore islands. The route skirts the edges of the Iveragh Peninsula to Kenmare, then circles back over the mountains via Moll's Gap and Ladies' View to Killarney. Make this a leisurely drive with an overnight stop in order to savour all the magnificent scenery along the way.

In mid-August, this rather quiet little town is abuzz with the three-day Puck (Poc) Fair. It dates from 1613, and things get off to a rousing start when a tremendous male (or puck) goat is crowned King of the Fair. In the somewhat rowdy atmosphere, pubs stay open around the clock, and every sort of street entertainment goes on non-stop. This is also a traditional gathering place for the country's travelling people, who come to engage in some hard-driving horse trading. The origin of the Puck Fair is a matter of dispute: some say a goat bleated to alert a shepherd boy of approaching enemy forces and he, in turn, alerted the town about impending attack. The argument that the festival dates back to the worship of the Celtic god, Lug, gains credence when linked to the Gaelic word for August – Lughnasa, or festival of Lug.

▶ *Turn southwest on to the **N70** to Glenbeigh.*

2 Glenbeigh, Co Kerry
On the main street of this little village, look for the bog village adjoining the Red Fox Inn. Bogs have always played an important role in Ireland, and this re-creation is an authentic depiction of the lives of the peatbog communities

▶ *Follow the **N70** southwest to reach Caherciveen.*

3 Cahersiveen (Cahirciveen), Co Kerry
The drive along the southern banks of Dingle Bay from Glenbeigh to this small town at the foot of the Bentee Mountain is one of island-dotted coastal scenery and fields studded with prehistoric stone ringfort ruins, with clear views of the Dingle Peninsula across the water. At Cahersiveen, Valentia Island comes into view. There is a ferry service, and it is accessible by car via a causeway at Portmagee. The island is noted for its superb scenery of cliffs, mountains, seascapes and vivid-

Brooding mountains – and the weather – overwhelm the pretty village of Waterville

ly coloured subtropical flowers.

One mile (1.5km) northeast of Cahersiveen, on the N70, Carhan House was the birthplace of Daniel O'Connell (1775); Cahersiveen's Heritage Centre includes displays on Ireland's beloved 'Liberator'.

Sheltered by encircling hills, Sneem nestles at the head of an inlet of the Kenmare River

BACK TO NATURE

If the seas are calm and you are a birdwatcher, join one of the cruises that take you out to the rocky islands that make up the Skelligs. Landings are limited by erosion and because this is a bird sanctuary. The smaller of the two islands, Little Skellig, is a major breeding ground for gannets. More accessible is Puffin Island which, as its name suggests, has breeding puffins as well as Manx shearwaters. Boats go from Valentia Island. The Skellig Experience Heritage Centre focuses on monastic and birdlife on the Skelligs.

▶ *Drive 10 miles (16km) south on the **N70** to Waterville.*

4 Waterville, Co Kerry

Set on a strip of land that separates Ballinskelligs Bay from the island-sprinkled Lough Currane, this popular resort and angling centre is also internationally known for its superb golf course. Mountains rise from the lake's eastern and southern shores, and on Church Island there are ruins of a 12th-century church that was dedicated to the 6th-century holy man, St Fionan.

SCENIC ROUTES

From Waterville, the N70 follows the coast, then lifts you some 700 feet (215m) above sea level at Coomakista Pass, with breathtaking views of the bay, the offshore Skellig Islands, and the coastline. It was on Skellig Michael, a massive rocky hulk that rises 700 feet (215m) above the sea, that a colony of early Christian monks built a retreat of stone beehive huts. From Castlegrove, the road turns away from the coast through wild and gorgeous scenery before coming back to the sea at Sneem.

▶ *Continue south, then east on the **N70** for 22 miles (35km) to reach Sneem.*

5 Sneem, Co Kerry

On the drive east on the N70 from Waterville to Sneem, just east of Caherdaniel, is Castlecove, where, about 1½ miles (2km) north of the road you will see Staigue Fort, one of the country's best-preserved Iron-Age stone forts. The circular stone walls, 13 feet (4km) wide and 18 feet (5.5km) high, have held over the centuries without the benefit of mortar, and along their interior are several flights of stairs in near perfect condition.

Just beyond the Coomakista Pass on the N70, about 1 mile (1.5km) beyond Caherdaniel on the Derrynane road, is Derrynane House, set in the wooded National Park. This is where 'The Liberator', Daniel O'Connell, lived for most of his political life, and the house is now maintained as a museum containing all sorts of O'Connell memorabilia.

The National Park covers some 320 acres (130 hectares),

incorporating semi-tropical plants and coastal trees and shrubs, as well as fine coastal scenery. There is a well-marked nature trail, and sea bathing is accessible to visitors. The pretty little town of Sneem, situated where the Ardsheelaun river estuary joins the Kenmare river, is a popular angling centre for brown trout and salmon, and its fine sandy beaches provide safe swimming. George Bernard Shaw wrote part of his play *St Joan* here. Sneem is also the last resting place of Father Michael Walsh, who was a parish priest in the area for 38 years in the 1800s and has been immortalised as 'Father O'Flynn' in a well-known Irish ballad.

Two miles (3km) to the south in Parknasilla, the elegant Great Southern Hotel is famed for its rock gardens and colourful sub-tropical blooms.

▶ *Continue east on the **N70** for 17 miles (27km) to Kenmare.*

6 Kenmare, Co Kerry

The drive from Sneem along the banks of the Kenmare river has lovely views of the Caha and Slieve Miskish mountains on the opposite shore. Kenmare faces the broad Kenmare river estuary, with impressive mountains at its back.

Known as Ceann Mara (Head of the Sea) by the ancients, today it is a lively resort and heritage town, particularly noted for its fine salmon, brown trout and sea fishing, safe swimming, local walks and climbs, homespun woollen industry, and lace. (See Tour 6.)

i *Kenmare Heritage Centre*

▶ *Turn north on to the **N71** to reach Moll's Gap.*

7 Moll's Gap, Co Kerry
The drive north to Moll's Gap is one of rugged mountains and stone-strewn valleys. The viewing point at this gap affords sweeping views of Macgillycuddy's Reeks and of Ireland's highest mountain, 3,414-foot (1,040m) Carrantuohill. The restaurant and craft shop make this a good refreshment stop.

▶ *Follow the* ***N71*** *northeast for 3 miles (5km) to Ladies' View.*

8 Ladies' View, Co Kerry
This mountainside viewing point overlooks the broad valley of the Killarney lakes. Queen Victoria and her ladies-in-waiting so enthused about this view that it was promptly named in their honour.

Nine miles (14.5km) north on the return to Killarney, the well-preserved ruins of Muckross Abbey are situated. The abbey dates from 1448 and was built on the site of an earlier religious establishment. About a 10-minute walk from the abbey, Elizabethan-style Muckross House is surrounded by landscaped gardens that slope down to the lake. Built by a wealthy Kerry MP in 1843, it was sold to Americans in 1911, and presented as a gift to the Irish people in 1932. The first two floors are furnished in the manner of the great houses of Ireland, while its upper floors hold fascinating exhibits of maps, prints and other documents, as well as a small wildlife and bird collection. In the basement there is a folk museum with a country pub, print shop, dairy, carpentry shop and weaving shop. Craftspeople are at work in some, and you can purchase their products in the gift shop. A light, airy tea shop is just off the courtyard. Take time to visit the adjoining Muckross Traditional Farms, a working museum which farms the land in the methods which were used in the 1930s.

About 1 mile (1.5km) before Muckross House, a signpost on the N71 directs you to a scenic footpath up a mountain slope to the 60-foot (18m) Torc Waterfall in a beautiful wooded area. Continue upwards to the top of the falls for magnificent views.

▶ *Continue for 11 miles (18km) northeast on the* ***N71*** *to Killarney.*

FOR CHILDREN

Most children love being on the water, so what better way for them to see the Lakes of Killarney than aboard one of the watercoaches that leave the Ross Castle slipway several times daily to cruise the Lower Lake. They are sure to be fascinated by the mystical legends of the lake related by the boatmen as they glide past Innisfallen Island, O'Sullivan's Cascade, Tomies Mountain, Darby's Garden, the old copper mines, Library Point and many other points of interest.

The lakes and woodland of the Killarney National Park stretch out below Ladies' View

Kenmare & The Beara Peninsula

The attractive town of Kenmare, at the head of Kenmare Bay, is a thriving market town and tourist centre, and an excellent base for exploring the Iveragh and Beara peninsulas which extend westwards on either side of the bay. Its own attractions include The Kenmare Heritage and Lace Centre and one of Ireland's most impressive stone circles, known locally as the Druid's circle, which stands beside the River Finnehy.

1/2 DAYS • 96 MILES • 154KM

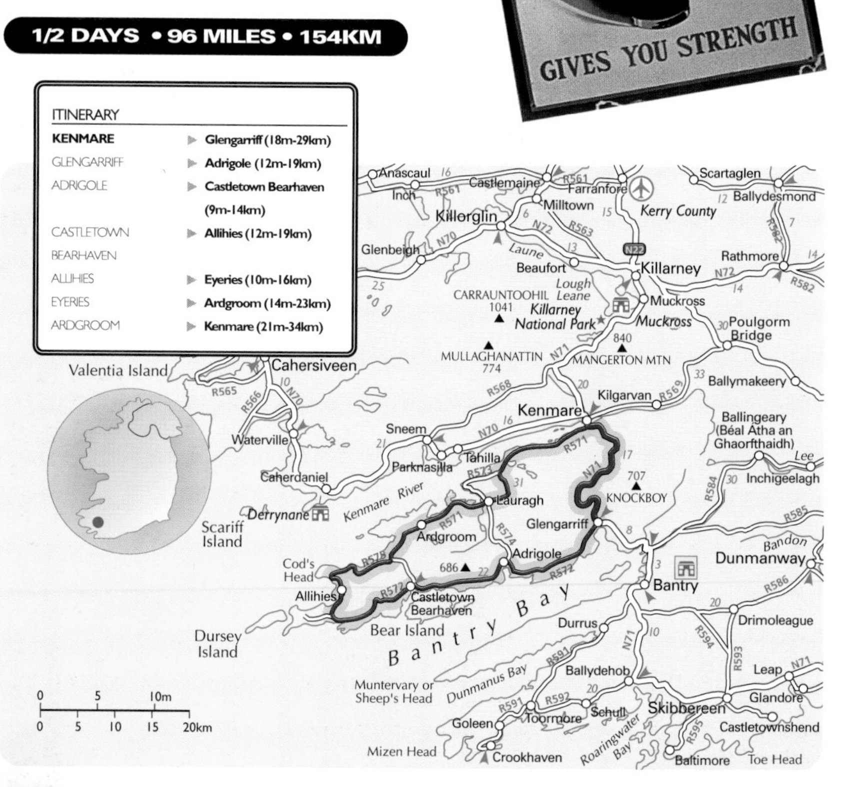

ITINERARY	
KENMARE	▶ **Glengarriff (18m-29km)**
GLENGARRIFF	▶ **Adrigole (12m-19km)**
ADRIGOLE	▶ **Castletown Bearhaven (9m-14km)**
CASTLETOWN BEARHAVEN	▶ **Allihies (12m-19km)**
ALLIHIES	▶ **Eyeries (10m-16km)**
EYERIES	▶ **Ardgroom (14m-23km)**
ARDGROOM	▶ **Kenmare (21m-34km)**

Stormy skies add an extra touch of mystery to the ancient standing stones at Kenmare

i *Heritage Centre, Kenmare*

RECOMMENDED WALKS

Walk out along the Glengarriff road (N71) from Kenmare and turn right at the signpost for the pier. Try to go when the tide is in as the views of the Kenmare river are at their most impressive then. The river, with its backdrop of surrounding mountains and drifts of graceful swans, presents a view of tranquility and natural beauty that provides ample reward for the short walk.

FOR HISTORY BUFFS

Cross the bridge over the River Finnehy at Kenmare to find an impressive stone circle and dolmen. There are 15 stones in the circle, which measures about 50 feet (15m) across. In its centre is the dolmen, a megalithic tomb where upright stones support a large, flat capstone. Kenmare has been designated a Heritage Town as a 'planned estate town'. There is a visitor centre in the square which includes exhibitions of lacework and the story of the Nun of Kenmare.

▶ *Drive south for 18 miles (29km) on the* **N71** *to reach Glengarriff.*

1 Glengarriff, Co Cork

The 18-mile (29km) drive from Kenmare to Glengarriff (Rugged Glen) is known as the Tunnel Road. Two tunnels, one the longest in Ireland, bore through the Caha Mountains, and the road alternately climbs around mountain heights and dips into deep valleys. The sky in these parts seems to expand to the edges of eternity, and the play of light and shadow from ever-shifting clouds is nothing short of spectacular.

Lying in the heart of a secluded valley surrounded by mountains, Glengarriff's sheltered position nurtures luxuriant Mediterranean flowers and plants such as fuchsia and arbutus. Its harbour is dotted with wooded islands, on one of which – Garinish Island – are the world-famous Italian gardens, laid out between 1910 and 1913 by John Annan Bryce and Harold Peto. The lovely little island was a favourite of George Bernard Shaw, who came here to write much of his *St Joan*. Only the strongest-willed visitor will be able to resist the entreaties of the bold boatmen who line the main street hawking a trip to the gardens; those who pass on by will be the poorer for it.

Glengarriff is also one of the few places in the country that preserves some specimens of ancient mixed forests, best seen at Glengarriff Forest Park, on the northern edge of the village. Here there are oak, elm, pine, yew, mountain ash, rowan and holly trees reminiscent of the woodland that once covered much of Ireland.

Along with the boatmen hawking trips to Garinish Island, the main street is lined with shops offering Irish crafts.

Glengarriff lies at the head of the Beara Peninsula, a 30-mile (48km) long, mountainous

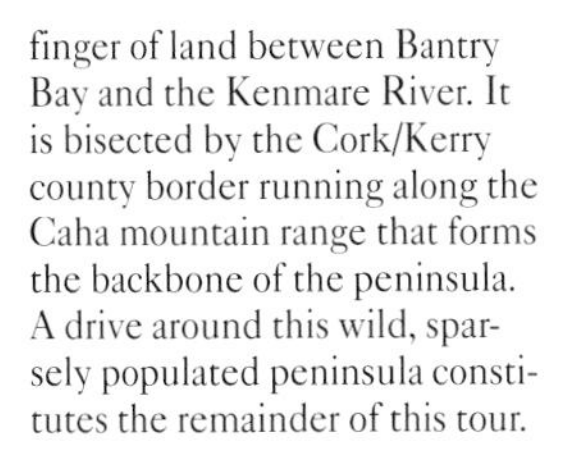

finger of land between Bantry Bay and the Kenmare River. It is bisected by the Cork/Kerry county border running along the Caha mountain range that forms the backbone of the peninsula. A drive around this wild, sparsely populated peninsula constitutes the remainder of this tour.

[i] *Eccles Car Park*

FOR CHILDREN

A delightful bonus for children on the short boat ride from Glengarriff Pier to Garinish Island, about 1 mile (1.5km) offshore in Bantry Bay, is the sight of seals cavorting through the waters. The island's beautiful Italian gardens are a riot of colour in season, with subtropical plants in gorgeous bloom. Turn the children loose to wander along the woodland pathways, through the formal gardens, and down to the shores of the bay, or to explore the Grecian temple and old Martello tower.

RECOMMENDED WALKS

Scenic walks in Glengarriff include the Blue Pool, via a pathway west of the post office; Lady Bantry's Lookout, 2 miles (3km) southwest of the village on the Castletownbear road, returning by Shrove Hill viewpoint; or continue past Lady Bantry's Lookout to Eagle's Nest, and from there to Biddy's Cove on the shores of the bay.

▶ *Drive southwest on the* ***R572*** *to Adrigole.*

2 Adrigole, Co Cork

From Glengarriff, the road follows the shoreline of Bantry Bay, winding along the rocky coastal strip at the foot of the Caha Mountains, with 1,887-foot (575m) Sugarloaf Mountain on the right. At Adrigole Bridge, the spectacular Healy Pass (named after Tim Healy, the first Governor-General of the Irish Free State) crosses the mountains and is an alternative (and shorter) route to Kenmare and Killarney.

Some 3 miles (5km) west of Adrigole, Hungry Hill, highest of the Caha range, rises 2,251 feet (686m), with a rocky shelf halfway up its face on which are two lakes that feed a 700-foot (214m) cascade into the valley below – especially spectacular after rain.

Lush vegetation cloaks the hillsides around Glengarriff, in a sheltered corner of Bantry Bay

SCENIC ROUTES

At Adrigole Bridge, turn right for the Healy Pass road. Begun during the famine, the road – after years of stopping and starting, and a high death-rate during its construction – was completed in 1931 and named for Tim Healy, the first Governor-General of the Irish Free State when it became a dominion in 1922. This spectacular drive, about 10 miles (16km), climbs right across the spine of the Caha mountain range and across the Cork/Kerry border, with magnificent views of Glanmore Lough, the forests of Tousist, Kenmare Bay and Macgillycuddy's Reeks. There is a viewing point and Crucifixion shrine at the top.

▶ *Continue southwest for another 9 miles (14km) on the* ***R572*** *to Castletownbear.*

3 Castletownbear, Co Cork

Sheltered by the elongated Bere (Bear) Island just offshore, Castletownbear, now a fishing port, was once a British naval base. There is a regular ferry service out to the island, where some forts still remain, manned from time to time by Irish forces. On a hillside near the old waterworks, look for a group of boulder burials and a fine stone circle, the latter on the western side of the hill.

Less than 2 miles (3km) west of town, facing Bere Island, are the remains of 16th-century Dunboy Castle, in spacious grounds overlooking the inlet. Its star-shaped fort was the stronghold of O'Sullivan Bere, the last Irish leader to hold out with Spanish allies against the British forces led by Sir George Carew in 1602. After a long siege, during which the garrison refused to surrender until the walls were completely shattered, the fort was all but destroyed. The ruins have been excavated for easy exploration.

The grandiose ruined mansion sited between the castle and Castletownbear was the home of the Puxley family, copper-mining moguls whose family and mining history form the basis of Daphne du Maurier's novel *Hungry Hill.*

Fifteen miles (24km) further west, Ireland's only cable-car connects Dursey Island with the mainland. The beautiful, long, mountainous island is rimmed by high cliffs and is the site of a gannetry.

▶ *Continue southwest on the* ***R572*** *to its junction with the* ***R575****, which turns north to Allihies, a total of 12 miles (19km).*

4 Allihies, Co Cork

The road from Castletownbear continues southwest to Black Ball Head before turning northwest to reach Allihies through a gap in the hills. This was once a rich copper-mining centre that provided the basis for the Puxley family fortunes. The 19th century was their most prosperous period, although some work continued right up to 1962. There are picturesque ruins on the scarred hillsides, but they should be explored with extreme caution, since the

old workings, with unguarded shafts, can be very dangerous.

Seascapes seen from the hills are breathtaking, the strand is safe for swimming, and just north of the village there is an old Mass rock.

▶ *Follow the **R575** northeast to Eyeries.*

5 Eyeries, Co Cork

From Allihies, the road leads northeast along the wide sea inlet of the Kenmare River through rugged scenery to the little village of Eyeries, set back from the sea on a pretty bay.

A little to the east, at Ballycrovane, there is an inscribed Ogham pillar stone thought to be the tallest in western Europe, at more than 17½ feet (5.18m) high. In general, Ogham stones served as gravestones and the script on them records details of the person who is buried.

One of Ireland's most striking wayside shrines looks south from the summit of the Healy Pass over the Caha Mountains

▶ *Continue northeast on the **R571** for 14 miles (23km) to Ardgroom.*

6 Ardgroom, Co Cork

Just beyond the little village of Ardgroom, you cross into Kerry, where there is yet another fine stone circle in Canfie, on the Lauragh road.

Lauragh, at the northern end of the Healy Pass, has a scenic ridge walk along a horseshoe of peaks surrounding the valley in which the village stands. Near by is almost totally enclosed Kilmakilloge harbour, where boats can be hired to sail the safe harbour waters. A little beyond Lauragh, look for signposts directing you inland to Cloonee and Inchiquin loughs, both worth a detour. Rejoining the main road, the R571, the drive into Kenmare follows the shores of Kenmare Bay, with scenic views along a striking section of the journey.

▶ *Remain on the **R571** for 21 miles (34km) back to Kenmare.*

BACK TO NATURE

About 8 miles (13km) southwest of Kenmare on the R571, signposts point into a valley of exceptional botanical interest. Inchiquin Lough, one of the chain known as the Cloonee Loughs, has marvellous views and a lovely waterfall. In the early summer, the large-flowered butterwort (Pinguicula grandiflora) flowers freely, and across the lake, Uragh Woods holds primeval oakwoods, which have all but disappeared from Ireland, along with saxifrages, Irish spurge, strawberry tree and rhododendrons. For the best view of the lake, waterfall and Uragh Wood, follow the tarred road along the edge of Inchiquin Lough.

SPECIAL TO...

As you might expect from this watery area, the seafood is outstanding. From local lakes, rivers and surf comes bass, conger, pollock, ray, mullet, mackerel and shellfish. These are, of course, supplemented by deep-sea fish brought in by fisherman who ply these waters for a livelihood. The elegant, late Victorian-style Park Hotel, whose cuisine has earned it a Michelin star, specialises in the best local seafood. With lovely views of the estuary and mountains, the hotel has a garden setting. The Purple Heather Bistro is an old-fashioned pub/restaurant that also serves superb seafood in a casual setting.

Island City, Magic Stone

Spreading out along a long valley, Cork is the Republic's second city, with an atmosphere and character all of its own. It has a lively arts scene, excellent shopping and such attractions as the Crawford Art Gallery, the Old Gaol and the famous St Anne's church at Shandon. (See also Tour 8).

ITINERARY

CORK	▶ **Blarney (6m-10km)**
BLARNEY	▶ **Kanturk (30m-48km)**
KANTURK	▶ **Mallow (13m-21km)**
MALLOW	▶ **Mitchelstown (21m-34km)**
MITCHELSTOWN	▶ **Cahir (18m-29km)**
CAHIR	▶ **The Vee (14m-23km)**
THE VEE	▶ **Lismore (8m-13km)**
LISMORE	▶ **Youghal (21m-34km)**
YOUGHAL	▶ **Cork (28m-45km)**

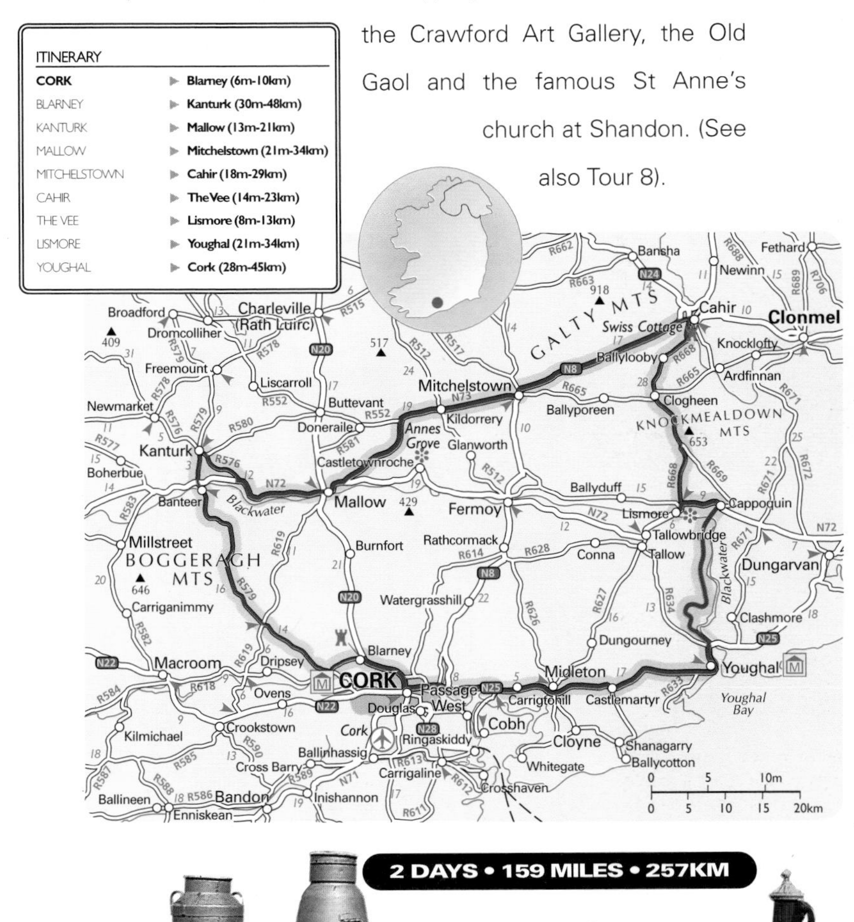

2 DAYS • 159 MILES • 257KM

Grand Parade, Cork

FOR HISTORY BUFFS

Between 1848 and 1950 over six million people emigrated from Ireland; 2.5 million left through the port of Cobh, 15 miles (24km) east of Cork, making it the most important point of emigration. The Queenstown Story, a multi-media exhibition at Cobh's Victorian railway station, details the life of the port. Convict ships, trans-atlantic steamers, the ill-fated *Titanic* and other ocean liners all departed from here.

RECOMMENDED WALKS

There is a fine riverside walk in Cork which leads between rows of old trees, with seats and rustic shelters sprinkled along the way. The river widens into Cork Harbour, and on the opposite bank fine town houses climb up the hills of the Montenotte and Tivoli residential sections. The small fishing village suburb of Blackrock is at the end of the marina, with Blackrock Castle (now a restaurant) on a little promontory jutting out into the River Lee.

*Cross Patrick Street bridge and turn left for the sign-posted 6-mile (10km) drive northwest on the **R617** to reach Blarney.*

0 Blarney, Co Cork

The well-preserved ruins of Blarney Castle, built in 1446, draw visitors not just for their history, but also for the magical powers attributed to the famous stone embedded in its parapet wall. The legend of its powers rose from Queen Elizabeth I's frustration in dealing with Cormac MacCarthy, Lord of

The climb to kiss the Blarney Stone renders many visitors more speechless than eloquent

Blarney, and his smiling flattery that veiled wiliness with eloquence. Her declaration that 'This is nothing but Blarney – what he says, he never means!' added a new word to the English language and probably gave rise to the legend of the 'gift of eloquence' associated with the stone. Kissing the magical stone, however, involves climbing 120 steep steps to lie on your back and hang over an open space.

About 200 yards (180m) from the castle is the superb Scottish baronial mansion, Blarney Castle House, set amidst lovely 18th-century gardens.

Blarney Woollen Mills are also worth a visit.

i Village centre

*Leave Blarney on the **R617** and a few miles from the village turn northwest on to the **R579** for the drive to Kanturk.*

2 Kanturk, Co Cork
One mile (1.5km) south of town, unfinished Kanturk Castle was begun in 1609 by Irish chieftain MacDonagh MacCarthy, who planned it as the largest mansion in Ireland, with a large quadrangle and four-storey towers at each corner. Alarmed at its size and strength, the English Privy Council ordered work to cease, declaring that it was 'much too large for a subject'. The roofless, stout walls and towers have survived in remarkably good condition.

At Mealehara there is a fascinating farm museum.

*Drive southeast on the **R576** to its junction with the **N72**, then turn east for 9 miles (14km) to reach Mallow.*

3 Mallow, Co Cork
Set on the Blackwater river, Mallow was a popular spa town during the 18th and early 19th centuries; its lively social life prompted the famous song, The Rakes of Mallow. The fine fortified house built in the 16th century to replace 12th-century Mallow Castle, itself burned in 1689 on the orders of James II, now stands in fairly complete ruins in its own park by the river crossing.

From the Tourist Office in Cork or Youghal ask for the Blackwater Drive map and chart that shows a wealth of historic relics.

About 9 miles (14km) north of Mallow, via the N20, the little town of Buttevant saw the world's first steeplechase in 1752, run between its church steeple and the one in Doneraile. Buttevant was the model for 'Mole' in Spenser's *The Faerie Queene*.

On the outskirts of town are the remains of Ballybeg, an Augustinian Canons' Regular House, enclosed by low stone walls, that dates back to 1237. The ruins include a dovecot with ranks of stone nesting boxes inside.

*Take the **N73** northeast for 21 miles (34km) to Mitchelstown.*

4 Mitchelstown, Co Cork
This is a tidy, attractive landlord-planned town founded in the early 19th century. Ten miles (16km) northeast of town via the N8, the signposted

Mitchelstown Caves are thought to be the largest system of river-formed caves in Ireland

Mitchelstown Caves are an underground wonderland of passages and high-ceilinged chambers, including the biggest chamber in the British Isles. The Old Caves were used as a refuge for a 16th-century Earl of Desmond, with a price on his head. There are escorted tours through 2 miles (3km) of the fantastic netherworld, with its fine stalactite formations.

*Follow the **N8** for 18 miles (29km) northeast to Cahir.*

5 Cahir, Co Tipperary
Cahir Castle occupies a small islet in the River Suir, a natural site for fortifications as far back as the 3rd century. The present castle was built in the 13th century by the de Berminghams and was held by the Anglo-Norman Butlers until 1599, when the Earl of Essex captured it after a three-day siege that left gaping breaches in the east walls. Oliver Cromwell made a fierce show of force before the walls in 1650 and sent in surrender terms. Historians differ as to whether the garrison accepted the terms immediately or held out until they saw the heavy ordnance ranged against them. They did,

however, surrender before the walls were battered again, and the castle thus remained in sound condition. It has been restored almost to its original condition, and there is an excellent audio-visual show in the 1840 courtyard cottage. (See also Tour 10.)

▶ *Head south on the **R668** through the village of Clogheen to begin The Vee mountain pass road en route to Lismore.*

6 The Vee, Co Tipperary and Waterford
The viewing points along this drive through a gap in the Knockmealdown Mountains provide spectacular panoramic views of Killballyboy Wood, Boernagore Wood, the Galtee Mountains, the Golden Vale of Tipperary, Bay Lough and the Comeragh mountain range. (See also Tour 10.)

▶ *Continue south on the **R668** for 8 miles (13km) to Lismore.*

7 Lismore, Co Waterford
This historic little town, site of an ancient monastic centre of learning, is beautifully situated on the Blackwater River. Its most outstanding sightseeing attractions are Lismore Castle, whose gardens are open to the public, the Protestant cathedral, with grave slabs from the 9th and 11th centuries, and the modern Romanesque-style Catholic cathedral. An outstanding audio-visual show in The Heritage Centre depicts the town's history. The Centre has booklets tracing the interesting Town Walk and the riverside Lady Louise's Walk. (See also Tour 10.)

SCENIC ROUTES

About a mile (1.5km) from the Cappoquin bridge, the scenic 10-mile (16km) route to Youghal follows the Blackwater River, with deeply wooded stretches as well as superb views of the broad river and the opposite banks. Great houses of the 19th century and earlier are dotted along the route, and about 2 miles (3km) south of Cappoquin, the large house high above the east bank is the remodelled wing of ancient Dromana Castle, where traces of the old gardens sloping down to the river can still be seen.

The fairy-tale appearence of Lismore Castle is second only to the fascinating facts of its history and illustrious occupants

▶ *Take the **N72** east for 4 miles (6km) to the bridge on the outskirts of Cappoquin and turn right on to an unclassified road to a T-junction. Turn right on to the road signposted Youghal that follows the Blackwater River south to the sea, then turn right on to the **N25** south for the short drive into Youghal.*

i *Town centre*

8 Youghal, Co Cork
This picturesque fishing harbour and seaside resort is filled with mementoes of its past. Sir Walter Raleigh lived here, and legend has it that this is where he first smoked tobacco from the New World and planted the first potato in Irish soil. Myrtle Grove, his Elizabethan house, is at the top of Nelson Place.

A Tourist Trail booklet available from the tourist office details a signposted walking tour of the town, which includes the historic Clock Tower in the town centre that was erected in 1771 as a gaol and now holds an

art gallery and museum featuring the works of local artists, ancient town charters and Sir Walter Raleigh memorabilia. A short distance away, there are fragments of the old town walls, constructed in 1275 and added to up until 1603. During summer months there are harbour and river cruises as well as deep-sea fishing charters.

As the Blackwater River broadens near its entrance to the sea north of Youghal, look for the extensive ruins of 13th-century Molana Abbey, situated on what was once an islet. Although it has become rather overgrown, the site holds ruins of a church, cloisters and conventual buildings, as well as what is believed to be the burial place of the Norman knight Raymond le Gros.

Eight miles (13km) east of Youghal, via a signposted turnoff from the N25, the pretty little seaside village of Ardmore grew from the 7th-century settlement founded by St Declan and has a fine group of ecclesiastical remains, including one of the most perfectly preserved round towers in Ireland. There are also bracing cliff walks along the sea's edge.

[i] *Heritage Centre, Market Square*

Follow the ***N25*** *west for 28 miles (45km) to return to Cork.*

Sunset over a deserted Youghal beach, on the south coast

BACK TO NATURE

About 5 miles (8km) west of Youghal on the N25, the entrance to Glenbower Wood is at the Thatch Inn in Killeagh village. Its nature trail is a 1½-mile (3km) loop that can be walked in about half an hour, or fully savoured for an hour or two. The wood is set in a glen through which the River Dissour rushes, and at one point an earthen dam was built to power the village corn mill, forming a lovely lake. Native trees include hazel (considered to have magical powers to ward off evil), sessile oak, alder, scrub oak, holly, birch and rowan. Tree plantations are mostly Norway spruce, Western hemlock and Sitka spruce. The profusion of ferns includes hard fern, bracken fern, hart's tongue and the male shield fern.

FOR CHILDREN

The Fota Island Wildlife Park, just to the east of Cork, is a child's paradise, inhabited by an engaging animal population that includes zebras, cheetahs, kangaroos, giraffes, ostriches, antelopes, gibbons and monkeys, as well as rare and endangered species. There are pools for flamingos and penguins, and swans float serenely on the lake. A tour train is great fun, and there is a children's corner and playground.

SPECIAL TO...

Cork's high-spirited International Jazz Festival in October attracts some of the world's most outstanding musicians, with concerts all around the town, as well as impromptu jam sessions breaking out in pubs, B&B drawing rooms, and wherever two jazz devotees happen to meet. The Cork Film Festival in late September or early October enjoys a worldwide reputation as a showcase for independent film-makers.

Cork's Coastal Villages

Its great age and its location in a long, marshy valley have fashioned Cork City into what a native son once aptly described as 'an intimate higgledy-piggledy assemblage of steps, slopes, steeples and bridges'. Parallel to the Western Road is the Mardyke, a mile-long (1.5km) tree-shaded walk bordered by Fitzgerald Park, the site of the Cork Museum. (See also Tour 7.)

2 DAYS • 143 MILES • 229KM

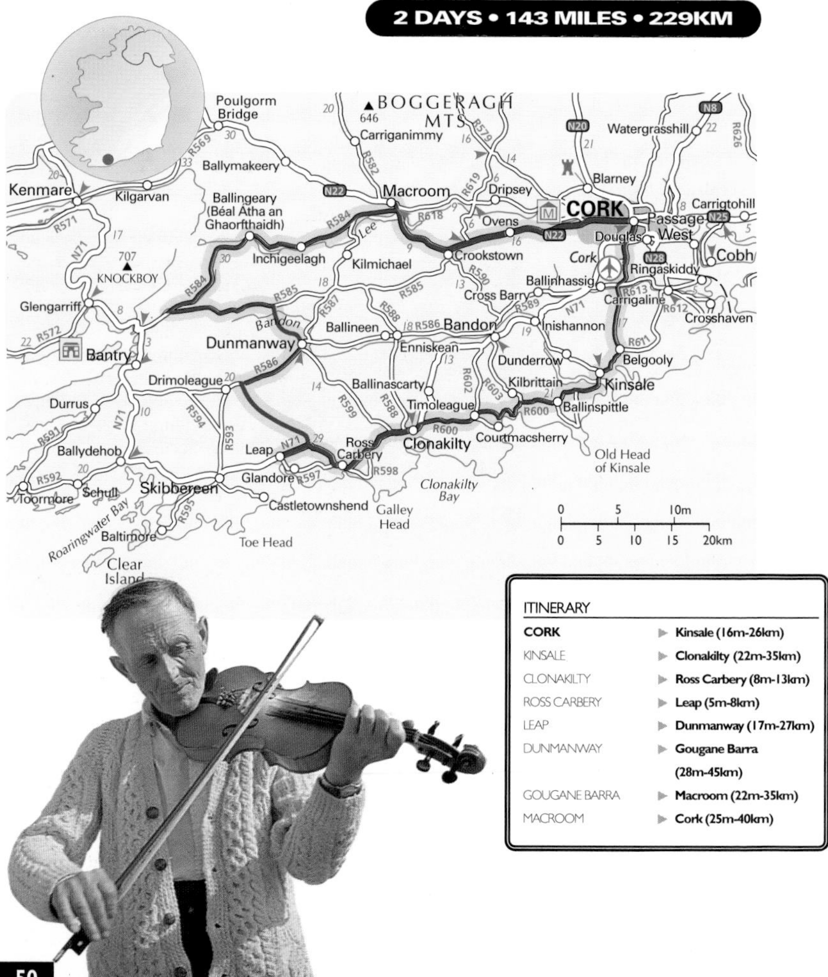

ITINERARY

CORK	▶ **Kinsale (16m-26km)**
KINSALE	▶ **Clonakilty (22m-35km)**
CLONAKILTY	▶ **Ross Carbery (8m-13km)**
ROSS CARBERY	▶ **Leap (5m-8km)**
LEAP	▶ **Dunmanway (17m-27km)**
DUNMANWAY	▶ **Gougane Barra (28m-45km)**
GOUGANE BARRA	▶ **Macroom (22m-35km)**
MACROOM	▶ **Cork (25m-40km)**

The narrow promontory of the Old Head of Kinsale shelters the popular yachting centre of Kinsale Harbour, to the east

i *Grand Parade, Cork*

RECOMMENDED WALK

Cork has a Tourist Trail marked out for visitors and a copy can be obtained from the Tourist Information Office.

FOR CHILDREN

Treat the children to a cruise of Cork harbour. Departing from Kennedy Pier in nearby Cobh (see Tour 7), the cruiser passes harbour forts, Spike Island, the naval base, and ships of all descriptions from freighters to pleasure-boats.

► *Take the **R600** south for 16 miles (26km) to Kinsale.*

1 Kinsale, Co Cork

The fishing and boating village of Kinsale has figured prominently in Ireland's history since it received its charter in 1334. A decisive British victory here in 1601 led to a mass exodus of Irish royalty known as the 'Flight of the Earls'. Twelfth-century St Multose Church displays the old town stocks, and there are ruins of a 12th-century Carmelite friary and 15th-century Desmond Castle. The Seanachie Pub in Market Street has traditional music, and The Spaniard is a haunt of yachtsmen and local fishermen.

FOR HISTORY BUFFS

When Don Juan d'Agila arrived in Kinsale from Spain in 1601 with a large force to assist the Irish rebels against the English forces, an Irish victory seemed certain, even though the English Lord Deputy, Mountjoy, threw some 12,000 soldiers into the siege of the town. Irish chieftains O'Donnell and O'Neill marched their troops down from the north to mount a rear offensive against the English. This might well have succeeded had not word reached Mountjoy of their strategy, enabling him to successfully rout both Irish and Spanish. South of the town the remains of King James Fort (or Old Fort), which housed the Spanish, can be visited.

Near Summer Cove, there are extensive, well-preserved remains of Charles Fort, built around 1677, with spectacular views of Kinsale harbour.

Seven miles (11km) south via the R600 and R604 is the Old Head of Kinsale, where a ruined clifftop castle overlooks the spot where the *Lusitania* was sunk in 1915 by a German submarine.

i *Pier Road*

SPECIAL TO...

The lively town of Kinsale is internationally known for its gourmet restaurants featuring cuisines from around the world, with local seafoods and meats in various guises starring on all menus. For the ultimate dining experience, look for restaurants displaying the Kinsale Good Food Circle emblem. Or come for the Gourmet Festival in October.

The gentle hills and tranquil waters of Rosscarbey

▶ *Continue on the* ***R600*** *for 22 miles (35km) southwest to Clonakilty.*

> **SCENIC ROUTES**
>
> For a scenic alternative route from Kinsale to Clonakilty, turn southeast at Timoleague on the R601 and drive along Courtmacsherry Bay. The fishing village of Courtmacsherry nestles between the bay and the thick woods at its back. Continue south to Butlerstown, where there are marvellous seascapes and views of the Seven Heads, a rugged peninsula with seven jutting headlands. Follow the unclassified road west to North Ring, then north along the shores of Clonakilty Bay, to reach Clonakilty.

2 Clonakilty, Co Cork

Ten miles (16km) from Kinsale, on the Clonakilty road, Timoleague Castle Gardens were laid out more than one and a half centuries ago. Timoleague Abbey is a well-preserved ruined Franciscan friary, which in its day was an important religious centre. At Clonakilty, castles dot the shores of the bay, the Catholic church is a fine example of Gothic architecture, and the West Cork Regional Museum displays archaeological relics and town corporation minute books going back to 1675, along with memorabilia of Irish resistance leader Michael Collins. The Michael Collins Memorial Centre is about 2 miles (3km) west at Woodfield.

Two miles (3km) south of town, Inchydoney is just one of many fine beaches in the area.

i *25 Ashe Street*

> **FOR CHILDREN**
>
> Clonakilty Animal Park at the Agricultural College not only has birds and animals to enjoy, there is also 'Noahs Ark', the 'Old Woman's Shoe', the houses of the 'Three Little Pigs', and more.

▶ *Continue southwest on the* ***N71*** *to Rosscarbery.*

3 Rosscarbery, Co Cork

At the head of Rosscarbery Bay, this picturesque little town was the site of a medieval Benedictine monastery in the 6th century, founded by St Fachtna, and was famous for its school. A few remains of its foundation can be seen near the church which stands on the site of an ancient cathedral.

One mile (1.5km) east of town are the ruins of Benduff Castle, and a little further on, the beautiful demesne of Castlefreke. Two miles (3km) west of town, the fine Drombeg stone circle can be seen from the Glandore road, R597, and near by is Fulacht Fiadh stone trough, an ancient Celtic cooking pot in which water was brought to the boil with stones heated in a fire.

▶ *Take the* ***N71*** *west to Leap.*

4 Leap, Co Cork

This pretty little village sits at the head of a narrow inlet where the River Leap (pronounced 'lep') enters Glandore harbour. Stop in at the Leap Inn in the main street to experience an authentic Irish country inn that has been run by the same family for generations, and has a cosy bar and lounge enlivened by the colourful conversation of locals and a dining room that serves good, solid, traditional Irish favourites.

Climb the hill above the

village for beautiful harbour views, and drive to nearby Unionhall on a scenic road that follows the harbour as it widens to enter the sea.

*Take the **N71** east to Connonagh, then turn northwest on an unclassified road to reach the **R586**. Turn northeast for Dunmanway.*

5 Dunmanway, Co Cork

The famous Gaelic Athletic Association figure, Sam Maguire, was born near this early 17th-century linen industry plantation town and is buried in St Mary's cemetery. The town pitch bears his name.

There are fine forest walks at Clashnacrona Woods, 3 miles (5km) southwest of the town on the R586, and at Aultagh Wood, which lies 4 miles (6km) north on the R587.

*Take the unclassified Coolkellure road northwest, then turn left on meeting the **R585** and continue to Kealkill. Turn northeast on the **R585** through the Pass of Keimaneigh to reach the Gougane Barra road.*

6 Gougane Barra Forest Park, Co Cork

Gougane Barra was Ireland's first forest park. The River Lee rises in Gougane Barra lake, a corrie lake surrounded by thickly wooded crags. Before moving on to the marshes of Cork, St Finbar had a hermitage in this remote spot. St Finbar's Holy Island, connected to the shore by a causeway, holds a tiny Romanesque chapel built in 1901. Pilgrimages are made to the hermitage each September.

*Drive northeast on the **R585** to Macroom, turning left on to the **N22** to enter the town.*

BACK TO NATURE

Gougane Barra Forest Park is one of the few forest parks to have a drive-around trail, but the best way to experience it is to walk along the numerous signposted paths or the nature trail. Picnic tables are provided to make this an ideal day's outing. The 350-acre (140-hectare) park was virtually bare until the government planted it with lodgepole pine, Sitka spruce and Japanese larch. Along the nature trail there are specimens of trees native to the area, silver birch, ash, holly and hawthorn.

7 Macroom, Co Cork

This is the main market town for the Gaelic-speaking region to the west. Macroom Castle, off the square, dates from the 13th century and was a seat of the MacCarthys of Muskerry. Oliver Cromwell granted it to Admiral Sir William Penn, whose son William spent much of his childhood here and later founded the US state of Pennsylvania. Little now remains of the castle, although its impressive entrance has been restored. There is an interesting museum in Castle Street.

*Take the **N22** east for 25 miles (40km) and return to Cork.*

On the remote inland border between Cork and Kerry, the Gougane Barra Forest Park is a haven of peace and wildlife

Unspoiled Peninsulas

Bantry sits at the head of one of Ireland's most beautiful bays, with a sheltered harbour that reaches right into the town centre, where the narrow streets and lovely broad square are lined with shops and houses that have changed little over the centuries.

Bantry House, a magnificent Georgian mansion in beautiful landscaped grounds, is open to the public. Its French Armada Interpretive Centre, holds items from the disastrous invasion of 1796.

1/2 DAYS • 96 MILES • 156KM

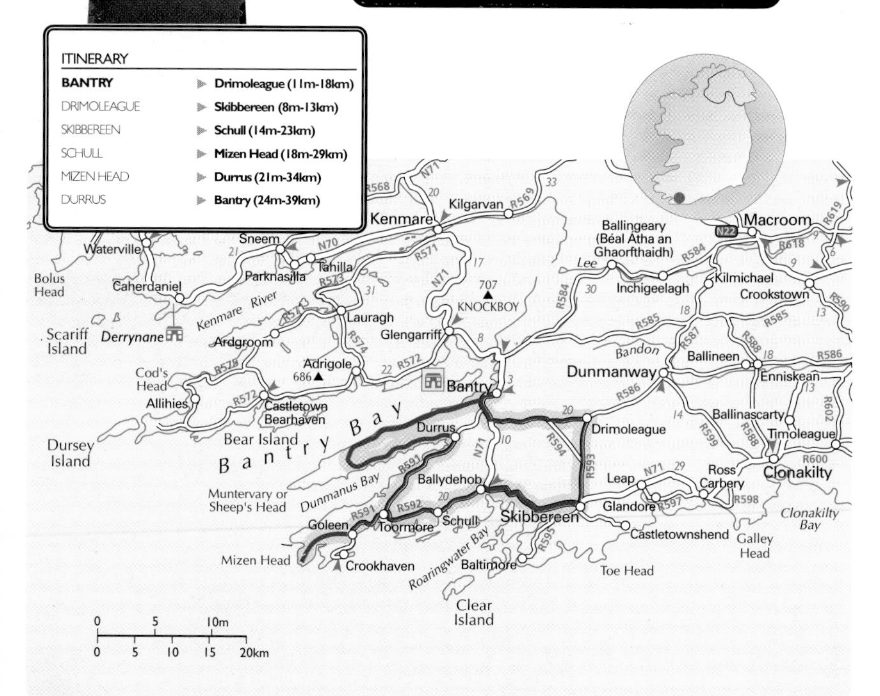

FOR HISTORY BUFFS

High seas and storm conditions spelt defeat for the French Armada that anchored in Bantry Bay on 21 December, 1796. Fired with the fervour of their own successful revolution, they had responded eagerly to the entreaties of revolutionary Wolfe Tone to join with United Irishmen to end the British occupation of Ireland. Tone, aboard one of the ships, was dismayed when the fleet lost its flagship and commanding officer in a storm at sea. Eventually, gale-force winds drove 20 of the great ships back down the bay and out to sea. When there was no let-up in the weather, the Armada and a heartbroken Tone sailed back to France.

RECOMMENDED WALKS

There are fine forest walks in Barnegeehy Woods, about 3 miles (5km) south of Bantry via the Ballydehob road (N71).

i *The Old Courthouse, The Square, Bantry*

▶ *Take the* **N71** *south and turn off to Drimoleague, 8 miles (13km) east via the* **R586**.

1 Drimoleague, Co Cork
The Roman Catholic church in this small town is noteworthy for its architecture, a modern box-like structure with a solid, unbroken wall on one side, and glass on the other. Castle Donovan, north of town and now in ruins, is a relic of the late 15th and early 16th centuries.

▶ *Turn south on to the* **R593** *to Skibbereen.*

SPECIAL TO...

This West Cork region is alive with festivals and special events during summer months. There are regattas in Castletownshend and Schull in July, and Baltimore, Schull and Crookhaven in August. In July and August Castletownshend holds its Festival of Music; Skibbereen celebrates its 'Welcome Home' Festival in August, with an emphasis on greeting returning family and friends, as well as new visitors. The entire area is also a mecca for anglers, with sea and shore angling, and salmon fishing in the River Ilen at Skibbereen. Trout are the prize at lakes Garranes and Driminidy near Drimoleague.

2 Skibbereen, Co Cork
This progressive town sits on the River Ilen just where it broadens and then empties into

Beautiful Bantry House enjoys an unparalleled setting on the shores of Bantry Bay

Abbeystrewery is a sad and atmospheric place, with its mass famine graves amidst the overgrown abbey ruins

Baltimore Bay. Its long history of independence has produced two battling bishops – one who died fighting Elizabethan forces in 1602 and another who was hanged in 1650 during the Cromwellian conflicts. The Maid of Erin monument in the town square was erected in 1904 by the Young Ireland Society. The Pro-Cathedral, a fine Grecian-style edifice built in 1826, is well worth a visit, while arts and crafts take centre stage at the West Cork Arts Centre.

Abbeystrewery Abbey, dating from the 14th century, lies in ruins 1 mile (1.5km) west of town, the setting for mass famine graves that bear silent witness to one of Ireland's most tragic eras.

Castletownshend, 5 miles (8km) southeast of Skibbereen via the R596, is a pretty little village with only one street that slopes rather steeply down to the sea. The tree that sits in the middle of that street was spared by roadmakers. This was home to Edith Somerville and Violet Martin Ross, two Victorian ladies whose humorous *Experiences of an Irish RM* has kept the entire English-speaking world chuckling. They lay buried in the Church of Ireland grounds, their lively spirits no doubt still haunting the halls of their beloved Drishane House at the upper end of the village. Just outside town, on a ridge overlooking the sea, Knockdrum ringfort has an underground passage (souterrain) and a stone with megalithic cup marks.

Eight miles (13km) southwest of Skibbereen, the little fishing village of Baltimore also has a stormy history, attested to by the ancient castle of the O'Driscolls, now in ruins, that still keeps a brooding eye on things from its perch on a rock overlooking the harbour. Despite the presence of that powerful clan, in 1631 Algerian pirates captured some 200 town residents for sale to North African slave traders and massacred most of those left behind. Poet Thomas Davis's *The Sack of Baltimore* gives a vivid account of the raid.

There are fine views of the bay and Sherkin Island from the tall whitewashed navigational beacon a short distance outside the village, and there is a regular boat service from Baltimore to Sherkin Island, which defines the westward side of Baltimore Bay. Silver Strand is typical of several good swimming spots among the island's many coves. Of special note is the outstanding Marine Research Centre on this island. Near the pier stand ruins of another castle of the O'Driscolls, destroyed in 1537, and on the eastern end of the island are remains of a friary founded by one of the O'Driscolls in the 15th century for the Franciscan Order of Strict Observance.

Southwest of Sherkin is Clear Island, one of the four

Gaeltacht (Irish-speaking) areas in the Cork/Kerry region, with a regular boat service from Sherkin and mailboat service from Baltimore. This large island holds one of Europe's few electricity-generating windmills, an innovative EU pilot scheme. You will be well rewarded by a visit to the Cape Clear Heritage Centre. There is also a small bird observatory that has tracked the migrations of a host of interesting species. Just south of the island, on the southernmost offshore point in Ireland, Fastnet Rock Lighthouse stands as a major navigational aid to mariners. This is the second lighthouse to occupy the rock, and was built in Cornwall in 1906 from local granite, disassembled and refitted on to Fastnet Rock, each block dovetailed into the next to withstand the fierce seas.

[i] *Town Hall*

BACK TO NATURE

About 4 miles (6km) southwest of Skibbereen is Lough Hyne, the country's most important marine nature reserve. Its pollution-free waters, warmed by the Gulf Stream, form a natural habitat for several thousand species of marine animals and plants. Many southern, or Lusitanian, species common to the Mediterranean and surrounding area thrive here, as do others peculiar to Ireland and Britain. At low tide, search the shore for intriguing marine creatures such as jewel anemones, sea squirts and gobies. From the lake shores, you can observe patches of different-coloured seabed, which change with the intensity of grazing by the fascinating marine population.

There is always activity on the water at Schull harbour

RECOMMENDED WALKS

At the head of Lough Hyne, look for the path that climbs steeply up through woodlands to reach the hilltop. The panoramic view is nothing short of breathtaking, looking down over the Hundred Isles, down the length of the peninsula to Mizen Head, and east as far as Kinsale.

▶ *Take the* ***N71*** *west to Ballydehob, then turn southwest on to the* ***R592*** *to reach Schull.*

3 Schull, Co Cork

The scenic drive west from Skibbereen follows the River Ilen and then the shore of

Roaringwater Bay to Ballydehob, a picturesque little harbour that has attracted scores of crafts-people, whose workshops may well prompt a shopping stop. During World War II a German war plane crashed on the slopes of Mount Gabriel, which is now topped by a tracking station. Beautiful Cuss Strand, 2 miles (3km) from Ballydehob, offers excellent swimming. Further on, Schull's harbour is virtually enclosed, making it a haven for fishing and pleasure boats. This delightful little town usually has music in the pubs and a variety of resort-type special events during summer months. In the village, the Church of Ireland church (no longer in use) incorporates interesting medieval remains, and in the grounds of the Community College, a 60-seat planetarium is the first of its kind in the Republic of Ireland. There is also a regular ferry service to Clear Island from Schull harbour.

▶ *Follow the* ***R592*** *to Toormore, then turn left on to the* ***R591*** *to Goleen. At Goleen take an unclassified road to Mizen Head.*

4 Mizen Head, Co Cork

This part of the peninsula route calls out for a leisurely drive as it sweeps around beautiful Toormore Bay to Goleen, where a lovely secluded beach invites a break for a swim. From Goleen, you can either proceed straight out to Mizen Head via a minor road off the R591 or make a short side trip to the village of Crookhaven, whose charming harbour is a favourite with yachtsmen, before proceeding on to land's end. The fine sandy beaches of Barley Cove are a strong point in favour of the side trip to this popular resort spot. The drive on to Mizen Head is one of breathtaking seascapes and high vertical cliffs against which breaking white-foamed waves beat ceaselessly. Exercise extreme caution, however, as the clifftops end abruptly and the fall is straight down. In 1993, the last keepers left the lighthouse and the Mizen Vision Visitor Centre is now housed in the keeper's house and engine room. Happily for sailors, all equipment is now automated.

▶ *An unmarked road strikes north at Barley Cove, but is rough driving. The recommended route is a return to Goleen, where you rejoin the* ***R591*** *north to Toormore, then*

The ever-changing seascapes of the Mizen Peninsula culminate in this spectacular headland

head northeast for the scenic drive to Durrus, 21 miles (34km).

FOR CHILDREN

While most children will take delight in the coastal scenery and wooded stretches along the drive, they will welcome stops for a swim and romp on the fine beaches at Goleen, Barley Cove, Ahakista, and Kilcrohane. Surfers will find good waves at Barley Cove.

5 Durrus, Co Cork

Situated at the head of Dunmanus Bay, this village is the gateway to the narrow, 15-mile (24km) long Sheep's Head Peninsula. A minor, unnumbered road leads southwest along the coast to the wooded inlet of Ahakista, where there is good swimming at sandy beaches, and the Air India Memorial commemorating the loss of the passengers and crew of the plane that crashed off this coast in 1985. Then on to Kilcrohane, which also has a good beach. Adventurous souls may want to continue southwest to the car park from which you can walk out across the rocky headland to Sheep's Head.

▶ *At Kilcrohane, take the road known as Goat's Path across Seefin (Fionn's Seat) Mountain, the highest on the peninsula, for the drive along the southern shore of Bantry Bay. Just past the village of Tedagh, turn left on to the **N71** for the short drive back to Bantry.*

RECOMMENDED WALKS

It is an easy walk from the summit of the Goat's Path road up to the top of Seefin Mountain. The small effort will be rewarded by even more extensive views of the peninsula and coastline, since Seefin is almost twice the height of the road summit.

The Sheep's Head Peninsula has a wonderful rocky coastline, backed on its sheltered southern slopes by luxuriant hedgerows and gardens

SCENIC ROUTES

The drive from Durrus down Sheep's Head Peninsula – especially the Goat's Path road just outside Kilcrohane that leads across the mountains – is the most scenic part of the route. When you reach the summit, stop to enjoy the extensive panorama east over County Cork and west to the Beara Peninsula and parts of County Kerry. The narrow but well-surfaced road is especially beautiful in autumn when gorse (dwarf furze/whin) covers the mountains and countryside with golden yellow flowers.

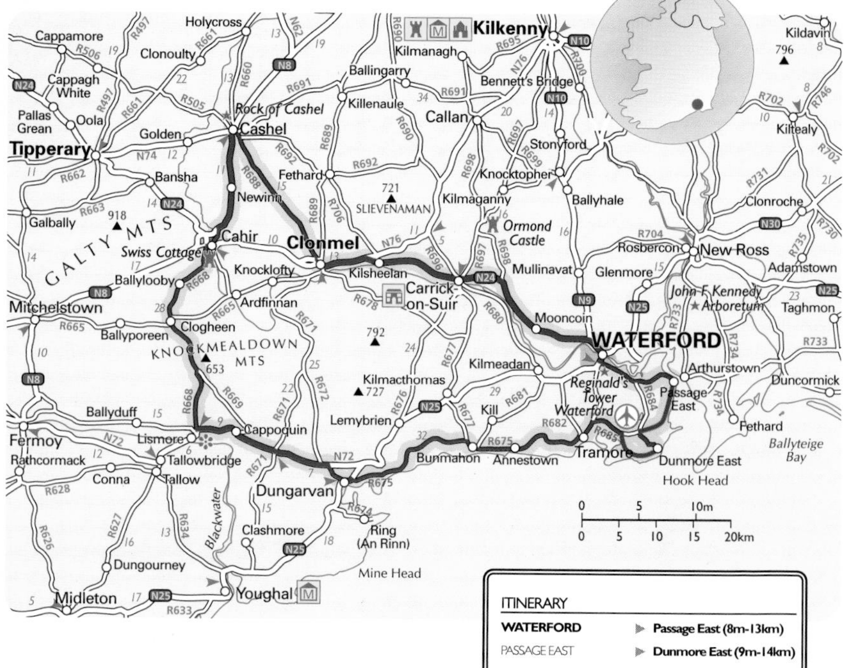

ITINERARY	
WATERFORD	▶ **Passage East (8m-13km)**
PASSAGE EAST	▶ **Dunmore East (9m-14km)**
DUNMORE EAST	▶ **Tramore (11m-18km)**
TRAMORE	▶ **Dungarvan (25m-40km)**
DUNGARVAN	▶ **Cappoquin (10m-16km)**
CAPPOQUIN	▶ **Lismore (4m-6km)**
LISMORE	▶ **Cahir (22m-35km)**
CAHIR	▶ **Cashel (12m-19km)**
CASHEL	▶ **Clonmel (15m-24km)**
CLONMEL	▶ **Carrick-on-Suir (14m-23km)**
CARRICK-ON-SUIR	▶ **Waterford (17m-27km)**

Rock of Cashel

2 DAYS • 147 MILES • 235KM

Waterford is an important seaport and cultural centre and also reflects much of the country's history. Reginald's Tower, on The Quay, dates back to 1003, and now houses a museum of Waterford's historical treasures. There are traces of the old Viking-built city walls, a fine cathedral and an excellent Heritage Centre. The famous Waterford Crystal Glass Factory and summer river cruises are great attractions.

[i] *41, The Quay, Waterford*

SPECIAL TO...

In September, a lighthearted gathering of amateur companies from around the world and from all parts of Ireland converges on Waterford for the annual International Festival of Light Opera. For 16 nights there are performances of such musicals as *Brigadoon* and *Showboat*, all to a very high standard.

▶ *From Waterford take the **R683** east to Passage East.*

1 Passage East, Co Waterford
This quaint riverside village with its whitewashed cottages, narrow, winding streets and a car-ferry service to Ballyhack, County Wexford, was the landing point for Henry II, who arrived in 1171 with 4,000 men in 400 ships to receive oaths of loyalty from Irish chieftains who wished to hold on to their lands. The hill just above the village provides splendid views of the head of Waterford harbour.

On the road to Dunmore East are the ruins of Geneva Barracks, relics of a colony of goldsmiths and silversmiths from Switzerland who sought refuge from religious persecution in 1782. Their planned town of New Geneva failed, and by 1785 was abandoned. The barracks became a prison for insurgents (or 'croppies') of the 1798 rising, subjects of the ballad 'The Croppy Boy'.

▶ *Follow an unclassified coastal road south, join the **R684** and turn left for Dunmore East.*

2 Dunmore East, Co Waterford
Neat thatched cottages perch on steep hills above the harbour in this pretty little village that is a popular summer resort and sea-angling centre. Pleasure boats and fishing vessels fill the picturesque harbour. The bay is divided into cliffs and coves, with good walks to Creadan Head to the north, Black Knob promontory to the south, and Swines Head at the southern end of the peninsula. There are also several safe sandy beaches in the area.

Dunmore East offers the Irish idyll in pretty, traditional-style holiday homes

▶ *Take an unclassified coastal road to the junction with the **R685**, turn left, then left again at the junction with the **R675** and continue to Tramore.*

FOR CHILDREN

There are exciting diversions for children in Tramore. Splashworld has water-based fun, with slides, flumes and white-knuckle rides, while Laserworld provides a high-tech game with special effects, set in a Celtic maze.

3 Tramore, Co Waterford
This lively seaside town is one of the southeast coast's most popular resorts, with a wide, 3-mile-long (5km) beach, its waters warmed by the Gulf Stream. Attractions include a 50-acre (20-hectare) amusement park, a race course, miniature golf, and an 18-hole golf course. Watersports, particularly surfing, are popular here, and there is good swimming at the pier,

Guillameen Cove and Newton Cove.

The giant clifftop 'Metal Man' statue at Great Newtown Head, was erected as a navigational landmark for sailors, and legend has it that any unmarried female who hops around it three times will hop down the aisle within 12 months.

On the coastal drive to Dungarvan, the little fishing village of Bunmahon has a good sandy beach surrounded by jagged cliffs that rise to about 200 feet (60m), with interesting rock formations at their base.

In Stradbally look for Stradbally Hall and its narrow gauge railway.

[i] *Railway Street*

▶ *From Tramore, follow the* ***R675*** *coastal drive via Stradbally southwest to Dungarvan.*

Sand and rocks between Dungarvan and Tramore

RECOMMENDED WALKS

At Tramore, the oceanfront promenade leads to a range of sandhills known as The Burrows. West of town, both the Garrarus Strand and the Kilfarrasy Strand offer pleasant seaside walks. To the southwest of town, there are lovely walks along the Doneraile cliffs.

SCENIC ROUTES

There is scarcely a mile of this tour that could not be described as a scenic route. The R675, the coastal road from Tramore to Dungarvan, dips and winds through the quaint little fishing villages of Annestown and Bunmahon, with spectacular seascapes of soaring cliffs and quiet little coves. A short detour to the wide, curving beach at Clonea Strand is worthwhile. The Vee drive (see also Tour 7) from Lismore to Clogheen, on the R668, winds and twists along mountainsides covered with heather to the V-shaped pass in the Knockmealdown Mountains, with lay-bys giving sweeping views of Tipperary's Golden Vale, before descending to the little town of Clogheen. Between the pass and Clogheen, look for the stone cairn on the northern slope, where Samuel Grubb of Grace Castle was interred upright overlooking his landholdings. This drive is especially spectacular in the spring when the mountainsides are ablaze with rhododendron flowers.

4 Dungarvan, Co Waterford

A busy market town, Dungarvan sits on the broad, natural harbour where the Colligan river meets the sea. Along the quays can be seen remnants of Dungarvan Castle, dating from 1186, surrounded by fortified walls. At the top of Main Street an excellent small museum, with prints, documents and artefacts of Dungarvan's turbulent history through colonial and revolutionary eras, is located in the old Market House, which dates from 1642. Five miles (8km) south of town on the R674 is the village of Ring, where Irish is the daily language and is taught in an acclaimed language college. Further east beyond Ring, impressive Helvick Head rises to 230 feet (70m) and shelters a picturesque small harbour.

i *Grattan Square*

FOR CHILDREN

Further south on the coastal drive, Clonlea Strand, some 2 miles (3km) east of Dungarvan, flies the European blue flag for cleanliness, and there are ample refreshment facilities.

▶ *Take the* **N72** *west to Cappoquin.*

5 Cappoquin, Co Waterford

The broad Blackwater River makes a 90-degree turn to the west at Cappoquin, and provides scenic riverside drives and some of the best salmon fishing, trout angling and coarse fishing in Ireland.

Cappoquin house and gardens command fine views over the River Blackwater. The house, built in 1779, used to face the town, but later the entrance was turned round and the façade is now enhanced by informal gardens and fine trees which extend towards the river.

Ballysaggartmore Gatehouse is a fitting entrance to romantic Lismore Castle

▶ *Follow the* **N72** *for 4 miles (6km) to Lismore.*

6 Lismore, Co Waterford

Set on the Blackwater River, Lismore's most prominent feature is Lismore Castle, which looms over the town and river, looking for all the world like a fairy-tale castle. It was built by King John in 1185 on the site of a 7th-century monastery that became one of Europe's most renowned seats of learning. After surviving devastating attacks by Viking raiders, the monastic university finally succumbed to the assaults of Raymond le Gros in 1173. The castle was presented to Sir Walter Raleigh, who sold it to Richard Boyle, Earl of Cork, in 1602. His son, Robert, the noted chemist and author of Boyle's Law, was born here. Since 1753 it has been the Irish seat of the Dukes of Devonshire, and the gardens are open to the public.

The medieval Protestant cathedral dates from 1633, although it was largely rebuilt around 1680. It has soaring Gothic vaulting and still

retains in its west wall 9th- and 11th-century grave slabs from an earlier church. The modern (1888) Catholic cathedral is Romanesque in style. Lady Louise's Walk along the river and the interesting Town Walk are well signposted.

Five miles (8km) south of Lismore, via the N72, the little town of Tallow was the birthplace of famed 19th-century sculptor John Hogan. Panoramic views open up from 592-foot (180m) Tallow Hill, less than 1 mile (1.5km) north-east of town, and there are ruins of an ancient fortified Fitzgerald keep located ½ mile (1km) west of Tallowbridge.

Six miles (10km) west of Lismore, via the R666, the village of Ballyduff is a popular angling centre and also holds the ruins of Mocollop Castle, another Fitzgerald fortress.

i *Courthouse*

▶ *At the eastern end of the bridge in Lismore take the* ***R668*** *which follows the Blackwater River, then climbs to the pass in the Knockmealdown Mountains known as The Vee and descends to Clogheen, then on to Cahir.*

7 Cahir, Co Tipperary

Cahir Castle, with its massive great hall, grim dungeon, and thick protective enclosing walls, is a superb restoration of the 1142 castle set on a rocky islet in the River Suir. It is also one of Ireland's best-preserved castles. Furnishings in the residential apartments are authentic reproductions of the period. The Articles ending the long Cromwellian wars were signed here, and in modern times it has served as the setting for such films as *Excalibur* and *Barry Lyndon*.

Other interesting buildings include the 13th-century abbey, founded by a Norman knight, which is being restored, and the delightful little Swiss Cottage. Cahir is a centre for walking and climbing.

A few miles northwest of Cahir, the N24 (the road to Tipperary town) leads to a left turnoff heading to the lush Glen of Aherlow, a secluded glen that was once a major route between the counties of Tipperary and Limerick and the scene of ancient battles. Later, Irish insurgents and outlaws took refuge in the thickly wooded valley that runs between the Galtee Mountains and Slievenamuck Hills.

Even the myths, legends and history pale beside the actual sight of the Rock of Cashel

BACK TO NATURE

The 1-mile (1.5km) nature trail in Glengarra Wood is a delight for those interested in rare and exotic trees and plants. To reach the wood, drive 8 miles (13km) southwest of Cahir via the N8, and turn right on to the signposted and unclassified road, then continue 2 miles (3km) to the car-park. There are nature walks along the Burncourt river and through forest groves, where Douglas fir, ferns and native heathers, Western hemlock, rowan, holly, birch, arboreal rhododendron, Bhutan pine from the Inner Himalayas of eastern India, and many other plants and trees can be seen. Native birds such as the treecreeper, the tiny goldcrest, wren, robin, chaffinch, magpie, jay and the introduced pheasant make this their home, as do a herd of fallow deer.

i *Castle Street*

▶ *From Cahir, follow the* ***N8*** *due north to Cashel.*

8 Cashel, Co Tipperary
Dominating the landscape for miles around is the awe-inspiring Rock of Cashel which soars 200 feet (60m) above the surrounding plains. Since ancient Celtic times, its 2-acre (0.8-hectare) summit has been connected with royalty and mysticism. Cormac's Chapel, the Round Tower, St Patrick's Cathedral, and a replica of St Patrick's Cross, (whose base may actually have been a pre-Christian sacrificial altar), are among the impressive ruins, all in good condition. At the foot of the Rock, a visitors' centre of stylised Celtic design presents traditional Irish entertainment.

i *Main Street*

▶ *Take the* ***R688*** *southeast for 15 miles (24km) to Clonmel.*

FOR HISTORY BUFFS

In the 5th century, a cashel, or stone fort, was erected on the lofty Rock of Cashel, and it was here, legend has it, that St Patrick came to preach to the King of Munster, using the humble shamrock as a symbol of the Christian Trinity. In 1101, Murtough O'Brien presented the Cashel of the Kings to the Church. In 1127, Cormac MacCarthaigh, King of Desmond, built the little chapel, a miniature gem of Romanesque style. King Henry II came here to receive homage from Irish princes; Edward the Bruce held a parliament here; and the first Protestant service was conducted here.

9 Clonmel, Co Tipperary
Set on the banks of the River Suir, Clonmel is the main town of County Tipperary, and is home to the Tipperary County Museum, where lively exhibits span prehistoric to modern times.

It was in Clonmel that the world's first public transport system was established by Charles Bianconi in 1815, based at Hearn's Hotel in Parnell Street. This aspect of Clonmel's history is reflected in a developing transport museum.

Parts of the Franciscan church in Abbey Street date back to the 13th centur, and 19th-century St Mary's Church near by has a fine high altar. The town's streets are lined with restored shopfronts.

i *Sarsfield Street*

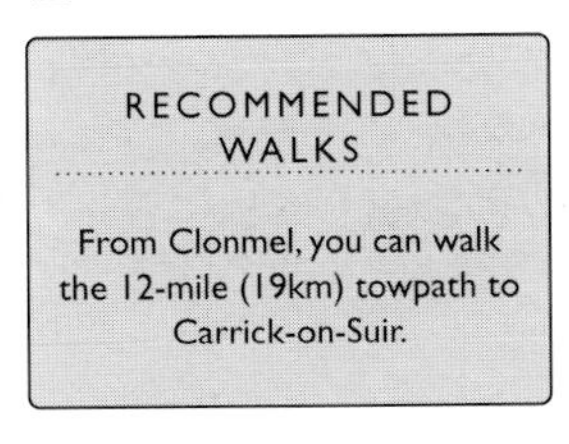
RECOMMENDED WALKS

From Clonmel, you can walk the 12-mile (19km) towpath to Carrick-on-Suir.

One of Clonmel's charming streets is framed by the arch of the great West Gate

▶ *Take the* ***N24*** *east to Carrick-on-Suir.*

10 Carrick-on-Suir, Co Tipperary
This scenic town is on the River Suir, and its Ormonde Castle is the only Elizabethan fortified mansion of its kind in Ireland. A principal seat of the Butlers, it is said to have been built by 'Black Tom', Earl of Ormonde, to host Elizabeth I, who subsequently cancelled her proposed visit.

Despite their influence with the Crown, the Ormondes were not able to prevent the arrest of the Archbishop of Cashel, who was taken prisoner here and martyred in Dublin in 1584.

The Tipperary Crystal workshop and showroom are out on the N24.

i *Main Street*

▶ *Take the* ***N24*** *back to Waterford.*

LEINSTER

Leinster might well be called the 'Royal Province' of Ireland. Its 12 counties have harboured rulers from the days of the prehistoric clans who constructed the great burial mound at Newgrange to the High Kings of Ireland who ruled from the Hill of Tara, from Viking and Norman conquerors, to appointees of English kings and queens. Indeed, with Irish chieftains battling against invaders and each other, it seemed best to concentrate beleaguered Crown forces in 'The Pale', a heavily fortified area around Dublin.

At Clontarf, just outside Dublin, the great Irish High King Brian Boru defeated the Vikings in 1014. In 1649, Oliver Cromwell arrived with his dreaded 'Ironside' forces and proceeded to march from Dublin to Drogheda, where he slaughtered thousands of men, women and children. And in 1690, William of Orange's decisive victory at the Battle of the Boyne had a profound effect on Ireland's history that echoes down the centuries to the present day.

South of The Pale, County Wexford bears the scars of Viking occupation followed by Normans, who first landed in Ireland along this county's coast. Cromwell and the insurgents of 1798 left their imprint too. The lush countryside of Kilkenny lured the Normans, who dotted the landscape with castles and built a dignified town that soon rivalled Dublin as an administrative centre.

Inland, Athlone stands guard over County Westmeath's rural, lake-dotted landscape and the River Shannon that divides it from Connacht. Along the banks of that great waterway in County Offaly are the remains of one of Ireland's most awe-inspiring ecclesiastical settlements, Clonmacnoise. Kildare's Hill of Allen is thought to have been the winter quarters of Fionn MacCumhail's legendary Fianna warriors, but these days the county is known for its stud farms and Curragh race course.

Kilkenny Castle reflects the history and importance of this lovely town (Tour 14)

The lushness and variety of Leinster's landscape are as much a delight to today's visitors as they were to past conquerors, many of whom sprinkled it with great mansions and gardens. The lake-filled midland counties draw avid anglers and boating enthusiasts on the Shannon, and the seemingly inexhaustible bogs of counties Laois and Offaly yield peat to fuel 40 per cent of the Republic's electricity. Along the coast are curving bays and sandy beaches, as well as nature reserves inhabited by a wide range of wildlife.

Mount Usher Gardens (Tour 13) on the River Vartry

Tour 11
From the historically important Athlone and its modern-day riverboating, this tour takes you to the former garrison town of Mullingar, whose proximity to good trout lakes makes it an excellent angling centre. Then you travel to Tullamore, home of a world-famous distillery, and on to Birr, with its castle and garden. The monastic ruins of Clonmacnoise lend a spiritual aspect to your travels, as do the ruins at Clonfert.

Tour 12
This is a historic drive through Ireland's past, in pleasant countryside rich in megalithic and early Christian monuments, including the intriguing passage grave of Newgrange, exquisite high crosses at Monasterboice, Slane and its associations with St Patrick and the Hill of Tara, redolent of the heroic age of the High Kings of Ireland. The tour ends with the site of the Battle of the Boyne in 1690, where King William met King James to finish a conflict of national and European significance.

Tour 13
From Dublin, the tour visits bright coastal towns which owe much of their character to Victorian enthusiasm for the seaside. The route winds its way into the mountains, and visits Glendalough, one of Ireland's most captivating combinations of history and landscape. The scenery which follows combines bog, lake and mountaintop, and a highlight of this tour is the profusion of glorious gardens, justifying the claim that this area is 'the Garden of Ireland'.

Tour 14
Norman castles, ecclesiastical ruins and tales of medieval witches haunt Kilkenny, starting point for this tour. History and active river commerce meld happily in New Ross on the River Barrow. Further along the river, prehistory has left its mark just outside Carlow town in the form of an impressive dolmen. Kildare's horse country will appeal to followers of the sport of kings, and beautiful gardens near Portlaoise have universal appeal. Celtic kings and St Patrick draw you on to Cashel.

Tour 15
Founded by Vikings, invaded by Normans, conquered by Cromwell's troops, and a hotbed of insurgence, Wexford is an excellent tour base: north to the country's famed beaches, then inland for more history, before turning south to the river town of New Ross. South to Waterford, another Viking stronghold and the east coast's most important port, then a ferry ride to the enchanting Hook peninsula takes you through villages virtually undisturbed by 'progress', and on to a noted bird refuge and a holy island.

Monastic Ruins & The Midlands

Athlone is an important commercial and holiday centre, and a junction for road, rail and river traffic. Its marina on the Shannon has fleets of smart river cruisers for hire, and Athlone also has good facilities for anglers and golfers. Athlone Castle, overlooking the bridge, provides marvellous town views and has an interesting visitor centre. Another attraction is the Athlone Crystal factory.

1/2 DAYS • 141 MILES • 227KM

ITINERARY	
ATHLONE	▶ **Mullingar (44m-71km)**
MULLINGAR	▶ **Tullamore (22m-35km)**
TULLAMORE	▶ **Birr (23m-37km)**
BIRR	▶ **Clonmacnoise (22m-35km)**
CLONMACNOISE	▶ **Ballinasloe (14m-23km)**
BALLINASLOE	▶ **Athlone (16m-26km)**

SCENIC ROUTES

Leave Athlone on the N55 northeast, and about 2 miles (3km) outside town turn right on to the R390. At Ballymore, some 12 miles (19km) north-east of Athlone, look for the slight remains of a 14th-century Anglo-Norman fortress. Continue on the R390 for 4 miles (6km) to the 602-foot (183m) high Hill of Ushnagh. This was a place of religious importance during pagan times, as it was the accepted centre of the universe, and from the summit there are fine views of Ireland's vast central plain. There are burial mounds and an earthen fort, and on the southwest side of the summit, Aill na Mireann (The Stone of Divisions) is thought to mark the boundaries of all five ancient provinces of Ireland.

Mullingar Cathedral is famous for its mosaics and its ecclesiastical museum

RECOMMENDED WALKS

On Lough Ree's western shore, about 8 miles (13km) from Athlone, Rinndown Peninsula juts out into the lake just east of the village of Lecarrow. Follow the unnumbered road from Lecarrow until it becomes a track leading to the lakeshore. The heavily wooded path passes ancient ruins from the 13th century that combine with the dense shade to create a somewhat spooky atmosphere. The walk takes in the remains of St John's Castle (so named for the Knights of St John who once occupied it) and a church with its outbuildings.

i *Athlone Castle, St Peter's Square, Athlone*

▶ *Take the **N55** northeast from Athlone to the town of Edgeworthstown, then turn southeast on to the **N4** for the drive to Mullingar.*

0 Mullingar, Co Westmeath

En route to Mullingar, stop by in Edgeworthstown, the village named after the Edgeworth family. The father of the family was a noted inventor and author, and his daughter Maria became one of Ireland's leading women writers. She holds a special place in Irish affections for her work among the suffering during the famine years. A friend of Sir Walter Scott, her best known work was *Castle Rackrent.*

If you plan to eat steak in Ireland, Mullingar is the place to do it, in the heart of Ireland's cattle-raising area. The county town of Westmeath, Mullingar's long history includes a position of prime importance as a barracks town for the British military. During the Williamite Wars, it was here that British commander de Ginkel rallied his forces for the 1691 siege of Athlone. The imprint of those years is stamped on the town's face even today in the form of large, grey, rather formidable buildings. The present-day personality of the town,

Tullynally Castle's rather grim exterior belies its splendid interior and works of art

however, in no way reflects its somewhat grim past, and Mullingar is an excellent base for seeing the Westmeath lakes, most of which offer excellent brown trout fishing.

The Cathedral of Christ the King, designed by Ralph Byrne, has outstanding mosaics of St Patrick and St Anne near the high altar that are the work of Russian artist Boris Anrep. Permission must be obtained from the sacristan to see the ecclesiastical museum.

Cloudy ancient mirrors, original order books and a little-changed interior are all reminders that Canten Casey's Pub is 200 years old – a unique look back into Ireland's past.

In July, Mullingar celebrates eligible bachelors from all round the world, with the International Bachelor Festival.

Travel in almost any direction from Mullingar and you can find the lakes that have made this region famous for trout. Lough Ennell is about 6 miles (10km) to the south, with a championship golf course overlooking the lake and the ruins of ancient Lynn Church on its northeastern shore. Three miles (5km) north of town, Lough Owel is a sailing and sub-aqua centre, and there are good swimming facilities. About 6 miles (10km) north of town, Lough Derravaragh is a beautiful, irregular-shaped lake with thickly wooded shores. It plays a central part in one of Ireland's most tragic and beloved legends, since it was one of three lakes on which the Children of Lir were doomed to spend 300 years when their wicked stepmother turned them into swans. Swans on Irish waters are still under the protection granted to all swans by the grieving father.

For good views of the lakes and plains, Rathconnell Hill is just 2 miles (3km) northeast of Mullingar off the N52. Lough Owel is part of the view from 499-foot (152m) Shanemore (Slanemore) Hill, 4 miles (6km) northwest of town. Thirteen miles (21km) north of Mullingar via the R394, Tullynally Castle and Gardens, in Castlepollard, are one of County Westmeath's chief attractions. Seat of the Earls of Longford since the 17th century, the turreted and towered Gothic-revival manor house has a two-storey Great Hall with a vaulted ceiling and impressive collections of art, china and furnishings. Life 'downstairs' in such a great house is depicted in the museum housed in the courtyard, Victorian kitchens and laundries. The 30-acre (12-hectare) grounds offer woodland walks, a water garden and Victorian grotto.

The village of Fore, about 3 miles (5km) east of Castlepollard, is the setting for an interesting group of antiquities. Before exploring, stop at the Abbey Pub to see paintings of the 'Seven Wonders of Fore'. Partly restored St Fechin's Church is a fine example of early church architecture, with a massive lintel stone on the west door that legend says was placed there by the saint himself. Then there is the Benedictine priory whose loophole windows and square towers give it the look of a castle; the 'Holy Trinity tree' that has never had but three branches; the spring beside the tree whose water never boils; and St Fechin's Mill, with a miraculous underground water supply. To the east of the village, there is a large motte thought to be an early Anglo-Norman fortification, and within a 1-mile (1.5km) radius there are nine ancient crosses.

i *Dublin Road (N4)*

▶ *Continue south for 22 miles (35km) on the* ***N52*** *for Tullamore.*

2 Tullamore, Co Offaly
On the drive from Mullingar, stop off at the village of Kilbeggan, 7 miles (11km) north of Tullamore, where a museum, antiques shop and café now occupy the restored 18th-century Locke's Distillery, once one of Europe's largest.

The chief town of County Offaly, Tullamore owes its development to the Grand Canal laid out in 1798 to connect Dublin to the Shannon. The canal carried huge cargoes of yellow brick made in the town to Dublin during its expansion in the 19th century.

Tullamore was the home of the Irish Mist Distillery, producers of Ireland's leading liqueur whiskey.

St Catherine's is the fine Gothic-style church you see perched on top of Hop Hill overlooking the town.

BACK TO NATURE

About 7 miles (11km) northwest of Tullamore, Clara Bog is one of the largest intact bogs of its type in Ireland. Its well-developed 'soak' system is considered to be the best in western Europe. Increased water flow from surface run-off or underground springs allows the growth of many more plant species than are normally found in a bog environment. Among those that thrive here are bog mosses, sundews, heathers, cotton grass, and bog rosemary. There are hummock/hollow complexes, bog pools and moss lawns. The bog is easily seen from the road, but is considered unsafe for exploration on foot.

▶ *Follow the* ***N52*** *for 23 miles (37km) southwest to Birr.*

3 Birr, Co Offaly
Plan a stop in the village of Kilcormac, about 12 miles (19km) south of Tullamore on the N52, for a look at the beautifully carved wooden pietà in the Catholic church, which is thought to be the work of a 16th-century artist. Attractive Georgian buildings and a world-famous castle and garden are the main attractions in the small town of Birr, just above the confluence of the Little Bronsa and Camcor Rivers.

Tullamore is a favoured starting point for narrowboat cruises on the Grand Canal

History and science combine at Birr Castle to provide a fascinating day out

Birr Castle is an impressive fortified manor house set in extensive grounds. Only the grounds are open to the public, since it has, for several centuries, been the residence of the Earls of Rosse. The 3rd Earl was a noted astronomer, whose giant 72-inch (180cm) reflecting telescope, built to his own design in 1845, was the largest in the world for an astounding 80 years. The telescope has been restored to full working order. The scientific museum at Birr Castle is being developed as Ireland's Historic Science Centre. The castle gardens cover 100 acres (40 hectares), laid out on the banks of the two rivers and around a lake. More than 1,000 species of plants and trees include magnolias, cherry trees, chestnut trees and weeping beeches, as well as box hedges named as the tallest in the world by the Guinness Book of Records.

[i] *Castle Street*

FOR CHILDREN

At Shannonbridge, north of Birr on the N62, is a narrow-gauge railway trip across a stretch of bogland, with a guide giving a commentary. A slide show precedes the tour.

▶ *Take the* ***N62*** *north to Cloghan, and turn west on to the* ***R357*** *to Shannonbridge. Then follow a signposted unclassified road north for 4 miles (6km) to Clonmacnoise.*

4 Clonmacnoise, Co Offaly

Set beside the River Shannon, this is one of Ireland's holiest places. St Ciaran's monastery, founded here in AD 548, became the most famous of Ireland's monastic cities and was one of Europe's leading centres of learning for nearly 1,000 years. It enjoyed the patronage of many Irish Kings, and Rory O'Conor, the last High King, lies buried here. Its great fame and wealth attracted plunderers from home and abroad, and the final indignity came in 1552 when the English garrison at Athlone carried off spoils that included even the glass from the windows, and the site was finally abandoned. Restoration began in 1647, but Cromwellian forces carried out yet another raid that put paid to the revival of its former glory. Today, the site holds a cathedral, one of

SPECIAL TO ...

Each year on 9 September and the following Sunday, great throngs, drawn from around the world, make the pilgrimage to Clonmacnoise to commemorate St Ciaran's feast day.

eight church ruins, two round towers, three sculptured high crosses (and parts of two others), over 200 monumental slabs and a ruined castle. St Ciaran's grave is said to be in the east end of 'The Little Church', a small 9th-century cell.

i *Clonmacnoise site*

*Return to Shannonbridge and turn northwest on to the **R357** for the 8-mile (13km) drive to Ballinasloe.*

5 Ballinasloe, Co Galway
In a strategic position of military importance in the past, Ballinasloe once centred around its castle, but today it is a thriving market town. Seven miles (11km) from town on the Athenry road is the Abbey of Kilconnell, founded in 1400. Its nave, choir, side aisles, south transept, and some of the cloisters are in perfect condition.

Clonfert, 13 miles (21km) southeast of Ballinasloe, was the site chosen by St Brendan in the 6th century for a monastic settlement, of which nothing remains today. The church has superb Romanesque decoration, with various motifs, including animal and human heads and intricate carvings of foliage.

i *Main Street*

*Take the **N6** northeast to return to Athlone.*

FOR HISTORY BUFFS

Following their defeat at the battle of the Boyne in 1690, Irish forces who supported King James withdrew to the town of Athlone to establish the Shannon as their last line of defence against the English. Their leader, Colonel Grace, held the castle for King James and withstood a week's siege from the pursuing Williamite army. In 1691, however, the English commander laid siege to the town. The Irish, retreating across the Shannon, destroyed the bridge, but the English started rebuilding it immediately. A heroic Irish Sergeant, Custume, then called for volunteers and with a handful of men managed to break down the hastily thrown-up structure. As a result, the town held out for another ten days, after which Irish Jacobite forces withdrew.

SPECIAL TO...

Ballinasloe's great Fair carries on for eight days of fierce trading, street entertainment, and non-stop revelry. It is one of the few such fairs still held in modern Ireland.

FOR CHILDREN

Children will enjoy the Lough Ree cruises from Athlone, as they slide by the romantic and slightly mysterious wooded islands in the lake, including Hare Island.

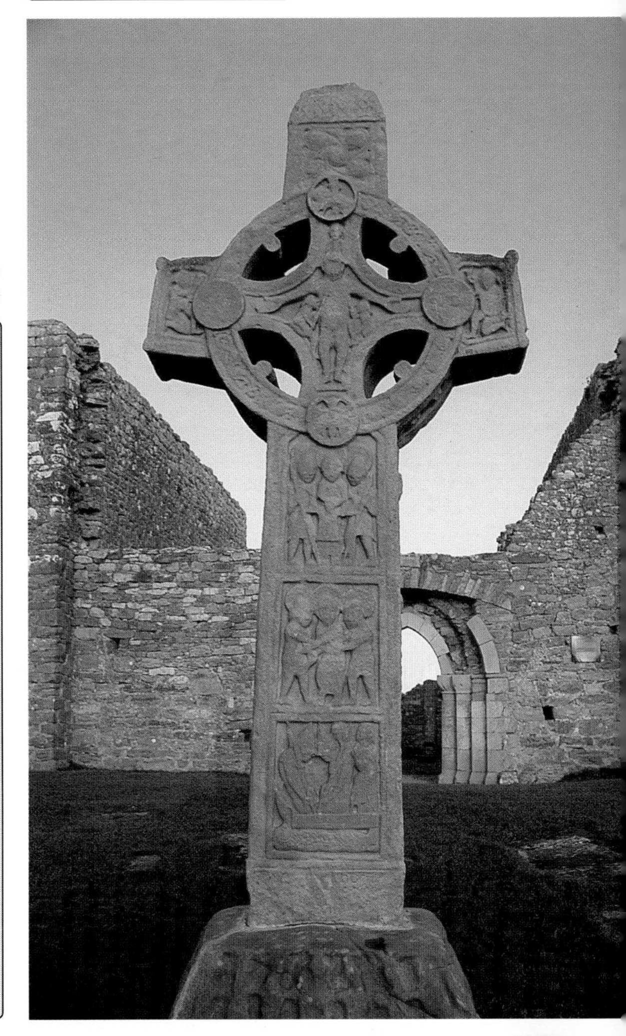

One of the three intact carved high crosses of Clonmacnoise

TOUR 12

The Boyne Valley

The great grassy mound of Millmount, which gives a panoramic view over Drogheda, was first a passage grave, then a Viking meeting place, a Norman motte, and an important military barracks in the 18th century, its history mirroring that of the town. Some of Millmount's buildings have been converted into a small museum. A view from any point of the town will show that Drogheda is a town of churches, including St Peter's which contains the head of martyred Oliver Plunkett.

2 DAYS • 84 MILES • 134KM

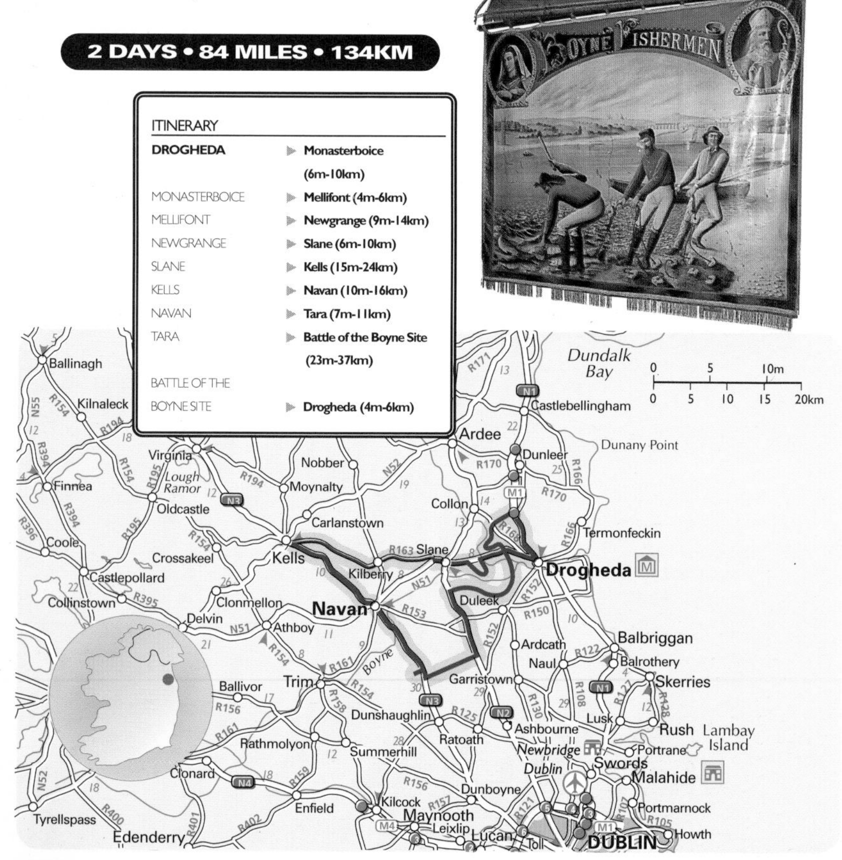

ITINERARY	
DROGHEDA	▶ **Monasterboice (6m-10km)**
MONASTERBOICE	▶ **Mellifont (4m-6km)**
MELLIFONT	▶ **Newgrange (9m-14km)**
NEWGRANGE	▶ **Slane (6m-10km)**
SLANE	▶ **Kells (15m-24km)**
KELLS	▶ **Navan (10m-16km)**
NAVAN	▶ **Tara (7m-11km)**
TARA	▶ **Battle of the Boyne Site (23m-37km)**
BATTLE OF THE BOYNE SITE	▶ **Drogheda (4m-6km)**

The superb frontage of St Peter's church in Drogheda

[i] *Drogheda*

BACK TO NATURE

Visit Mornington sand dunes, which lie close to Drogheda on the coast. The dunes grade from newly formed areas, colonised by marram grass close to the sea, towards mature 'slacks' inland. The latter support a rich variety of plants including many orchids in the spring.

SCENIC ROUTES

This part of the eastern coast of Ireland may lack the grandeur of the north and west, but there is pleasant, gentle scenery with sandy beaches and shingle shores on the road from Drogheda to Mornington, Bettsytown, Laytown and Julianstown. The road follows the estuary of the Boyne, close to the great railway viaduct.

▶ *Take the **N1** for Belfast. After 5 miles (8km) turn left, following signposts for Boyne Drive, Monasterboice. In ½ mile (1km) turn left again.*

0 Monasterboice, Co Louth

Pick your way between ancient and modern graves to see two of the finest high crosses. These free-standing carvings in stone are of a quality unparalleled anywhere in Europe at the time they were erected, and yet the very high round tower is a reminder that these remarkable works of art were executed in the midst of Viking plunder. The West Cross stands close to the round tower, while the Cross of Muiredach – so called because of the inscription on the base, which says 'A prayer for Muiredach by whom this cross was made' – is smaller and more perfect in appearance. The messages on these crosses follow coherent themes of God's grace to man and the parallels between Old and New Testaments. On Muiredach's Cross look for the stories of Adam and Eve, Cain and Abel, the Last Judgement and the Crucifixion of Christ.

An event of religious significance of more recent times was the visit of Pope John Paul in 1979, and the point where he celebrated Mass is marked on the main Belfast-Dublin road.

▶ *Continue on past Monasterboice. After a mile (2km), turn right for Mellifont. After a mile (2km) turn left on to the Drogheda road,* ***R168****, and after a further mile (2km) turn right for Mellifont.*

2 Mellifont, Co Louth

In a pleasant valley beside the River Mattock, Malachy, the former Archbishop of Armagh, founded the first Cistercian monastery in Ireland in 1142. A substantial square gate-house still stands, but only fragments of this great monastery now remain, including arches of a Romanesque cloister and a chapter house. An octagonal lavabo once equipped with water jets and basins is the most interesting structure.

▶ *Return to the crossroads and turn right. After 2 miles (3km) turn right. Go straight over the crossroads, following the signpost to King William's Glen. After 1 mile (1.5km) turn right on to the* ***N51****, then 2½ miles (4km) further on, turn left and follow signs for Newgrange.*

3 Newgrange, Knowth and Dowth, Co Meath

Irish architecture may be said to have begun in the Boyne Valley, when, in about 3000BC, people who had only stone and wood for tools created the most impressive monuments of their kind in western Europe. Little is known of these people, or of those interred in these prehistoric tombs, but excavations have shown that they were cultivators of crops and had cleared areas of forest.

The mound at Newgrange, constructed with water-rolled pebbles, rises to a height of 36 feet (11m), its mass retained by a kerb of great stone blocks lying end to end, topped by white quartz and granite boulders. The passage is lined by huge stones, and the central cross-shaped chamber is roofed with a vault untouched in five millenia. Standing around the mound is an incomplete circle of stones.

At Dowth, a larger passage-tomb has two chambers, while Knowth has two passage-tombs surrounded by 18 smaller ones. Knowth was used from the Stone Age, and in the early Christian era was a seat of the High Kings of Ireland. The significance of the Boyne Valley tombs is that here art combines with the engineering feats of the passage-tombs of Ireland. Spirals, lozenges, zigzags, sunbursts – figures cut in stone with stone implements – decorate the monuments.

At Newgrange the sophisticated structure incorporates the

St Patrick's conversion of Ireland to Christianity took a leap forward at Slane in 433

unique phenomenon of a roof-box, which, only at the winter solstice, allows the rays of the rising sun to penetrate the chamber and flood it with light. Newgrange is shown by guided tours, and at busy times you will have to arrive early in the day to ensure admission. Archaeological work continues, and important discoveries are still being made in the Boyne Valley which means that sites may be closed at times for excavation.

▶ *Return by minor roads to the **N51** and turn left for Slane.*

4 **Slane,** Co Meath

Slane occupies an attractive curve on the River Boyne and is overlooked by the Hill of Slane, where, tradition has it, St Patrick lit his paschal fire in AD433 in defiance of the orders of King Laoghaire. In his persuasive speech to the King, Patrick used the shamrock as his illustration of the Trinity. He won his argument and permission to preach Christianity throughout the land. From the viewpoint on the hill, the pleasant village can be seen running steeply down to the banks of the river.

Just to the east is the cottage of the poet Francis Ledwidge, who died during World War I.

Slane Castle on the banks of the River Boyne is the home of the Mount Charles family. Badly damaged by fire in 1991, it is not open to the public, but the magnificent amphitheatre in front of the house is used regularly to stage spectacular rock concerts.

[i] *Main Street*

▶ *Take the **N51** for Navan, and after 1 mile (2km) turn right on to the **R163** for Kells.*

5 **Kells,** Co Meath

Kells, or Ceanannus Mór, was one of the great religious centres of western Europe. You can pick out the circular ditch in the lie of the town, and see the round tower, an early church and the impressive Celtic crosses with their scriptural messages. The town is famous for the *Book of Kells*, the celebrated illuminated medieval manuscript, now on view in the library at Trinity College, Dublin.

[i] *Headfort Place*

▶ *Take the **N3** to Navan.*

6 **Navan,** Co Meath

Once a walled town, Navan marks the meeting of the waters of the Boyne and the Blackwater. Look out for the stocks outside the town hall, and a very modern blue sculpture, which is dedicated to 'the Fifth Province, the ideal of the cultural integration of all the people of Ireland.' The town has a good race course.

Close by are the ruins of Athlumney Castle, Dunmoe Castle and Bective Abbey.

[i] *Railway Street*

Tara, just a simple mound today, evokes a glorious past

FOR HISTORY BUFFS

Trim, south of Navan, is worth visiting for King John's Castle alone, the largest Norman castle in Ireland. It also has the Yellow Steeple, which was once part of an Augustinian monastery, a statue of the Duke of Wellington, who was educated here, and a small cathedral with a 15th-century tower. Richard, Duke of York, father of Edward IV, made Trim his Irish headquarters and initiated building projects in the town. Trim Castle, somewhat extended by set carpenters, featured in the film *Braveheart.*

▶ *Take the **N3** for Dublin, and after 6 miles (10km) turn right at the signpost for Tara.*

7 **Tara,** Co Meath

The seat of the High Kings of Ireland, the Hill of Tara commands majestic views over the fertile plains of Meath and beyond. This was the centre of Ireland's heroic age, a civilisation that had contact with the Roman Empire and was ruled by a king who was concerned with sacred rites and rituals as well as political matters. A *feis* at royal Tara was a renowned festivity, held at harvest, or for the crowning of a king, of which the dynastic O'Neills were the strongest.

Five chariot roads led here from all parts of Ireland. The Rath of the Synods is an elaborate trivallate earthwork. The Mound of the Hostages, a Stone Age passage-tomb that stands inside the Royal Enclosure, is an Iron-Age hillfort and encloses the Royal Seat, a ringfort. On Cormac's House is the Stone of Destiny, said to be the inauguration stone of the kings. Also here are the Banquet Hall, the Enclosure of King Laoghaire, the Sloping Trenches and Grainne's Enclosure. A statue of St Patrick recalls his profound influence, but it was the coming of Christianity that led to the eventual decline of Tara.

[i] *Hill of Tara*

▶ *Return to the* **N3** *and turn right. After 2 miles (3km) turn left following signs to Skreen Church and Cross, go straight over two sets of crossroads and follow a narrow, uneven road for 4½ miles (7km), then turn left towards Drogheda. After 1 mile (2km) turn left towards Slane on the* **N2** *and follow the marked route for the Battle of the Boyne Site.*

8 Battle of the Boyne Site, Co Louth and Meath

It does not take a great effort of the imagination to picture the field of battle in 1690, when the armies of William of Orange and James II met each other in a conflict that was significant for Ireland, Britain and Europe. A huge orange and green sign beside the deep waters of the Boyne marks the main site of the conflict, while helpful signs along the way show where the opposing armies camped, where battle was joined and where the river was crossed. The route passes along the Boyne Navigation Canal, once a link in Ireland's waterways system.

▶ *Take the* **N51** *to Drogheda.*

SPECIAL TO...

The pastures of Meath are among the richest in Ireland. Much of the land has not been ploughed for generations and provides excellent grassland for cattle and horses. In summer the pride of the country can be seen at many agricultural shows. As well as the show classes, you will find pony and horse jumping, home industries competitions, and get a real feel of the farming life at the heart of Ireland. Another part of the country's agricultural heritage is reflected in the Steam Threshing Festival at Moynalty, which recalls the harvesting methods of the past.

A cottage wall mural depicts Ireland's most famous battle

RECOMMENDED WALKS

At Townley Hall, the Forest and Wildlife Service has developed a waymarked trail that takes the walker close to the site of the Battle of the Boyne, and gives views over the valley. The walk up the wooded banks of the river is steep in places. A trail leaflet is available from the battle site.

FOR CHILDREN

As a complete antidote to the historical saturation of the Boyne Valley, try the ultra-modern attractions of Mosney Holiday Centre, south of Drogheda. The country's first subtropical funpool offers the Black Hole, the Swamp Experience and the Dragon Ride, as well as other popular amusements.

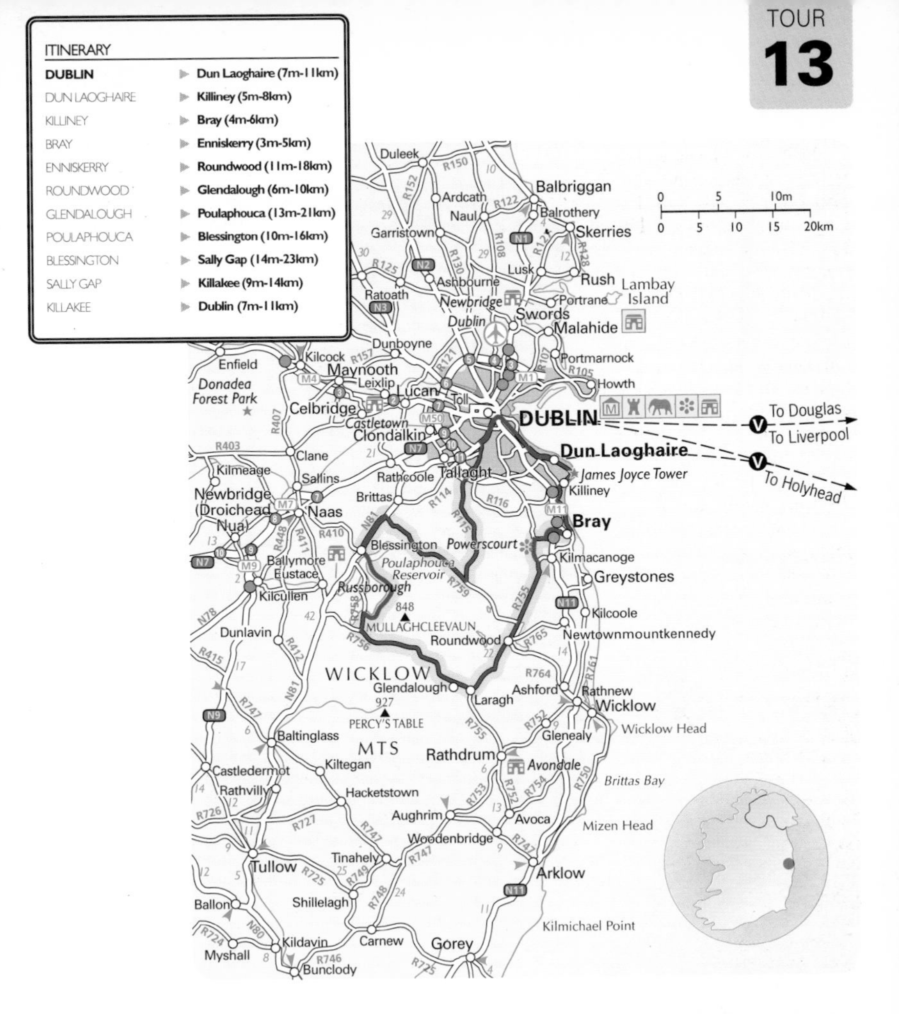

ITINERARY

DUBLIN	▶ Dun Laoghaire (7m-11km)
DUN LAOGHAIRE	▶ Killiney (5m-8km)
KILLINEY	▶ Bray (4m-6km)
BRAY	▶ Enniskerry (3m-5km)
ENNISKERRY	▶ Roundwood (11m-18km)
ROUNDWOOD	▶ Glendalough (6m-10km)
GLENDALOUGH	▶ Poulaphouca (13m-21km)
POULAPHOUCA	▶ Blessington (10m-16km)
BLESSINGTON	▶ Sally Gap (14m-23km)
SALLY GAP	▶ Killakee (9m-14km)
KILLAKEE	▶ Dublin (7m-11km)

Dublin & Wicklow

1/2 DAYS • 89 MILES • 143KM

Dublin is a lively and attractive city with a unique brand of Irishness. Easy to explore on foot, it has superb museums, galleries and shopping, elegant Georgian streets and the historic Temple Bar area, with its narrow lanes, pubs and restaurants. The River Liffey cuts the city in two, and the lovely Wicklow Mountains rise to the south.

i *Suffolk Street, Dublin*

SPECIAL TO...

If you have never ordered a Guinness in Ireland before, do not be surprised if you have to wait a while. It takes a good barman some time to pour the black porter or stout, let it sit, and then achieve a creamy head with perfect consistency. If you trace your initial on the top, it should still be on the cream by the time you are draining the glass. Drink it with champagne and it is 'Black Velvet', drink it with oysters and it is a festival. You can see where they have been brewing Guinness since 1759 at St James's Gate in Dublin.

Elegant Georgian houses add an air of distinction to the resort and port of Dun Laoghaire

▶ *Take the* ***R118*** *for 7 miles (11km) to Dun Laoghaire.*

1 Dun Laoghaire, Co Dublin

This is a place to promenade, along the extensive harbour piers, past the villas on the front, or through the parks. Savour the Victorian features of the place which was called Kingstown from the visit of George IV in 1821 until the establishment of the Irish Free State. When the granite piers were completed in 1859, the harbour was the biggest artificial haven in the world. Ships and ferries to England use the port and it is home to several yacht clubs, of which the Royal St George and the Royal Irish are the oldest. The town also boasts Ireland's National Maritime Museum, housed in the Mariners' Church.

Near by, at Sandycove, is a Martello tower, one of the distinctive squat round coastal defences erected in Napoleonic times. This one houses a James Joyce Museum (the writer stayed here briefly). The Martello tower and the nearby 'Forty foot' gentlemen's bathing place form a vividly described part of his novel *Ulysses*.

▶ *Take the* ***R119*** *coastal road to Dalkey and Killiney.*

2 Killiney, Co Dublin

With the broad sweep of a steeply dropping bay, elegant villas among tree-filled gardens and the two Sugar Loaf mountains to complete the vista, Killiney has been likened to the Bay of Naples. A good place to take in the full extent of the panorama is Sorrento Point.

Another good viewpoint is Killiney Hill, some distance inland from the beach, where an attractive park on the summit gives superb views of the hills and sea. Its 18th-century stone obelisk was built as a famine relief project.

▶ *Continue on the* ***R119****, then join the* ***N11*** *to Bray.*

3 Bray, Co Wicklow

A popular resort that retains much of its Victorian attraction, Bray's long beach stretches below the strong line of Bray Head, an extension of the Wicklow dome. From the promenade you can walk the outstanding cliff path for 3 miles (5km) to Greystones. Below the Head, fan-like fossils of the oldest known Irish animals have been found. In the town is an attractive Heritage Centre. Close by is Dargle Glen, a lovely wooded valley set in rugged mountains. Dargle Glen Gardens, which combine excellent planting with works of art, are occasionally opened to the public by their owner.

Kilruddery, by contrast, was one of the great set-piece landscape gardens of the 17th century. Very few of these early formal gardens, designed on a large scale with geometric patterns of water, avenues and plants, now survive.

*Return to and take the **N11** for Wicklow, then turn right for Enniskerry.*

4 Enniskerry, Co Wicklow
The first Irish Roman Catholic Gothic revival church was built in this pretty village in 1843. Its spire is an attractive feature in the lovely glen of Glencullen.

The superb mountain setting enhances Powerscourt, one of Ireland's great gardens, extravagantly created by the 6th and 7th Viscounts Powerscourt, and extensively altered between 1843 and 1875. A formal landscape of water, terraces, statues, ironwork, plants, flowers and ancient trees is stunningly contrasted with the natural beauty of Sugar Loaf Mountain, combining to form one of the most photographed vistas in the country. The house, a magnificent Palladian mansion, was destroyed by fire in 1974, but has been partly restored. Also in the estate is Powerscourt Waterfall where the Dargle river plunges over a face 400 feet (120m) high.

*Take the **R760** south, turning left to Killough. Take the **R755** for 8 miles (13km) to Roundwood.*

5 Roundwood, Co Wicklow
The highest village in Ireland, Roundwood sits amid lovely scenery. The Vartry Reservoir, which helps to serve Dublin, lies close to the village. To the northeast is the Glen of the Downs, a dry rocky gorge formed in the Ice Age, with an oak wood. The landscape gives an idea of what Ireland would have looked like in prehistoric times, before the clearance of the forests. Lough Dan and Lough Tay are dark loughs shadowed by granite.

Six miles (10km) southeast of Roundwood at Ashford is Mount Usher, one of the finest examples of the 'Wild Garden', an idea particularly suited to Irish gardens. In a sheltered valley, plants, which include many exotic species, grow naturally and in abundance in perfect harmony with the gentle landscape. They spread along the banks of a winding stream with cascades that are spanned by unusual suspension bridges.

*Continue on the **R755** to Laragh, then turn right on to the **R756** to Glendalough.*

FOR CHILDREN

Clara is the smallest village in Ireland, with two houses, a church and a school. It lies in a beautiful valley southeast of Glendalough. Children will enjoy the Clara Lara Funpark on the banks of the Avonmore river, which has boating, an adventure playground, picnic and barbecue sites and fishing at a trout farm.

Within the beautiful Powerscourt Demesne is this lovely waterfall, with woodland walks and picnic places near by

6 Glendalough, Co Wicklow

Glendalough, the glen of two loughs, is the loveliest and most historic of all its Wicklow rivals. Two beautiful loughs lie deep in a valley of granite escarpments and rocky outcrops. On its green slopes are the gentle contours of native trees, on its ridges the jagged outline of pines. Add to this picturesque scene a soaring round tower and ruined stone churches spreading through the valley, and you have a combination which makes Glendalough one of the most beautiful and historic places in Ireland. St Kevin came to Glendalough in the 6th century to escape worldly pleasures. He lived as a hermit, in a cell on a little shelf above the lake, but the settlement he founded flourished and grew to become a monastic city whose influence spread throughout Europe. The round tower was built when Viking raids troubled the serenity of Glendalough. Some of the little churches have fine stone carvings, and one has a good pitched stone roof. Guides will explain the full story of Glendalough, and a visitor

Glendalough's round tower is a prominent landmark in this very special valley

centre skilfully illustrates the life of a monastery.

To the south near Rathdrum is Avondale, the home of the great Irish leader Charles Stewart Parnell. The 18th-century house, now a museum, is set in a large beautiful forest park on the banks of the Avonmore river.

BACK TO NATURE

The wide open spaces of the Wicklow Mountains offer opportunities for seeing a variety of upland birds, including peregrines, merlins, hen harriers, ring ousels and red grouse. In the glens, wood warblers and the occasional redstart may be seen.

▶ *Follow the **R756** through the Wicklow Gap, then turn right on to the **R758** for Poulaphouca.*

FOR HISTORY BUFFS

Patrick Pearse, one of the leaders of the uprising in 1916, kept a school in St Enda's Park. The building has now been converted into a museum dedicated to his memory.

7 Poulaphouca, Co Wicklow

At Poulaphouca there are large lakes, now dammed to supply Dublin's water system and also forming part of the Liffey hydroelectric scheme. The proximity to the city and the abundance of lakeside roads make it a popular venue for Dubliners.

▶ *Follow the lakeside road by Lackan to Blessington.*

8 Blessington, Co Wicklow

An attractive village with a long main street, Blessington was an important coaching stop on the main road south from Dublin.

Just south is Russborough House, serenely placed in a beautiful landscape before a fine lake. It was built in the middle of the 18th century, the work of architect Richard Castle, for Joseph Leeson, the Earl of Milltown. A Palladian house constructed of granite, it sweeps out elegantly along curving colonnades to flanking wings and pavilions. Decorative features include superb plasterwork by the Francini brothers, and the house now contains the famous Beit Art Collection.

▶ *Take the **N81** for Dublin. After 4½ miles (7km) turn right on to the **R759** to the Sally Gap.*

FOR HISTORY BUFFS

Wicklow men played a large part in the 1798 rebellion, and in order to finally suppress the uprising and clear the mountains, the 'Military Road' was forged from Rathfarnham in the north through the Sally Gap to Aghavannagh in the south. Former barracks can be seen at Drumgoff and Aghavannagh.

9 The Sally Gap, Co Wicklow

The most complete stretch of blanket bog on the east of the country is the beautiful Sally Gap. There are many pools and streams here, as well as the characteristic bog plant, the bog rosemary.

SCENIC ROUTES

The road from Sally Gap to Laragh rises and falls wonderfully, with views across the Cloghoge Valley to War Hill. The road goes south through rugged mountain land, into forest plantations and passes Glenmacnass, a deep glen formed by glaciers, with a magnificent waterfall.

▶ *Turn sharp left on to the **R115** to Killakee.*

10 Killakee, Co Dublin

The view from Killakee gives an outstanding picture of Dublin, as George Moore put it, 'wandering between the hills and the sea'. It takes in the crescent of Dublin Bay, bounded by the twin bastions of Howth Head to the north and Killiney Head to the south. The River Liffey is clearly defined, and you can identify the green landmark of Phoenix Park.

South of Killakee is a sinister hilltop ruin, once a retreat of the Hell Fire Club which was formed by a group of rakes in 1735. There are colourful tales of their terrible wickedness, the worst involving a game of cards with the devil.

North of Killakee, towards Dublin, is Marlay Park, with a river, wood, miniature railway and craft centre. In the same area is Rathfarnham Castle, which dates back to 1583. It has been declared a national monument, and is presented to the public as a building undergoing active conservation.

▶ *Follow the **R115** for 7 miles (11km) back to Dublin.*

RECOMMENDED WALKS

The Wicklow Way is a long-distance walk that follows a course from Marlay Park in the north to Shillelagh and then through into County Kilkenny, on high ground on the east of the Dublin and Wicklow Mountains. The route is mostly waymarked through forests, along old bog roads and up steep mountain tracks. It is best to come equipped for wet weather and wear strong walking shoes. In addition, there are dozens of forest walks through Wicklow.

TOUR 14

Witches Castles & Horses

ITINERARY

KILKENNY	▶ Thomastown (11m-18km)
THOMASTOWN	▶ New Ross (16m-26km)
NEW ROSS	▶ Carlow (34m-55km)
CARLOW	▶ Kildare (34m-55km)
KILDARE	▶ Portlaoise (20m-32km)
PORTLAOISE	▶ Abbeyleix (9m-14km)
ABBEYLEIX	▶ Thurles (30m-48km)
THURLES	▶ Cashel (13m-21km)
CASHEL	▶ Fethard (10m-16km)
FETHARD	▶ Kilkenny (24m-39km)

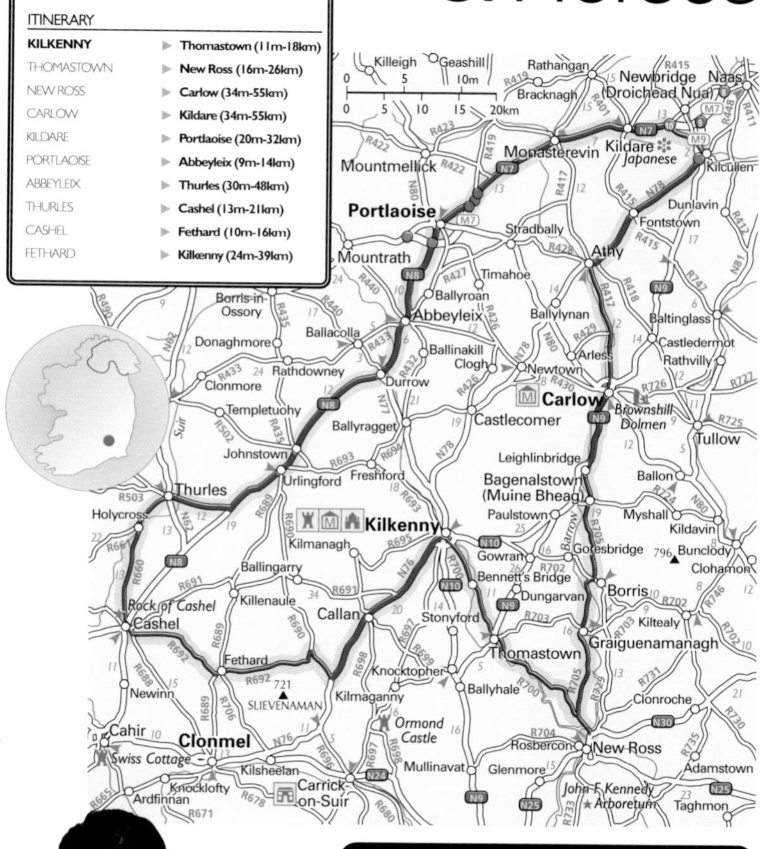

2/3 DAYS • 201 MILES • 324KM

Kilkenny is an ancient town that once rivalled Dublin in importance, and many of its historic buildings have been preserved, including the splendid 14th-century castle, perched above the river. Kilkenny is also the home of the Kilkenny Design Centre, promoting the best in Irish design and craftsmanship. The centre has craft workshops as well as the showroom.

SPECIAL TO...

Kilkenny was the home of Ireland's most famous witches. In 1324 Dame Alice Kyteler was the owner of Kyteler's Inn is St Kieran's Street. A beautiful woman who had become wealthy following the successive deaths of her four husbands, she was accused of witchcraft and condemned to a public whipping, followed by burning at the stake. She escaped, leaving her maid to be burnt in her place, and was never seen again. She is said to haunt the house still. Each August, Kilkenny Arts Festival takes place, when the town is host to world-class musicians and performers.

i Shee Alms House, Rose Inn Street

*Take the **R700** southeast for 11 miles (18km) to Thomastown.*

1 Thomastown, Co Kilkenny

This prosperous little market town on the banks of the River Nore is named after Thomas FitzAnthony Walsh, Seneschal of Leinster, who built a castle and walled the town in the early 13th century. Grennan Castle, about 1½ miles (2km) to the southwest, is now in ruins. The most impressive remains of ancient buildings in the town are those of a large church dating from the 13th century.

Jerpoint Cistercian Abbey, some 2 miles (3km) southwest of Thomastown on the N9, is one of Ireland's finest monastic ruins. Founded in the 12th century, it was dissolved and its lands given to the Ormonde family in 1540. The extensive remains are awe-inspiring, with the original Romanesque pillars, a fine chancel and the most decorative cloister arcade of any Irish church. The detailed secular and religious carved figures are an accurate portrayal of the armour and clothing of 15th- and 16th-century Ireland. A visitor centre provides information on the abbey's long history. Mount Juliet, signposted from the town centre, was once one of Ireland's largest private

Delightful formal gardens contrast with the forbidding stone walls of Kilkenny Castle

estates, covering 1,411 acres (570 hectares) of woodlands, pastures and landscaped lawns. Now a luxury hotel, the grounds provide an exceptionally beautiful drive off the main roads, and its public rooms are open to non-residents.

RECOMMENDED WALKS

From Thomastown walk along the banks of the River Nore for 1½ miles (2km) to the southwest to reach the remains of 13th-century Grennan Castle. The river walk is through woodland, with patches of rich pasture, and the lawn between the castle ruins and the river is covered with daffodils in spring.

SCENIC ROUTES

Leaving Thomastown by the R703 east, the 8-mile (13km) drive to Graiguenamanagh provides tremendous views of the River Barrow and the long ridge of the Blackstairs Mountains and 1,694-foot (516m) Brandon Hill which lies to the south.

▶ *Take the **R700** southeast for 14 miles (23m) to Mountgarret Bridge, where it joins the **N30** for the short drive to New Ross.*

2 New Ross, Co Wexford

There is much evidence of its medieval origins in the narrow streets of New Ross, climbing the steep hill on which the town is built, overlooking the River Barrow. The town invites exploration on foot, as many of the streets are stepped and inaccessible to vehicles. The long bridge in the town centre connects New Ross to County Kilkenny. The original bridge was built around 1200 and the town was soon walled. In 1643, it held off a siege by the Duke of Ormonde, but fell to Cromwell just six years later. It was captured and then lost by insurgents in 1798, leaving the town in flames and many of its inhabitants slain.

The Tholsel (Town Hall) had to be rebuilt in 1806 when the original 18th-century structure fell victim to subsidence. It has a fine clock tower and holds the maces of Edward III and Charles II and ancient volumes of the minutes of the old town corporation. The 1798 memorial at the Tholsel depicts a 'croppy boy', typical of the insurgents who assaulted the town.

River cruises depart from the quay during the summer months. (See also Tour 15.)

Jerpoint Abbey, once at the centre of its own small town, remains an impressive sight

Though worn by time, this decoration on a tomb shows Jerpoint's artistic heritage

i *Quay Street*

▶ *Head north on the **N30**, turn left on to the **R700**, then right after a short distance on to the **R705** for 23 miles (37km) to join the **N9** at Leighlinbridge for the 7-mile (11km) drive into Carlow.*

BACK TO NATURE

About 6 miles (10km) south of New Ross, signposted from the N25 east, is the 480-acre (195-hectare) John F Kennedy Park and Arboretum, the Irish government's tribute to the American president (1961–3) whose ancestral home is in nearby Dunganstown. Nearly 300 acres (120 hectares) are given over to an arboretum that holds more than 5,000 shrubs and trees from all over the world. Follow the signposts to the top of Slieve Coillte for a panoramic view of south Wexford and the splendid estuary of the rivers Barrow, Nore and Suir.

3 Carlow, Co Carlow

The village of Graiguenamanagh ('the Granary of the Monks'), between New Ross and Carlow, was once a place of great ecclesiastical importance. Occupying the site was the

Abbey of Duiske, built between 1207 and 1240. It was suppressed in 1536, but determined monks stayed on for many years afterwards before abandoning the extensive settlement. By 1774 it stood in ruins and the tower collapsed. A large part of the church was roofed in 1813 and Catholic services were resumed. In the 1970s, a group of dedicated locals undertook a major restoration, and today the completely restored abbey serves as the parish church.

The county town of Ireland's second smallest county, Carlow was an Anglo-Norman stronghold, strategically placed on the border of the English 'Pale', a protected area around Dublin and its environs. The 640 insurgents who fell here during their 1798 attack on the town are remembered by a fine Celtic cross.

The west wall and the two flanking towers of 13th-century Carlow Castle can be seen near the bridge across the Barrow. This Norman castle was destroyed not by Cromwell, who captured it in 1650, but by one Dr Middleton in 1814. In his zeal to convert it into an asylum, he tried to reduce the thickness of the walls with explosives, rendering itno more than a dang-erous shell, most of which had to be demolished.

The Cathedral of the Assumption, in Tullow Street, is a fine Gothic-style building erected between 1828 and 1833. Of special interest are its 151-foot (46m) high lantern tower and the marble monument by the sculptor John Hogan, of the 19th-century political writer Bishop Doyle. Adjacent to the town hall and housed in an old theatre, the Haymarket Museum contains a reconstructed forge and kitchen, military relics and local tools.

Browne's Hill Demesne, about 2 miles (3km) east of town, holds a mammoth dolmen, with a capstone that is the largest in Ireland.

RECOMMENDED WALKS

There is a pleasant walk in Carlow town along the banks of the River Barrow to the junction with its Burrin tributary. The meeting of the two rivers forms an attractive four-angled lake.

[i] *College Street*

*Follow the **R417** north to Athy. Turn northeast on to the **N78** for Kilcullen, then northwest on the **R413** to its junction with the **N7**, which takes you west to Kildare.*

Ireland is dotted with prehistoric remains. This ancient dolmen is at Brown's Hill, near Carlow

SCENIC ROUTES

The Carlow/Stradbally road (N8) takes you through Windy Gap, one of eastern Ireland's most famous scenic drives, with wide vistas of the surrounding countryside.

FOR CHILDREN

Take the children to see the National Stud, 1 mile (2km) east of Kildare off the N7. Some of the world's most renowned racehorses have been bred and trained on these grounds, and you can visit the stables and watch the thoroughbreds being exercised and groomed. There is a museum depicting the history of the horse in Ireland.

4 Kildare, Co Kildare

En route to Kildare, stop in Athy to view the Dominican church, a striking example of modern church architecture. Inside are George Campbell's outstanding Stations of the Cross. To the southeast of Athy Castledermot's ecclesiastical ruins include a round tower, two high crosses and the remains of a Franciscan friary church.

Kildare's beautiful 18th-century Church of Ireland St Brigid's Cathedral incorporates part of a 13th-century church.

In the heart of Ireland's horse-breeding and training country, Kildare sits on the edge of the vast Curragh plain, and the National Stud is near by. In addition to its equine interest (see For Children panel above), the stud features a superb Japanese garden and another which was laid out to celebrate the millennium.

East of town, horse racing has reigned supreme for centuries at The Curragh, where all the Irish Classics are run. The Curragh Camp, handed over to the Irish army in 1922, has been an important military station for a century, and there you can see the famous 1920 armoured car 'Slievenamon' in which Michael Collins was travelling when the fatal ambush of 1922 took place.

The Hill of Allen, legendary home of Irish folk hero Fionn MacCumhail and the site of three royal residences in ancient Leinster, is northeast of town and is crowned by a 19th-century battlemented stone tower.

i *Market Square*

▶ *Take the* **N7** *southeast to reach Portlaoise.*

A climb up the round tower beside the cathedral gives a wonderful view over Kildare

5 Portlaoise, Co Laois

Set at the junction of the Dublin/Limerick and Dublin/Cork main roads, Portlaoise is also the site of Ireland's national prison.

There is a well-preserved 12th-century round tower in the little village of Timahoe, about 7 miles (11km) southeast of Portlaoise via the R426. Four miles (6km) east of town, the Rock of Dunamase rises 200 feet (60m) above the plain, with the ruined 12th-century castle of Dermot MacMurrough, one time King of Leinster.

Emo Court, about 8 miles (13km) northeast of Portlaoise off the N7, is probably the premier attraction of County Laois. The grand house was

An eye-catching shopfront in Portlaoise leaves no doubt about the goods on offer

designed by the celebrated architect James Gandon, and is open to the public. The gardens are famous for their sweeping formal lawns, statuary and avenue of giant sequoia trees. The landscape of woodland and lake is undergoing careful restoration.

To the west of town, the many roads crossing the Slieve Bloom Mountains offer interesting and scenic drives.

▶ *Take the* ***N8*** *for 9 miles (14km) south to Abbeyleix.*

6 Abbeyleix, Co Laois
This attractive town, with tree-lined streets, is noted for the de Vesci Demesne, known as Abbeyleix House. The great house, which dates back to 1773, is not open to the public, but the splendid grounds are. They include formal terrace gardens to the west of the house, a 'wild garden' (called the Paradise Garden) that is carpeted with bluebells in spring, and an American garden with magnolia trees. There is also a magnificent avenue of lime trees.

The Heritage House in Abbeyleix is designed to be a focus for visitors to this historic town. Interactive multi-media displays tell the story of Abbeyleix and the surounding area.

▶ *Take the* ***N8*** *southwest to the* ***N75*** *turnoff to Thurles.*

7 Thurles, Co Tipperary
In ancient times, the O'Fogartys fortified this site on the River Suir, and although the Norman Strongbow's army was soundly defeated here in 1174, Anglo-Normans returned later to build a castle that would protect the crossing. Today it is a busy, well-laid-out marketing centre for the surrounding agricultural area. It is also the cathedral town of the archdiocese of Cashel and Emly.

▶ *Take the* ***R660*** *south for 13 miles (21km) to reach Cashel.*

8 Cashel, Co Tipperary
Look above the ground floor of the shop opposite the city hall to see the crenellated battlements and gargoyles of what was 15th-century Quirke's Castle, named after a family

who lived there in the 19th century. At the southwest end of Main Street, the ornamental fountain is in memory of Dean Kinane and his efforts in bringing an extension of the railway to Cashel in 1904. Cashel is best known for the Rock of Cashel, Folk Museum and Heritage Centre (see Tours 3 and 10.)

▶ *Take the **R692** southeast to Fethard.*

9 Fethard, Co Tipperary
Fethard was an important Anglo-Norman settlement in medieval times. Remnants of the old town walls and their flanking towers can still be seen. In the town centre, there are keeps of three 15th-century castles, including that of Fethard Castle. Well-preserved remains of a priory contain several 16th- and 17th-century tombs. More than a thousand exhibits of rural life in this area are on display at the Folk, Farm and Transport Museum.

▶ *Take the **R692** northeast to Mullinahone. Turn right for Callan, then turn north on the **N76** for the 11-mile (18km) drive back to Kilkenny.*

Holycross Abbey, near Thurles, was restored in 1975 after more than 200 years in ruins

FOR HISTORY BUFFS

The ancient name for Slievenamon, just southeast of Fethard, was 'The Mountain of the Women of Feimhinn' in honour of the fairy women of the area who, according to legend, enchanted Fionn and his Fianna warriors. It is also believed that it was here that Fionn decreed he would take as his bride the first women to reach him in a race to the summit. The winner was Grainne, who created a legend of her own when she later opted for Diarmuid as a mate.

By Hook or By Crooke

Founded in the mid-9th century on the River Slaney, Wexford retains much of its old Viking layout, with tiny lanes leading down to the river. The narrow main street, lined with traditional shopfronts and pubs, is the heart of this lively and prosperous little agricultural and tourist town.

3 DAYS • 163 MILES • 262KM

ITINERARY

WEXFORD	▶ **Courtown (25m-40km)**
COURTOWN	▶ **Gorey (4m-6km)**
GOREY	▶ **Enniscorthy (19m-31km)**
ENNISCORTHY	▶ **New Ross (21m-34km)**
NEW ROSS	▶ **Waterford (15m-24km)**
WATERFORD	▶ **Passage East (7m-11km)**
PASSAGE EAST	▶ **Ballyhack (ferry)**
BALLYHACK	▶ **Hook Head (11m-18km)**
HOOK HEAD	▶ **Fethard (7m-11km)**
FETHARD	▶ **Kilmore Quay (24m-39km)**
KILMORE QUAY	▶ **Lady's Island (13m-21km)**
LADY'S ISLAND	▶ **Rosslare (7m-11km)**
ROSSLARE	▶ **Wexford (10m-16km)**

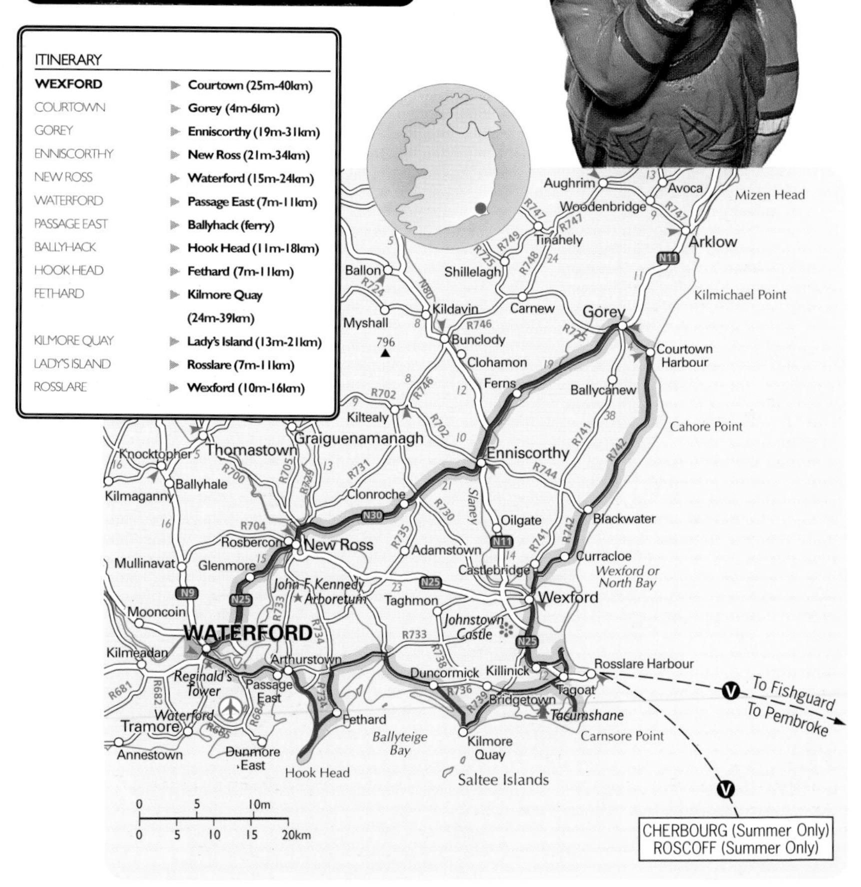

i *Crescent Quay, Wexford*

FOR CHILDREN

The Irish National Heritage Park, some 3 miles (5km) northeast of Wexford via the N25, has authentic reconstructions of Irish life including a campsite, farmstead and portal dolmen from the Stone Age; a stone circle from the Bronze Age; an Ogham stone, ringfort and souterrain, Viking boathouse and crannog from the Celtic and early Christian ages; and a Norman motte and bailey, the first Norman fortification in Ireland, and a round tower from the early Norman period. There is also a fine nature walk.

▶ *Take the **R741** north, then turn right on to the **R742** for Courtown.*

SCENIC ROUTES

The coastal drive via the R742 from Wexford to Courtown passes through charming little villages, countryside dotted with thatched cottages and stretches of wide sandy beaches.

1 Courtown, Co Wexford
This pleasant harbour town set in the wide sweep of Courtown Bay is a popular family resort, with a fine, 2-mile (3km) long sandy beach, amusements and a picturesque golf course. Its harbour piers were a part of famine relief work sponsored by the Earl of Courtown in 1847.

Ballymoney is a small resort with an excellent beach north of Courtown, and to the south, Ardamine and Pollshone are secluded coves with good swimming. At Ardamine, look for the little church by George Edmund Street, designer of the London Law Courts and restorer of Christ Church Cathedral in Dublin.

The wide sweep of Courtown Bay and its sandy beach make this one of the most popular resorts on the southeast coast

▶ *Follow the **R742** for 4 miles (6km) northwest to Gorey.*

2 Gorey, Co Wexford
Set against a backdrop of the Wicklow Mountains to the north, Gorey dates back to the 13th century. The wide Main Street and neat street plan give it a pleasant appearance. It figured prominently in the 1798 conflict, and insurgents camped at the western end of town at 418-foot (127m) high Gorey Hill before they marched on Arklow. A granite Celtic cross stands near the hill as a memorial to those who fell in battle. The Loreto convent, designed by Pugin, dates from 1839 to 1842.

i *Main Street*

▶ *Take the **N11** southwest to Enniscorthy.*

RECOMMENDED WALKS

Northeast of Gorey, on an unclassified road to Castletown, Tara Hill (not to be confused with the more famous Hill of Tara) rises to 833 feet (254m). There are lovely forest walks, and the view from the summit is spectacular.

SPECIAL TO...

In late June/early July, Enniscorthy celebrates the Wexford Strawberry Fair, with tons of the luscious, locally grown fruit and non-stop street entertainment, art exhibitions and musical events.

3 Enniscorthy, Co Wexford
Set on the steeply sloping banks of the River Slaney, Enniscorthy suffered several attacks following the arrival of

the Normans, and it was a veritable storm centre of the 1798 rebellion, when insurgents led by the revered Father John Murphy held the town for four weeks before being overthrown by Crown forces under General Lake. A bronze statue of Father Murphy and a pikeman stands in Market Square.

Wexford County Museum is housed in a Norman castle built in the 13th century by the Prendergast family, recalling the town's earliest history, while spectacular displays at the National 1798 Visitor Centre interpret the momentous events of the 1798 Rebellion and place them in an international context. Lively presentation techniques are used to illustrate the rebellion and the subsequent journey to modern democracy in Ireland.

The 390-foot (120m) high Vinegar Hill at the eastern edge of town is where the Wexford pikemen made their last stand in June 1798. Their defeat marked the end of any effective resistance in the county. Today, it is a peaceful vantage point from which to view the town and surrounding countryside. The battles of 1916 are commemorated by a memorial to Commandant Seamus Rafter that stands in Abbey Square.

St Aidan's Cathedral is an impressive Gothic-revival structure designed by Pugin.

[i] *Town Centre*

RECOMMENDED WALKS

At Dunamore Bridge, 3 miles (5km) south of Enniscorthy, Dunamore Forest Park is reached via an unclassified road to Killurin on the west side of the River Slaney. It is an ideal place to stop for a picnic, and has beautiful forest and riverside walks.

▶ *Follow the **N30** to New Ross.*

4 New Ross, Co Wexford

The busy port town of New Ross was founded by Isabella, granddaughter of the Irish King Dermot MacMurrough and daughter of the Norman leader Strongbow. The River Barrow that runs through the town, links up with Ireland's inland waterway system.

Old Ross, a tiny village east of town, lost its importance in ancient times with the development and growth of New Ross.

Eight miles (13km) south of New Ross via the R733, the extensive ruins of Dunbrody Abbey, founded in 1182, are near the village of Campile. They are among the finest in Ireland, with a well-preserved nave, aisles, choir and transepts. Each transept is joined by three vaulted and groined chapels. (See also Tour 14.)

[i] *The Quay*

▶ *Take the **N25** southwest for 15 miles (24km) to Waterford.*

5 Waterford, Co Waterford

The most important seaport in the southeast, Waterford's face is lined with traces of its past.

The massacre at nearby Vinegar Hill is among the displays in the museum at Enniscorthy Castle

The French Church in Greyfriars Street was built in 1240 for the Franciscan order, but the extensive ruins serve as a poignant reminder of the Huguenot refugees who fled religious persecution in France in the 17th century and were given use of the church, which had fallen into disuse. Near the City Hall, St Olaf's Church dates from the 11th century. The impressive Church of Ireland Christ Church Cathedral sits on the elevated site, one street off the quay, that once held a Viking church built in 1050. The original structure was replaced in 1773, and the present building has been enlarged and renovated.

Waterford's lively cultural scene includes the Waterford Arts Centre in O'Connell Street, which has permanent and visiting exhibitions, and the Garter Lane Arts Centre, also in O'Connell Street, is the venue for special events and exhibitions. (See also Tour 10.)

[i] *41,The Quay*

▶ *From Waterford take the* ***R683*** *east to Passage East.*

6 Passage East, Co Waterford
This picturesque village at the foot of the steep hill overlooking the Waterford harbour estuary was fortified in years gone by to control shipping on the river. These days, it is the County Waterford terminal for the car ferry across to County Wexford. (See also Tour 10.)

▶ *Take the passenger ferry from Passage East across the estuary to Ballyhack.*

7 Ballyhack, Co Wexford
The ruined castle overlooking the estuary was part of the Preceptory of the Knights of St John, founded in the 11th century. Today, it is the County Wexford terminal for the car ferry from County Waterford and is noted for salmon fishing and boat building.

The Hook Head lighthouse is a distinctive landmark, night or day, for passing ships

SCENIC ROUTES

The road leading southeast out of Ballyhack gives extensive and beautiful views of Waterford harbour estuary as far as Hook Head on the Wexford side and the bulk of Creadan Head on the Waterford side.

▶ *Turn southeast from Ballyhack on to the* ***R733,*** *then just past Arthurstown turn right for Duncannon. Shortly turn on to an unclassified signposted road south for about 7 miles (11km) to Hook Head.*

8 Hook Head, Co Wexford
Perched on a craggy sea-carved peninsula, the striking black-and-white lighthouse called the Tower of Hook is thought to date from the 12th century. The tradition of a light to guide ships through the treacherous waters of this dangerous point began long before then, however. Legend has it that it was the Welsh monk, St Dubhann, who first tended a cauldron of burning pitch, which he hoisted to the top of a high platform each night. The practice continued right through the 10th to 12th centuries as first the Vikings and then the Normans occupied the Hook area. Raymond le Gros, an important Norman leader, is believed to have built the tower some 800 years ago on the site of the beacon of St Dubhann, and it was this structure that was renovated in 1677, when an oil lamp was installed. Nowadays, the lamp is electrically powered with a standby generator, a flashing light and a powerful fog horn. While special permission must be obtained to visit the lighthouse, the drive along the peninsula is spectacular, with secluded beaches and coves.

▶ *Return north on the unclassified road to the point where it branches right on to another unclassified road and take this road to Fethard.*

FOR HISTORY BUFFS

Hook Head gave to the English language one of its most frequently used expressions when the Norman leader Strongbow, Earl of Pembroke, declared in 1170 that 'I will take Waterford by Hook or by Crooke'. He was referring to the Tower of Hook on the Wexford side and to Crooke Castle on the Waterford shore near Passage East, both of which were heavily fortified. Strongbow made good his vow and thus changed the course of Irish history.

9 **Fethard,** Co Wexford

This pleasant little resort on the eastern shore of the Hook Peninsula has a fine sandy beach. In ancient times, there was woodland here, and traces of fossilised tree trunks have been found buried in the sands. The monument in the village centre is in memory of nine members of the Fethard lifeboat crew who drowned in 1914 as they made a gallant attempt to save the crew of a Norwegian vessel that had gone aground.

Fethard Castle, now in ruins but with its round tower still intact, was built in the mid-14th century. Tintern Abbey, 3½ miles (6km) north of Fethard between Wellington Bridge and Duncannon, dates from about 1200 and was built by the Earl of Pembroke in thanksgiving for having survived a fierce storm at sea. The long drive into the wooded estate is signposted at the gate. In 1540, following the dissolution of the monasteries, the land and buildings passed into private hands, and parts of the church and tower were used as a residence until 1963. The domestic alterations have now been removed.

▶ *Take the **R734** north for about 4 miles (6km), then turn east on the **R733** to Wellington Bridge. Turn right on to the **R736** to Duncormick, then right again via unclassified roads to Kilmore Quay.*

10 **Kilmore Quay,** Co Wexford

The charming little fishing village of Kilmore Quay is noted for its lobsters and deep-sea fishing, and is also the port of departure for the Saltee Islands to the south.

Between the Quay and the village of Kilmore, look for Brandy Close and the mound of wooden crosses at the roadside – tradition decrees that mourners place a small cross on the heap each time a funeral passes. The outstanding feature of the village of Kilmore, further along, is its concentration of fine thatched cottages.

▶ *Take the **R739** northeast, through Kilmore, to the*

BACK TO NATURE

The Saltee Islands, 4 miles (6km) offshore from Kilmore Quay, harbour huge seabird colonies including razorbills, kittiwakes, puffins and thousands of gulls. Negotiate with local boatmen for a trip out, or arrange for one of the fishing trawlers to drop you on their way out to sea and pick you up on their return.

Fethard, now a quiet little resort, is close to the place where the first Anglo-Normans landed

*junction with the **R736**. Turn right on to this road and proceed to its junction with a signposted unclassified road south (at Twelveacre) to Lady's Island.*

11 Lady's Island, Co Wexford
Lady's Island is at the head of a saltwater lagoon, Lady's Island Lake. Its ancient name translates to 'Meadow of the Women', and it may well have been inhabited by druidesses. With the coming of Christianity, it became one of the first shrines of the Blessed Virgin and an important place of pilgrimage. The church was destroyed and the holy men of the island were savagely butchered by Cromwellian forces in 1649, but pilgrimages began again at the end of the Cromwellian era and continue to this day.

▶ *Return to Twelveacre via the unclassified road north, then turn northeast on to the **R736** to its junction with the **N25**. Turn right to reach Rosslare Harbour, and straight across to reach Rosslare.*

BACK TO NATURE

Lady's Island Lake is itself an important habitat for many bird species. However, on the lake's two islands all five species of terns have established the largest breeding colonies of these birds in Ireland. It is also the only known site at which all species breed together The islands and terns are easily viewed from the pathway around Lady's Island Lake, but during late spring and summer, access to the islands themselves is restricted to prevent disturbance.

12 Rosslare, Co Wexford
Car and passenger ferries arrive daily at Rosslare Harbour, from Wales and northern France. Five miles (8km) to the north, Rosslare is a popular seaside resort with a fine 6-mile (10km) curving beach and good restaurants and accommodation.

i Rosslare Harbour, Kilrane

▶ *From Rosslare take the **R740** to the **N25** and turn right to return to Wexford.*

SPECIAL TO...

The Wexford Opera Festival is a gala October/November event of music and festivity, featuring local and international opera companies presenting lesser-known operas as well as standard classics. There are three performances during each week, along with music recitals, workshops, art exhibitions, and many other related activities. Throughout the town, there are peripheral events, competitions and street performances.

Kilmore Quay is at the heart of an area where traditional thatched roofs are still maintained

CONNACHT

The counties that make up the province of Connacht seem to fit the popular image of Ireland more than any other region. It is a land of stony fields, brooding mountains, windswept cliffs along a rugged coastline dotted with offshore islands, and wide skies alive with the shifting light and shadow of clouds moving inland from the Atlantic.

County Galway's eastern landscape stretches along flat, fertile plains from Lough Derg and the Shannon Valley north to Roscommon. The streets and lanes of Galway town are filled with medieval architecture and a lively creative arts-and-crafts culture. Poet William Butler Yeats drew inspiration from the surroundings of his beloved Thoor Ballylee tower home near Gort, and Lady Gregory, the moving force behind Dublin's Abbey Theatre, gathered some of Ireland's most distinguished writers around her hearth at nearby Coole Park. In western Galway, peaks of the Twelve Pins (Bens) face the misty heights of the Maumturk range across a lake-filled valley in rock-strewn Connemara, whose jagged coastline has a stark, silent beauty punctuated with rocky fields and tiny hamlets. The three Aran Islands, some 30 miles (48km) offshore, are a repository of antiquities left by prehistoric peoples and the language, customs and dress of a Celtic Twilight heritage.

County Mayo holds reminders of a great prehistoric battle on the plain of Southern Moytura near Cong. Christianity came with St Patrick, and pilgrims still follow his footsteps to the summit of Croagh Patrick on the shores of island-studded Clew Bay. Achill Island, connected to the mainland by a bridge, is ringed by mighty cliffs and tiny coves, with a flat, boggy interior.

Boyhood visits to his uncle's home in Sligo nurtured W B Yeats's deep love for the west, and some of his best works celebrate Sligo landmarks. Lough Ree was the haunt of early Christians, who had churches and monasteries on many of its islands. Lough Key lies in a luxurious forest park, with the remains of a great abbey at Boyle.

Dominated by inland lakes and the River Shannon, County Leitrim has its fair share of mountains and hills. Carrick-on-Shannon, which grew up at one of the traditional fords of the Shannon, is home to a vast flotilla of cruisers for exploring the river and lakes.

A long, narrow inlet, Killary Harbour, cuts into the hills of Connemara at Leenane (Tour 19)

Typical Connemara landscape near Roundstone (Tour 19)

Tour 16

This tour, which starts in the bright town of Sligo, is steeped in echoes of Ireland's greatest poet, William Butler Yeats, passing his grave beneath the majestic profile of the mountain, Benbulben, and visiting places which inspired some of his finest lyric poetry. This corner of Ireland is a happy unison of wooded lakes, bare mountain-tops and Atlantic seascapes, and abounds in history from prehistoric times.

Tour 17

The majestic ruins of its 12th-century abbey and the beauties of its riverside setting and nearby Lough Key Forest Park make Boyle an attractive touring base. The Shannon, with its cruiser-filled marina at Carrick-on-Shannon, lures you onward, with perhaps a stop or two along the way for fishing in the trout-filled waters of this region. Roscommon's ruined castle speaks of the town's turbulent history, while Clonalis, the 'great house' of Castlerea, is a relic of more gracious times.

Tour 18

The ghost of Grace O'Malley will follow you on this tour after a visit to magnificent Westport House, with its museum and zoo. After a side trip to her Clare Island home, the route travels to Newport and one of her numerous strongholds before heading for Achill Island, Ireland's largest and most scenic, with yet another castle of the sea queen. At Knock, a huge basilica honouring a miraculous vision of the Blessed Virgin dominates the town. Monastic ruins and impressive Ashford Castle lie along the route as you make your way back to Westport through the county town of Castlebar.

Tour 19

Galway town's many historic and cultural attractions may tempt you to tarry before setting out on this tour. A trip out to the very special Aran Islands beckons before embarking on the swing through Connemara's starkly beautiful landscape. This Gaeltacht (Irish-speaking) region is one of rocky, untillable fields, where the Twelve Bens mountain range faces the Maumturk range across a lake–filled valley. The jagged coastline is a solitary place of rocks and tiny hamlets and stark, silent beauty.

Sligo & Yeats Country

The busy town of Sligo has good shops, traditional public houses, thriving art galleries and a theatre. There are fine 18th- and 19th-century buildings and 13th-century abbey ruins, all set against the distinctive backdrop of Benbulbin, an extraordinary flat-topped and rugged-faced mountain profile.

1/2 DAYS • 98 MILES • 157KM

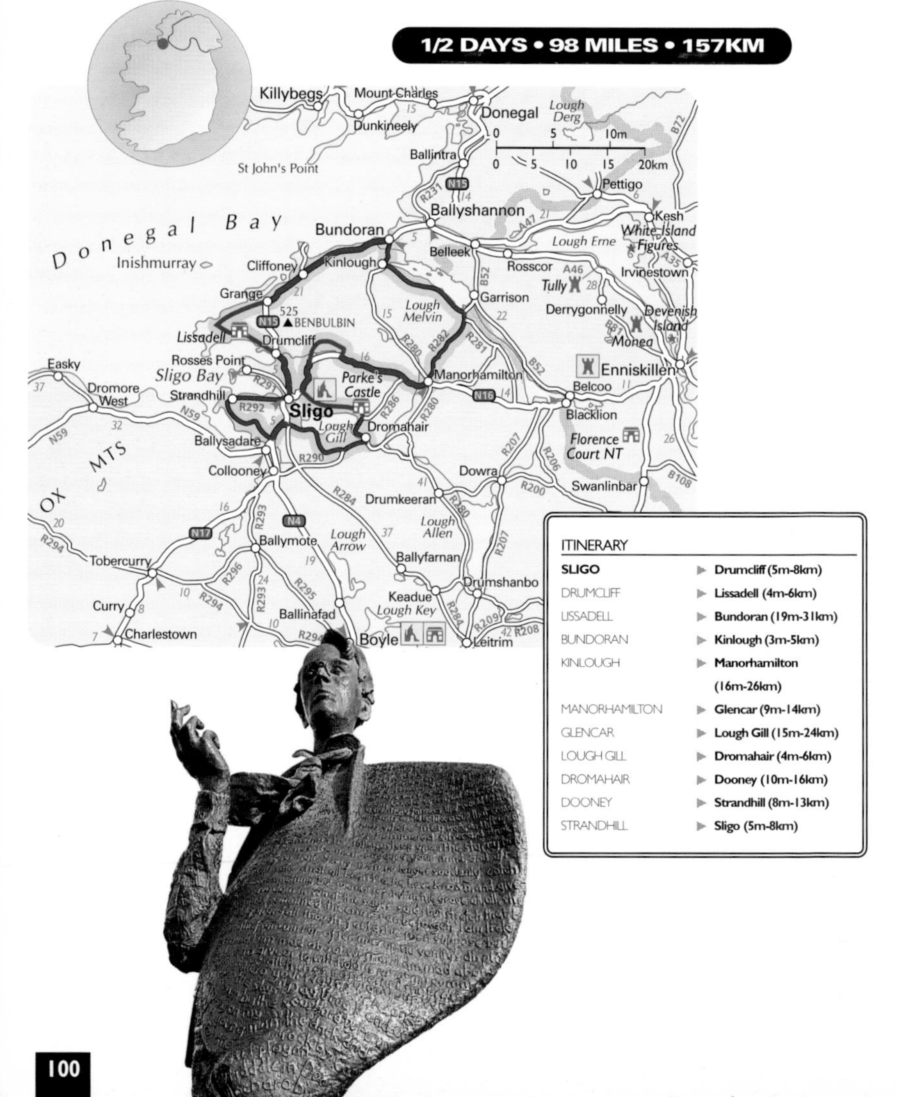

ITINERARY	
SLIGO	▶ **Drumcliff (5m-8km)**
DRUMCLIFF	▶ **Lissadell (4m-6km)**
LISSADELL	▶ **Bundoran (19m-31km)**
BUNDORAN	▶ **Kinlough (3m-5km)**
KINLOUGH	▶ **Manorhamilton (16m-26km)**
MANORHAMILTON	▶ **Glencar (9m-14km)**
GLENCAR	▶ **Lough Gill (15m-24km)**
LOUGH GILL	▶ **Dromahair (4m-6km)**
DROMAHAIR	▶ **Dooney (10m-16km)**
DOONEY	▶ **Strandhill (8m-13km)**
STRANDHILL	▶ **Sligo (5m-8km)**

[i] *Temple Street, Sligo*

FOR HISTORY BUFFS

Carrowmore, 2 miles (3km) from Sligo, is the largest group of megalithic tombs in Ireland. Over 60 tombs have been located by archaeologists – the oldest predate Newgrange (see Tour 12) by 700 years.

*Take the **N15** for 5 miles (8km) to Drumcliff.*

1 Drumcliff, Co Sligo

'Under bare Ben Bulben's head
In Drumcliff churchyard Yeats is laid
An ancestor was rector there
Long years ago; a church stands near,
By the road an ancient cross,
No marble, no conventional phrase;
On limestone quarried near the spot,
By his command these words are cut:
Cast a cold eye
On life, on death,
Horseman, pass by!'

Yeats's poem describes Drumcliff completely, and his grave can be found easily in the Protestant churchyard. The road runs through a monastic site, to the church, where the poet's grandfather was rector.

*Continue on the **N15** and almost immediately take a turn left for 4 miles (6km) to Lissadell.*

2 Lissadell, Co Sligo

The slightly forbidding classical façade of Lissadell hides the romantic background of the Gore-Booths. Yeats was a regular visitor here and his poem in memory of the two sisters, Eva and Constance, begins:
'The light of evening, Lissadell,
Great windows open to the south,
Two girls in silk kimonos, both
Beautiful, one a gazelle.'

Lissadell House would ring to the romanticism of poetry and patriotic fervour

Constance became the Countess Markievicz, a leader in the Easter Rising of 1916, and the first woman to be elected to Westminster, although she never took her seat. The 1830s mansion is of Ballisodare limestone, and has a charming music room and a dining room with interesting murals. The house is set in fine parkland with small car parks beside the sea, supposedly the warmest bathing water in the country. It certainly seems to suit the seals, which can be spotted basking on the sand-banks. In the estate is the Goose Field, where Ireland's largest mainland colony of barnacle geese winter.

▶ *Drive through the parkland to rejoin the road and turn left, then right at the fork. Shortly turn right and continue to Grange. Turn left, to rejoin the* ***N15*** *for Bundoran.*

BACK TO NATURE

At Streedagh, there is a dune system based on a shingle ridge, which is of international importance and which supports the plant, insect and bird life associated with dunes. The limestone rocks are laced with varieties of fossil coral. Bunduff Lake, near Creevykeel, is a salt-water marsh, where whooper and Bewick swans, Greenland white-fronted geese and many species of duck spend the winter.

SCENIC ROUTES

From the main Sligo-Donegal road, the Gleniff Horseshoe is a signposted loop that passes the jagged summits of Benwisken and Truskmore.

FOR HISTORY BUFFS

Creevykeel Court Tomb, southwest of Bundoran, is regarded as the finest example of a classic court tomb in Ireland. The cairn has a kerb of large stones surrounding a ritual court, also with a boundary of upright stones. In the two burial chambers, which were originally roofed, a Harvard archaeological expedition found four cremated burials, as well as decorated neolithic pottery and stone weapons. These are now held in the National Museum in Dublin.

3 Bundoran, Co Donegal
Bundoran is a busy seaside resort, and presents quite a contrast to the placid towns and coastal villages of the northwest, offering a wide variety of attractions, as well as a 'blue flag' beach and cliff walks.

Glencar Waterfall plunges 30 feet (10m) through a ferny chasm into Glencar Lough

To the southwest of Bundoran, at Streedagh, is a small park that commemorates the place where three vessels of the Spanish Armada foundered in 1588. Members of the crew who struggled ashore from the overladen ships found little succour on land.

i *Main Street*

▶ *Take the **R280** for 3 miles (5km) to Kinlough.*

4 Kinlough, Co Leitrim
Sitting at the north end of Lough Melvin, this attractive village is a good place for coarse and salmon fishing. The ruins of Rossclogher Abbey stand on the shore, and on an artificial island are the remains of the MacClancy Castle (known as Rossclogher Castle), where nine survivors of the Armada were given refuge.

▶ *Follow the **R281** along the shore of Lough Melvin for 8 miles (13km), then turn right on to the **R282** for Manorhamilton.*

5 Manorhamilton, Co Leitrim
This unassuming village stands in an area of untouched mountain valleys and grey cliff walls. Lush fertile slopes, steep clefts and lofty peaks characterise this part of Leitrim. Glenade Lough and the valley where the River Bonet rises have a special quality. The ruined castle that overlooks the town was built at the meeting of four mountain valleys by the Scottish 17th-century planter Sir Frederick Hamilton, who gave his name to the village.

▶ *Take the **N16** for Sligo. After 7 miles (11km) turn right on to an unclassified road for Glencar Lake.*

6 Glencar, Co Leitrim
Glencar is a beautiful lake; the steep slopes of the valley are generously clothed with mixed woodland and topped with cliffs. Plants grow here in profusion, including rare species, while the mountaintops are luxuriantly covered with heather. Glencar waterfall cascades down from a rocky headland to a deep pool, white with spray. Yeats immortalised the waterfall in his poem *The Stolen Child.*

Parke's Castle, built in 1609, looks out over the tranquil waters of Lough Gill

RECOMMENDED WALKS

This is a region well provided with walks, many of them waymarked. Two good town trails can be found in Sligo and Dromahair. There are fine walks from the picnic site beside the village of Kinlough through Kinlough Forest, by Lough Melvin. A spectacular walk takes you from the Glencar Lake up a mountain road into Swiss Valley, a steep-sided cleft surrounded by peaks. The route then returns to the point where the waterfall cascades into the lake below.

Echoes of England are still in evidence in the purpose-built village of Dromahair

▶ *At the end of the lakeside road turn right towards Sligo on the **N16**, then turn left to Parkes Castle Visitor Centre on the **R286**.*

7 Lough Gill, Co Leitrim
From Parkes Castle there is a superb view of Lough Gill, one of the loveliest loughs, dotted with islands and wooded with native trees like yew, arbutus, white beam, oak and birch. The bare mountain reaches down deep ferny glens to the lake below. Parkes Castle is an impressively reconstructed fortified manor house, originally a stronghold of the O'Rourkes, but gaining its present name from the English family who were 'planted' here. An audio-visual show and tea-room will enhance a visit. If you explore the lake you will find a sweat-house, medieval Ireland's answer to the sauna.

FOR CHILDREN

Although they were not conceived with children in mind, the Hazelwood Park wooden sculptures have proved to be a delight to young visitors. Along paths in the woods by Lough Gill are huge works of art, hewn, constructed and carved in wood. A walk here is a voyage of discovery, to meet 'Fergus rules the Brazen Car', 'The Old Woman' or 'The Fisherman' among many.

▶ *Continue on the **R286**, then turn right on to the **R288** for Dromahair.*

8 Dromahair, Co Leitrim
This area is O'Rourke country, overlooked by a rock plateau called O'Rourke's Table. Dromahair enjoys hosting gatherings of the O'Rourke family, as well as a Wild Rose Festival, but it was an English family, the Lane-Foxes, who laid out the pretty village around the River Bonet on a plan based on a Somerset village. In Thomas Moore's song *The Valley Lay Smiling Before Me*, the tale is told of the elopement from Dromahair in 1152 of Dervorgilla O'Rourke and the King of Leinster (her husband was away on a pilgrimage of penitence for beating her).

To the west is the Isle of Innisfree. You can take a cruise from Parkes Castle (including one at sunset), and see the island for which Yeats yearned – 'where peace comes dropping slow'.

▶ *Take the **R288** for Carrick-on-Shannon, then turn right on to the **R287** for Sligo. After 2½ miles (4km) turn right again with the **R287**, and follow the road past the sign for Innisfree to Dooney Rock Forest, before rejoining the **N4**.*

9 Dooney, Co Sligo
This beautiful corner of Lough Gill has forests and paths to satisfy any enthusiastic walker, offering great views of the lough. Dooney Rock Forest bears the vestiges of a once important oak forest. You can see the 'twining branches', two linked oaks. Yeats wrote of 'the Fiddler of Dooney', who made folk 'dance like the waves of the sea'. The poem has inspired a Fiddler of Dooney competition

for the champion fiddler of Ireland, held in Sligo in July.

Slish Wood, or Sleuth Wood as Yeats knew it, has a lovely stream. Cairns Hill Forest Park marks the two cairns on Belvoir and Cairns peaks. A legend tells of two warriors, Omra and Romra. Romra had a daughter, Gille, meaning beauty, and Omra fell in love with her. When a mortal battle ensued after the lovers were discovered by Romra, Gille drowned herself, and Lough Gill was formed from the tears of her nursemaid. The legend holds that the two cairns are the burial places of the warriors.

Cashelore stone fort is a large oval stone enclosure, once the settlement of an important Celt. The tranquil Tobernalt is a holy well where Mass was said in penal times. A stone altar was erected in thanksgiving when the town was spared the worst ravages of a fever at the turn of the century.

> *Travel south on the* ***N4****, then turn right on to the* ***R292*** *for Rathcarrick and Strandhill.*

SPECIAL TO...

Sligo and the surrounding district is an important centre of traditional music in Ireland, and in recognition of this, it has hosted the All-Ireland Fleadh, or festival of traditional music and dancing, in recent years. You will come across music throughout the region.

10 Strandhill, Co Sligo
Great Atlantic breakers crash on to the beach at Strandhill, making the small seaside village a favoured place for surfing championships. Lifeguards watch bathers, but if you prefer calmer waters, drive round to the beach at Culleenamore, which is safer and quiet. Culleenamore nestles under the mountain of Knocknarea, which is capped by a cairn visible for miles round. It is known locally as the grave of Queen Maeve, the warrior queen of Connacht. If you climb to the summit of Knocknarea, Sligo tradition suggests that you add a stone to the cairn, as a protection against the fairies.

Among the fields below Knocknarea at Carrowmore is Ireland's largest group of megalithic tombs; more than 60 can be found here, mostly passage graves and dolmens. The best place to start to discover Carrowmore is from the Interpretive Centre, where a map is on display.

> *Take the* ***R292*** *for 5 miles (8km) back to Sligo.*

SCENIC ROUTES

The Knocknarea scenic drive gives spectacular views to the south, and to the Ox mountains and Croagh Patrick in the north.

Firm sand and rolling waves attract bathers and surfers to the resort of Strandhill

Boyle & The Lake Country

Lakes dotted with small wooded islands are the main characteristic of County Roscommon. Beautifully situated on the bank of the River Boyle at the foot of the Curlew Hills, the town of Boyle offers excellent fishing. Close to the river at the north end of town are impressive ruins of the Cistercian abbey, and the King House has excellent displays and presentations.

1 DAY • 87 MILES • 140KM

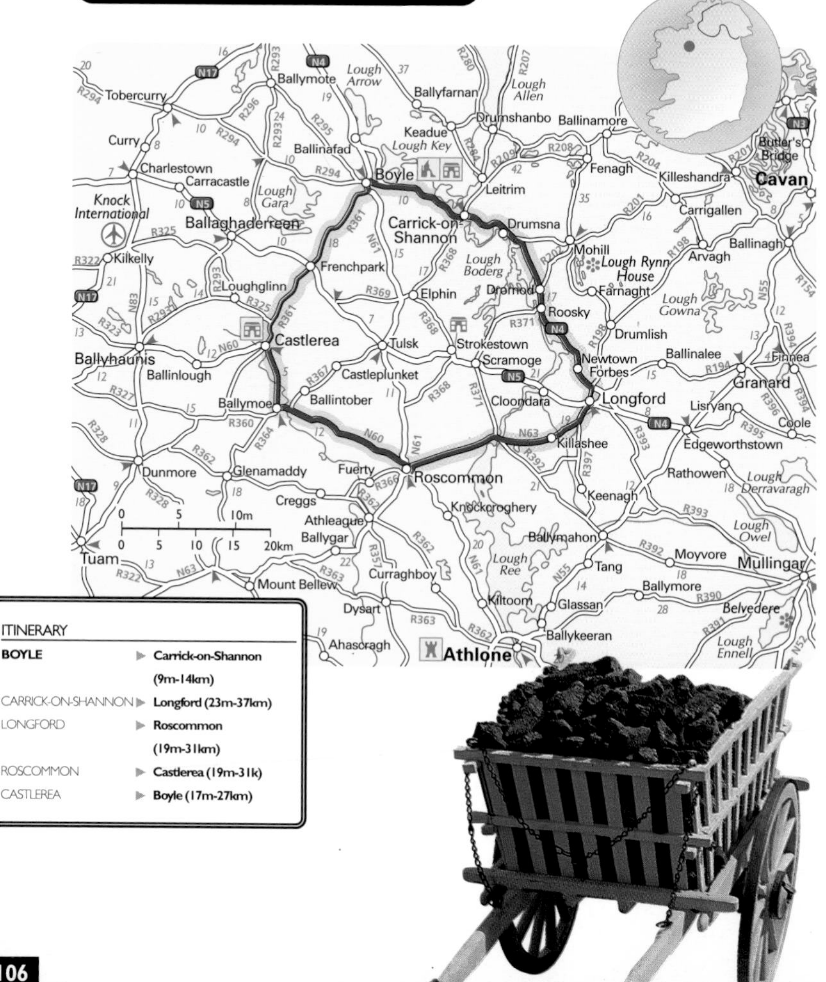

ITINERARY		
BOYLE	▶	**Carrick-on-Shannon (9m-14km)**
CARRICK-ON-SHANNON	▶	**Longford (23m-37km)**
LONGFORD	▶	**Roscommon (19m-31km)**
ROSCOMMON	▶	**Castlerea (19m-31k)**
CASTLEREA	▶	**Boyle (17m-27km)**

BACK TO NATURE

Lough Key Forest Park, 2 miles (3km) east of Boyle on the N4, is one of Ireland's most beautiful scenic spots. The bog gardens are brilliant with rhododendron and azalea blooms in early summer, complemented by a wide variety of plants and shrubs that thrive in the peaty soil. The nature trail that winds through extensive forests is well marked with information on the many trees and plants along the way. Moylurg Tower tops a hill that once held a stately mansion, Rockingham House (destroyed by fire), with fine views of the lake and woodlands.

RECOMMENDED WALKS

At Carrick-on-Shannon, the walk from the centre of the town to the riverbank and colourful marina is both interesting and scenic.

i *Boyle*

▶ *Take the* ***N4*** *for 9 miles (14km) southeast to Carrick-on-Shannon.*

1 Carrick-on-Shannon, Co Leitrim
Chief town of Ireland's most sparsely populated county, Carrick-on-Shannon is also the smallest county town in the country, and was first given its charter by James I. When river traffic was superceded by road and rail, it hit the town hard, but the growing demand for pleasure boating gave it a reprieve. Its situation on Shannon's navigational system makes this attractive town a major river-cruising and fishing centre.

Among the best preserved buildings in the town are the 19th-century Court House and the Protestant church.

SPECIAL TO...

Drumshanbo, 8 miles (13km) north of Carrick-on-Shannon on the R280, celebrates everything Irish – music, song, dance and pub events – in the An Tostal Festival each June. It is now possible to cruise up the River Shannon, along the Ballinamore-Ballconnell Canal and up intoLough Erne in Co Fermanagh, thanks to an enlightened cross-border initiative.

i *The Marina*

▶ *Follow the* ***N4*** *southeast for 23 miles (37km) to Longford.*

2 Longford, Co Longford
Set on the south bank of the River Camlin, the market town of Longford dates back to 1400, when a Dominican priory was founded here. Nothing remains of that ancient establishment, but the slight ruins of a castle built in 1627 are incorporated into the old military barracks. In the town centre is the grey limestone, Renaissance-style St Mel's Cathedral, a classical building of the 19th century by

The riverside abbey ruins provide a peaceful haven right in the centre of Boyle

SCENIC ROUTES

Heading south from Carrick-on-Shannon on the N4, leave the main road to divert to Jamestown on the Shannon and visit Drumsna, a small town in an exceptionally scenic setting. As you continue southeast to Longford, the landscape is dotted with many small lakes that are part of the Shannon system. Two miles (3km) beyond Aghamore, an unclassified road to the right leads to the wooded Derrycarne promontory, which projects into Lough Boderg.

J B Keane. Close by is Carriglas Manor, a romantic Gothic revival house, still occupied by the Lefroy family. A Palladian stable yard, a costume museum and delightful woodland walks add to the charm of Carriglas.

Longford was a terminal of a branch of the Royal Canal, called the 'Shoemaker's Canal'.

i *Town centre*

► *Take the **N63** southwest to Roscommon.*

FOR HISTORY BUFFS

Ireland's last hangwoman, the legendary 'Lady Betty', is commemorated by a plaque on the 18th-century gaol where she worked, and which was disused after 1822. A former prisoner, her own death sentence had been commuted when she agreed to take on the unwanted job of the hangman.

3 Roscommon, Co Roscommon

Situated at an important road junction, Roscommon is the county's chief town, named after St Coman, founder of an early 8th-century Christian monastery here. The ruin of the Dominican friary is mainly 15th-century and includes the 137-foot (42m) long, 23-foot (7m) wide church, with four pointed arches separating the aisle of the northern transept. A tomb in a burial niche in the north wall of the chancel is thought to be that of Felim O'Conor, King of Connacht, who founded the abbey in 1253. His effigy is perhaps the most interesting figure within the ruins. The eight gallowglasses (figures of mail-clad warriors) who support the tomb belonged originally to a much later tomb of about 1500.

Built in 1269 by Robert d'Ufford, the English Justiciar, but much altered since, Roscommon Castle was captured by the Irish four years later and razed to the ground. It was rebuilt in about 1280 and was besieged many times until the English Civil War, when it was held for the King by Sir Michael Earnley. It was surrendered to Cromwellian forces in 1652, who promptly dismantled it. The ruins form a large quadrangular area, with a round bastion tower at each corner. The gateway is protected by two similar towers that project from the eastern wall. These appear to have been connected to the inner court, which contained the state apartments.

i *Town centre*

► *Take the **N60** to Castlerea.*

FOR CHILDREN

There are sports facilities and a swimming pool at Castlerea's Demesne Park.

4 Castlerea, Co Roscommon

This pretty little town was the birthplace, in 1815, of Oscar Wilde's father, Sir William Wilde, who was an antiquarian and oculist. Just west of town the fine 'great house' of Clonalis, rebuilt in the 19th century, was the seat of the O'Conor Don, a direct descendant of the last High King of Ireland, who abdicated after the Anglo-Norman invasion of 1169. Ownership of such a manor house by a Gaelic family is unique, and Clonalis's furnishings reflect a more informal elegance than many other houses. The drawing room, for example, although beautifully furnished with Victoriana, is also a warm, comfortable room. Nineteenth-century portraits hang in the library, which also holds many fine books. There is a private chapel, and the highlight of the museum is the harp of Ireland's last great bard, Turlough O'Carolan (1670–1738), whose portrait is displayed. Among his many compositions was the tune to which the Star Spangled Banner is now sung.

Priceless Gaelic manuscripts, Victorian costumes, Sheraton furniture, porcelain and glass are also featured in the museum.

► *Take the **R361** to Boyle.*

FOR CHILDREN

Swimming, boating and other water sports are on offer at Lough Key Forest Park, 2 miles (3km) east of Boyle on the N4. Those who prefer to keep dry can enjoy the scenic lake cruises.

SPECIAL TO...

In August, the little town of Keadue (northeast of Boyle and Lough Key) rings with musical and sports events during the ten-day O'Carolan Festival, in memory of the last of the Irish bards, Turlough O'Carolan, who is buried in Kilronan Church cemetery, just northwest of the village.

The modest proportions of Clonalis House give no hint of the fascinating items within

TOUR
18

Achill Island & County Mayo

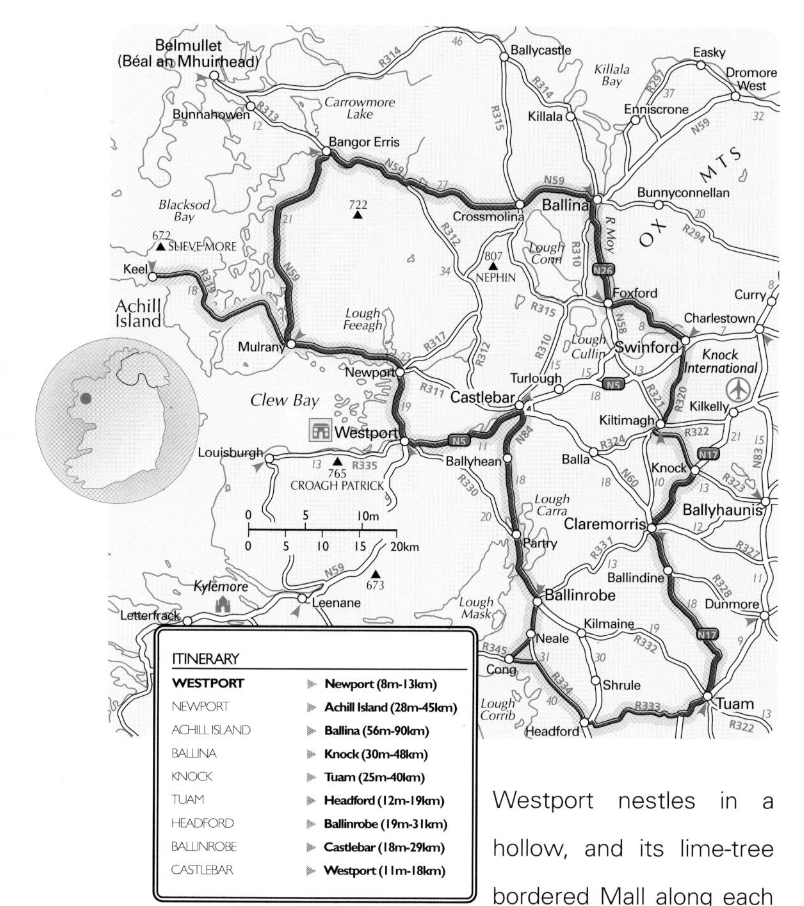

ITINERARY

WESTPORT	▶ **Newport (8m-13km)**
NEWPORT	▶ **Achill Island (28m-45km)**
ACHILL ISLAND	▶ **Ballina (56m-90km)**
BALLINA	▶ **Knock (30m-48km)**
KNOCK	▶ **Tuam (25m-40km)**
TUAM	▶ **Headford (12m-19km)**
HEADFORD	▶ **Ballinrobe (19m-31km)**
BALLINROBE	▶ **Castlebar (18m-29km)**
CASTLEBAR	▶ **Westport (11m-18km)**

Westport nestles in a hollow, and its lime-tree bordered Mall along each side of the Carrowbeg river is an attractive main artery. The town has splendid Georgian houses, traditional shopfronts, and lovely Westport House, a castle of the O'Malley clan, which dates back to the 1730s and is a major attraction.

2 DAYS • 207 MILES • 333KM

Westport is a lively and attractive town, with some splendid Georgian houses and colourful gardens

[i] *The Mall, Westport*

RECOMMENDED WALKS

Croagh Patrick, 5 miles (8km) west of Westport via the R335, rises some 2,510 feet (765m) above the shore of Clew Bay near the little town of Murrisk. This is Ireland's Holy Mountain, on which St Patrick is said to have spent the 40 days of Lent in 441, and where legend says he lured all the snakes in Ireland to the summit, then rang his bell as a signal for all to throw themselves over a precipice. It is an easy climb that takes only about an hour by way of a path from Murrisk.

► *Take the **N59** north for 8 miles (13km) to Newport.*

1 Newport, Co Mayo
This picturesque little town, which dates from the 17th century, faces Clew Bay and is sheltered by mountains. It is a noted angling centre, with fishing on loughs Furnace, Beltra and Feeagh as well as in the rivers Burrishoole and Newport. Its neo-Romanesque Catholic church was built in 1914 and features a superb stained-glass window of the Last Judgement designed by Harry Clarke.

Four miles (6km) west of town, off the N59, Rockfleet Castle, sometimes called Carrigahowley Castle, is another of Grace O'Malley's strongholds. Dating from the 15th and 16th centuries, the tower dwelling has four storeys with a corner turret. The indomitable pirate queen came to live here permanently after her second husband died in 1583.

FOR CHILDREN

While you explore the glories of Westport House and browse through its museum and shops, the children can spend time in the playground, where play equipment is guaranteed to keep them occupied. You may, however, want to accompany them on a walk through the zoo.

► *Follow the **N59** west to Mulrany, then the **R319** to Achill Island, 28 miles (45km).*

2 Achill Island, Co Mayo
The largest of Ireland's islands, Achill Island is connected to the mainland by a bridge. Only 15 miles (24km) long and 12 miles (19km) wide, its landscape is one of dramatic cliffs and seascapes, with a boggy, heather-covered interior. Fishing for shark and other big-game fish is excellent, with boats and guides for hire. There are also very good bathing beaches, and the beautiful Atlantic Drive around the island climbs from gently rolling mountain foothills, past stretches of sandy beaches, and

through tiny picturesque villages with excellent views of the sea, Clew Bay and the mainland. At Kildownet, another Grace O'Malley castle is well preserved, and ruins of a small 12th-century church are near by. At the centre of holiday activities is Keel, which has a fine sandy beach and a small harbour with fishing and sightseeing boats for hire. Seen from a boat, the sea-carved rocks below the Menawn cliffs at the eastern end of the beach take on fanciful shapes.

At Doogort, nestled at the foot of Slievemore, boatmen take visitors to the fascinating Seal Caves cut far into the cliffs of Slievemore.

*Take the **R319** back to Mulrany, then turn north on the **N59** for the drive to Ballina, passing through Ballycroy and Bangor Erris (where the **N59** turns sharply east).*

3 Ballina, Co Mayo

An important angling centre on the River Moy and near Lough Conn, Ballina is County Mayo's largest town. Founded in 1730, it is also a cathedral town, and near its 19th-century Cathedral of St Muiredach, which has a fine stained-glass window, are ruins of a 15th-century Augustinian friary. About 3 miles (5km) north of Ballina, the 15th-century Rosserk Friary sits peacefully on the shore of Killala Bay. The ruins include a tower, a small cloister, nave, chancel, a fine arched doorway and east window.

Beautiful Achill Island is remote yet easily accessible

SCENIC ROUTES

An alternative route from Achill Island to Ballina takes you on a 48-mile (77km) loop around the north coast of County Mayo, through some of the finest scenery in Ireland. Follow the N59 north to Bangor Erris, then take the Belmullet road, the R313, and just past Bunnahowen turn east on the R314 to Glenamoy, where an unclassified road turns left to reach the harbour of Portacloy. Returning to Glenamoy, proceed northeast on the R314 through Belderg and Ballycastle. Following the R314 south, you reach Killala, and 2 miles (3km) southeast of town, on a road to your left, is 15th-century Moyne Abbey. The R314 south takes you straight into Ballina.

Eight miles (13km) north of Ballina via the R314, Killala, the small harbour where General Humbert and his French forces landed in 1798, has a wealth of antiquities in the immediate vicinity, as well as one of the finest round towers in the country. Nearby Franciscan Moyne Abbey was founded in the mid-15th century. Although burned in 1590, the well-preserved ruins include a six-storey square tower, vaulted chapter room, and a partially vaulted sacristy.

i *Cathedral Road*

▶ *Take the **N57** south, then southeast through Foxford to Swinford. Follow the **R320** south to Kiltimagh, then turn southeast on the **R323** for 5 miles (8km) to reach Knock.*

4 Knock, Co Mayo

This small town was the setting of an apparition in 1879, the central figure of which was the Blessed Virgin. After intensive investigation by Catholic authorities, it was declared authentic and named a Marian shrine. A large, circular church was built to accommodate the huge number of pilgrims, with 32 pillars in the ambulatory contributed by all counties in the country, and four windows in medieval style that represent the four provinces of Ireland. In 1979 Knock was visited by Pope John Paul II.

The Knock Folk Museum exhibits relics of rural and small-town life in this part of Ireland.

i *Town centre*

▶ *Take the **N17** south to Tuam.*

5 Tuam, Co Galway

A thriving commercial and agricultural centre under James I's charter of 1613, the layout of Tuam was altered to include a diamond-shaped town 'square' on which all roads converged. St Mary's Cathedral, founded in 1130 and rebuilt largely in the 19th century, is a fine example of Gothic-revival architecture and incorporates a 12th-century chancel with magnificent windows. The town's 12th-century High Cross, well adorned but incomplete, now stands in its grounds. A slightly earlier Roman Catholic Cathedral of the Assumption is a marvellous neo-Gothic building with fine window and tower carvings. Tuam can claim Ireland's first industrial museum, the Mill Museum, an operational corn mill with millwheel and other interesting industrial exhibits.

A tangible representation of the vision that made Knock famous over 100 years ago

Just outside the town, on the Ryehill road, there is an interesting medieval lake dwelling, known as Loughpark Crannóg. Seven miles (11km) to the southeast, on the shores of a small lake, is the 12th-century Knockmoy Abbey. The tomb of its founder, Cathal O'Connor, King of Connacht, can be found within the ruins, as well as traces of ancient murals.

i *Town centre*

▶ *Leave Tuam on the **N17** southwest, and about 3 miles (5km) from town turn west on the **R333** for 9 miles (14km) to reach Headford.*

6 Headford, Co Galway

This popular angling and market centre is very close to Lough Corrib, and there are boats for hire at nearby Greenfield. Two miles (3km) northwest of town, Ross Abbey is a large 1498 Franciscan friary that fell victim to Cromwellian forces in 1656. Its original size can be judged by its two courtyards, around which are the domestic buildings. These include a refectory with reader's

At the heart of Castlebar, the courthouse overlooks this delightful leafy green

FOR HISTORY BUFFS

About 10 miles (16km) north of Ballinrobe, on the N84, Ballintubber Abbey is unique in the English-speaking world in that Mass has been celebrated continuously since its foundation in 1216. It was suppressed by Henry VIII in 1542, the roof was removed by Cromwellians in 1653 and the central tower collapsed. Then there were the Penal Laws in the 18th century, but despite all this, celebrants continued to worship here.

An excavated 5,000-year-old, 12 sq mile (31 sq km) rural landscape, the Ceide fields, lies 22 miles (35km) northwest of Ballina.

desk, dormitories, and a kitchen with a surprising forerunner of modern fish tanks.

▶ *Take the* ***R334*** *northwest for just over 6 miles (10km), then turn left to Cong via the* ***R346****. From Cong take the* ***R345*** *northeast to rejoin the* ***R334*** *and turn left to reach Ballinrobe.*

7 Ballinrobe, Co Mayo
Beautifully situated in the vicinity of three good fishing lakes (loughs Corrib, Mask and Carra), this small town is surrounded by mountains and woodlands. At the north end of town are the ruins of a 1313 Augustinian friary, and about 3 miles (5km) to the southwest is Killower Cairn, one of the most impressive in Connacht.

Just 7 miles (11km) south of Ballinrobe (take the R334 and turn west on the R345), the little town of Cong was the setting for most of the popular film *The Quiet Man*. That, however, is the least of its claims to fame. More notable are the ruins of the Royal Abbey of Cong, built by Turlough Mor O'Conor, High King of Ireland in the 12th century, on the site of a 7th-century monastic community, and burial place of Ireland's last High King, Rory O'Conor, who died in 1198; the impressive Ashford Castle, now

a luxury hotel, whose rather eccentric architecture incorporates several styles and periods; and the 14th-century inscribed stone cross in the main street.

▶ *Follow the **N84** to Castlebar.*

8 Castlebar, Co Mayo
The county town of Mayo, Castlebar has figured in several major Irish insurrections, most notable in 1798, when Irish–French forces routed British cavalry, causing such a hasty retreat to Hollymount, Tuam and Athlone that the campaign gained the nickname 'The Race of Castlebar'. The present Imperial Hotel was known as James Daly's Hotel in 1879 when the Land League was founded there.

Clydagh Bridge, northeast of the town, is the starting point for an idyllic forest walk.

i Town centre

SPECIAL TO...

Castlebar's International Walking Festival is a highlight of each June.

▶ *Take the **N60** southwest back to Westport.*

SPECIAL TO...

Westport's Street Festival in July features street performers and folk singers from all over Ireland.

BACK TO NATURE

Ten miles (16km) west of Westport, 2 miles (3km) east of Louisburgh and ½ mile (1km) on a signposted road off the R335, the National Forest Old Head Wood provides a refreshing stop. There is a car park and also picnic grounds, with well-marked pathways through the small reserve. Oak is the dominant species, but shares the territory with native birch, willow and rowan. Beech and sycamore trees, not native to the area, have also been introduced. There are fine views over Clew Bay.

Ashford Castle at Cong is now a sumptuous hotel

TOUR
19

Region of Stony Beauty

Galway is a thriving commercial and university city with a particularly lively cultural scene. The heart of the city is a maze of colourful medieval streets and the famous Spanish Arch is a relic of the old city walls. Attractions include the impressive modern cathedral and, on a much smaller scale, Nora Barnacle's House.

2/3 DAYS • 136 MILES • 218KM

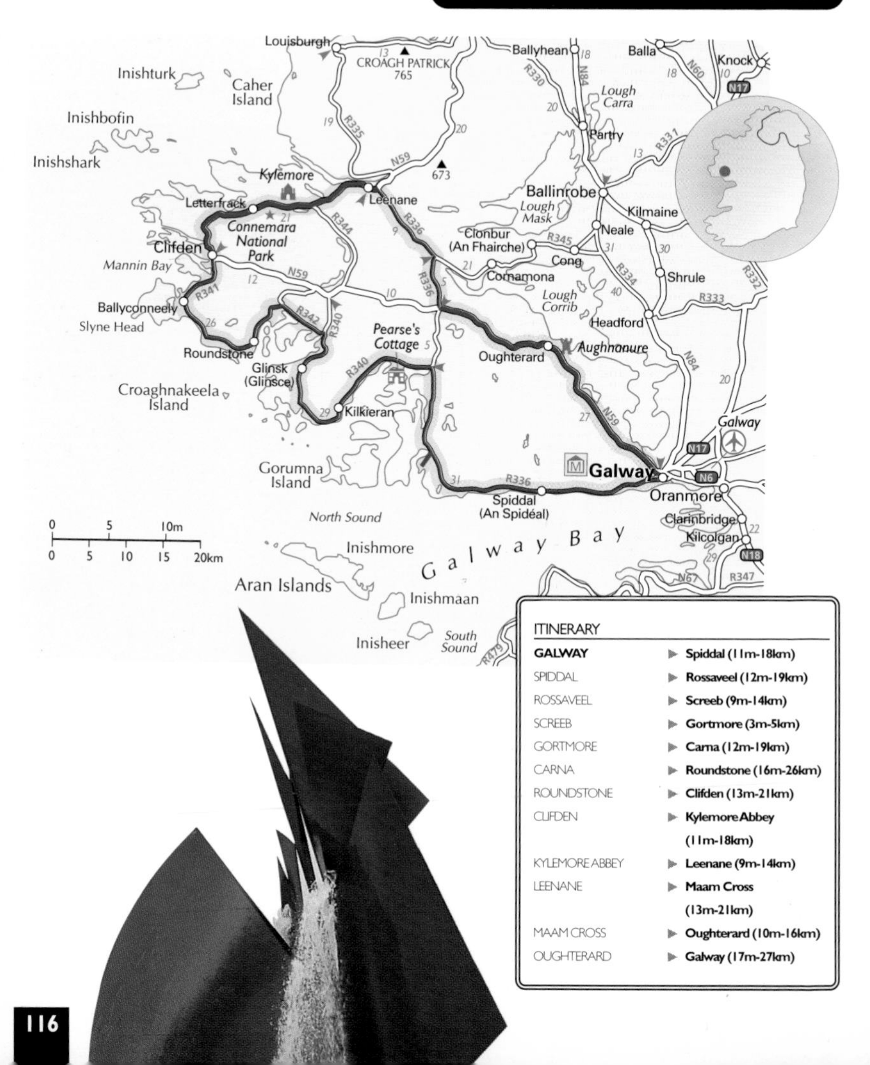

ITINERARY	
GALWAY	▶ **Spiddal (11m-18km)**
SPIDDAL	▶ **Rossaveel (12m-19km)**
ROSSAVEEL	▶ **Screeb (9m-14km)**
SCREEB	▶ **Gortmore (3m-5km)**
GORTMORE	▶ **Carna (12m-19km)**
CARNA	▶ **Roundstone (16m-26km)**
ROUNDSTONE	▶ **Clifden (13m-21km)**
CLIFDEN	▶ **Kylemore Abbey (11m-18km)**
KYLEMORE ABBEY	▶ **Leenane (9m-14km)**
LEENANE	▶ **Maam Cross (13m-21km)**
MAAM CROSS	▶ **Oughterard (10m-16km)**
OUGHTERARD	▶ **Galway (17m-27km)**

The lovely Eyre Square in the centre of Galway has many interesting monuments

[i] *Victoria Place, Eyre Square, Galway*

FOR HISTORY BUFFS

Take a look at the Lynch Memorial Window in Galway's Market Street, and the inscription above the doorway. The story goes that Lord Mayor James Lynch FitzStephen's popular 19-year-old son murdered one of his closest friends, who he thought paid undue attention to a young lady they both admired. Overcome with remorse, the son turned himself in, and his father sat as magistrate in the case, returning a death-by-hanging sentence. When the executioner refused to perform his duty, the father carried out the sentence himself.

▶ *Take the coast road, the **R336**, west to Spiddal.*

1 Spiddal, Co Galway
This charming little resort town has a marvellous beach, the Silver Strand, and shore fishing is especially good here. Its Roman Catholic St Eanna's Church is an architectural delight, completed in 1904 in Celtic Romanesque style by William A Scott. A favourite pastime during the summer are races between local curraghs (lightweight wood and canvas boats). The Spiddal Craft Centre, a complex of craft workshops and showrooms, is well worth a visit.

FOR CHILDREN

West of Galway, Salthill is a children's paradise. In addition to a good beach and pedal buggies for riding along the promenade, attractions at Leisureland Amusement Park are guaranteed to please. The huge complex includes a heated indoor pool, a superb water slide and just about every ride known to humankind.

▶ *Continue west on the **R336** for 12 miles (19km) to Rossaveel, which lies just off this road.*

2 Rossaveel, Co Galway
There are still thatched cottages scattered about this small harbour village, from which peat for fuel is shipped by barge to the Aran Islands. The passenger boat trip out to the islands takes just 40 minutes from Rossaveel, rather than the 1½-hour voyage from Galway.

The Aran Islands group consists of three inhabited islands: Inishmore, with the only safe harbour for steamers; Inishmaan and Inisheer, where curraghs meet incoming boats to take passengers or freight to the docks.

Prehistory has left its mark on the faces of all three islands – promontory forts, ringforts and beehive huts speak of the 'Celtic Twilight' era – while lofty round towers, oratories and tiny churches are reminders of the early days of Christianity in Ireland.

A visit to Aran is an easy, delightful day-trip from Rossaveel, and accommodation

can be arranged in advance for those who want to stay longer. Steamers to Inishmore, the largest of the islands, dock at the main port of Kilronan, and jaunting cars are waiting to take visitors exploring. Rented bicycles are also available, and walkers will delight in following the one main road around the island, with an occasional stop to chat with its local inhabitants. Dun Aengus is an 11-acre (4.5-hectare) stone fort perched on a cliff some 300 feet (91m) above the sea, one of the finest prehistoric monuments in western Europe. Its three concentric enclosures are surrounded by drystone walls, and from the innermost rampart there are outstanding views of the islands and accross the sea to the Connemara coast.

Near the village of Cowrugh, the grounds of a small 15th-century church hold four great flagstones marking the graves of saints, and south of the church there is a holy well. The area surrounding this village is littered with ancient monuments. But, then, it is literally impossible to go very far on this large island or the two smaller ones without encountering a vivid reminder of centuries past in one form or another.

Among the remains on Inisheer are the medieval tower of O'Brien's Castle which is situated on a prominent rocky hill, St Gobnet's Church and the Church of St Cavan.

The oval fort of Dun Conor rises from a steep-sided hill on Inishmaan; there is also a fine dolmen. Visits to Inishmaan and Inisheer can be arranged with boatmen in Kilronan.

▶ *Turn north on the **R336** for 9 miles (14km) to Screeb.*

3 Screeb, Co Galway
There is excellent game fishing from this small town. One of Ireland's peat-burning electricity generating stations is in the near vicinity.

▶ *Turn west on to the **R340** to Gortmore.*

4 Gortmore, Co Galway
From this village, a left turn will take you to the town of Tuar Loch, site of Padraig Pearse's cottage. It was in this small thatched cottage that the great Irish leader, who was executed in 1916, spent his holidays and wrote his most important works.

▶ *Follow the **R340** southwest to Carna.*

5 Carna, Co Galway
Lobster fishing is still the main occupation in this picturesque village. Three miles (5km) to the south, a bridge connects Mweenish Island to the mainland. The beautiful beaches and interesting University College Galway marine biology station make this a worthwhile detour from the route.

A boat trip is available from Carna to St Macdara's Island, named after the 6th-century saint who lived here.

▶ *Take the **R340** north for about 7 miles (11km), then turn west on to the **R342** (signposted Cashel) for 5 miles (8km) and at Toombeola turn south on to the **R341** for the 4-mile (6km) drive to Roundstone.*

6 Roundstone, Co Galway
This pretty village on the west side of Roundstone Bay is a quiet holiday resort that in recent years has attracted a host of artists and craftspeople as permanent residents, with workshops and showrooms. The settlement here was originally established in the early 19th century for Scottish fishermen.

About 2 miles (3km) out on the Ballyconneely road is a fine sandy beach at Dog's Bay (Port-na-Feadog).

▶ *Continue on the **R341** northwest to Clifden.*

RECOMMENDED WALKS

About 2 miles (3km) from Roundstone on the Ballyconneely road (R341), leave the car at Dog's Bay and walk its beautiful sandy beach around the coast to Gorteen Bay, which also has a lovely sandy beach. Errisbeg Mountain, which hovers over this part of Connemara, is an easy climb, with magnificent views of the lakes and stony landscape to the north and fine seascapes that reach as far as Clifden to the northwest and the Twelve Pins to the northeast.

7 Clifden, Co Galway
Nestled between the mountains and the Atlantic, with the Twelve Pins (or Bens) rising to its east, Clifden is often called 'The Capital of Connemara'. It lies at the head of Clifden Bay. Built in the 19th century, the town has managed to keep its Georgian character. Its two churches dominate the skyline, and the 1830 Catholic church is built on the site of an ancient monastic beehive stone hut, a clochan, which gave the town its name. The 1820 Protestant church is also a fine structure and holds a silver copy of the Cross of Cong. Clifden Castle was built by John d'Arcy in 1815. Its grounds give a fine marine view.

Clifden is the very centre of Connemara pony-breeding country, and you are in luck if you arrive in August during the annual Connemara Pony Show. The sturdy little Connemara ponies are native to the area, and are much in demand. It is great fun to watch the trading, and the festivities also include many exhibitions of Irish arts and crafts.

About 4 miles (6km) south of Clifden (1½ miles (2.5km) north of Ballyconneely), look for signposts to the Alcock and Brown Memorial, the spot in

The Twelve Pins (or Bens) are rarely out of view on the Connemara horizon

Derrygimlagh Bog where intrepid aviators Alcock and Brown crash-landed at the end of the first non-stop flight across the Atlantic from St John's, Newfoundland, in 1919. About 1½ miles (2.5km) away a limestone aeroplane commemorates the event. Near by are masts and foundations of the first transatlantic wireless transmitting station, set up here by Marconi, the Italian pioneer of radio.

i *Market Street*

SCENIC ROUTES

Almost every mile of this tour can be described as scenic, but without doubt one of the most striking stretches is Clifden's Sky Drive. The 9-mile (14km) narrow cliff road circles the peninsula to the west of the town and opens up vast seascapes. The drive is well signposted from Clifden.

▶ *Take the **N59** northeast for 11 miles (18km) to Kylemore Abbey.*

8 Kylemore Abbey, Co Galway

Situated in the scenic Pass of Kylemore, palatial Kylemore Abbey looks less like an ecclesiastical institution than any other in Ireland. Not surprising, since this magnificent gleaming white castellated mansion was built in the late 1800s as a private residence for millionaire MP Mitchell Henry. Its setting is enhanced by the castle's shimmering image reflected in the waters of one of the three Kylemore lakes. Now a convent of the Benedictine nuns of Ypres, it also houses a pottery and a restaurant run by the nuns. Visitors are welcomed to both, as well as to the lovely grounds and the Gothic chapel.

The gleaming fairy-tale towers of Kylemore Abbey are reflected in the lake

BACK TO NATURE

The Connemara National Park covers some 4,940 acres (2,000 hectares) that encompass virtually all varieties of this unique region's geology, flora and fauna. Four peaks of the Twelve Pins mountain range are here, surrounded by boglands, heaths and grasslands. The bogs are dotted with clumps of purple moor-grass, bog asphodel, bog myrtle and bog cotton. Insect-eating sundews and butterworts, milkwort, orchids and a variety of lichens and mosses are grown here. Birds of prey such as sparrowhawks, merlins, peregrines and kestrels are seen from time to time. Red deer, once native to the hills of Connemara, are being reintroduced, and there is a well-established herd of Connemara ponies. Detailed literature on the park is available at the visitor centre.

En route to Leenane, the Maamturk mountain range comes into view, with loughs Fee and Nacarrigeen on your left. Further on, the road follows the southern shore of Killary harbour, a 10-mile (16km) long fiord-like inlet from the sea that runs between steep mountains.

▶ *Continue northeast on the **N59** for 9 miles (14km) to Leenane.*

9 Leenane, Co Galway
Set near the head of Killary harbour, Leenane is a popular angling centre and mountain-climbing base. This is the western end of the Partry Mountains, and the 2,131-foot (650m) Devil's Mother is the most striking feature of the landscape around this lovely village, location of the film, *The Field*. Close to Leenane (on the road to Louisburgh) is the beautiful Aasleagh waterfall, which is well worth a short detour.

Aughnanure Castle is a fine ruin on Lough Corrib's shores

▶ *Turn southeast on to the **R336** to Maam Cross.*

10 Maam Cross, Co Galway
This crossroads between north and south Connemara runs through some of the region's most beautiful scenery. Local mountain peaks are relatively easy to climb and provide marvellous views. For good views of Lough Corrib and its fabled Castlekirk (the Hen's Castle), a 13th-century keep built by Rory O'Connor, take the road north signposted Maam and turn right at the T-junction. According to legend, Castlekirk was built overnight by a witch and her hen.

▶ *Continue southeast on the **N59** to Oughterard.*

SCENIC ROUTES

The 10-mile (16km) drive from Maam Cross to Oughterard passes through a landscape of amazing variety, encompassing lakes, moorland, mountain scenery and bogland.

11 Oughterard, Co Galway
This lively town on the upper shores of Lough Corrib is also a popular salmon- and trout-angling resort. Views along the loughside road are especially impressive, and local boatmen take visitors on excursions to the many islands. You can see the beautiful Hill of Doon by following the loughside road north. Aughnanure Castle, built by the O'Flahertys in about 1500, is a six-storey tower house by the shores of Lough Corrib.

Ross Lake and Ross Castle lie southeast of Oughterard. Here Violet Martin collaborated with her cousin Edith Somerville on *Experiences of an Irish RM* and other novels.

i *Town centre*

▶ *Follow the **N59** southeast for 17 miles (27km) to Galway.*

SPECIAL TO...

Galway town seems always to be celebrating one thing or another with a festival. Among the most important are the Race Week in late July or early August, six days of horse racing, music and feasting; and the International Oyster Festival in late September, which attracts people from around the world to participate in oyster-opening competitions and non-stop feasting on these bi-valves.

ULSTER

Ulster is a beautiful place, rich in history, rare in scenery, a province of mountains, loughs, coast and countryside, with tranquil villages and friendly people. The ancient province of Ulster had nine counties: Antrim, Down, Londonderry, Fermanagh, Tyrone and Armagh, which now form Northern Ireland; and Donegal, Cavan and Monaghan, which are part of the Republic of Ireland.

When Patrick came to Celtic Ireland, he chose Armagh for his ecclesiastical capital, because of the strength of Emain Macha, the Palace of the Red Branch Knights. Ulster made a contribution to Ireland's claim to be a land of saints and scholars. Great monasteries and educational establishments were founded, like that at Bangor, in County Down, which sent out missionaries to light up the Dark Age of Europe.

Since Patrick's time the province, like the rest of Ireland, has had successive waves of invaders. Vikings, Normans, English, Scots, Huguenots and refugees have settled here. However, in Ulster it was the number of Scots and Celts, but mostly Presbyterians, that created the special blend of Planter and Gael in Ulster. The hardy race of Scots-Ulster had a temperament tough enough to cope with the frontiers of the New World of America, and enterprising enough to leave a land where non-Conformists were at a disadvantage. A dozen American presidents came from this stock. These were the men who defended Derry in the siege, fought with William at the Boyne, won glory for their bravery at the Somme and rejected an independent Ireland in the 1920s.

The lovely Mourne Mountains include great forests, remote lakes and scenic coast (Tour 25)

There is evidence of the two distinctive traditions in Ulster – fife and drum, uillean pipes and bodhran, paintings of King Billy or Mother Ireland on gable walls (most likely drawn by the same man). However, you may be surprised at how little difference there is between the two. Ulster people are delighted to see visitors and very anxious to show them the best of their province. Local councils have worked hard to provide fine amenities in even the most out-of-the-way places. Small villages are festooned with hanging baskets, and window boxes and flower-filled carts give the best impression. When Ulster people are really enjoying themselves – and they do, often – they say 'It's great crack'. 'Crack' is fun, music, laughter and story-telling, often washed down with a drink or two, and they will be happy to share 'the crack' with visitors.

Tour 20
From historic walled Derry, a proud city rich in song and humour, the tour enters Donegal, whose incomparable scenery is world-renowned – empty beaches stretching for miles are commonplace, amid a landscape of rugged hills, stone walls and white cottages crouching against the Atlantic. The tour passes through fishing and farming communities where the Irish language and traditions are cherished, and ends with Donegal's treasure, Glenveagh National Park.

Tour 21
The Antrim Coast road, which clings to the shore between glens and mountains, headlands and villages, begins a drive of stunning variety. The Giant's Causeway is an essential destination, but the tour takes in lesser-known delights, as well as dramatic castles and historic landscapes, returning to Larne through pleasant countryside.

Tour 22
Belfast, a city of character, is the starting point for a tour that is full of interest for those who love history and wildlife or who simply enjoy discovering quiet villages in beautiful settings. The route takes in the Ulster Folk and Transport Museum, the two fine country houses of Mount Stewart and Castle Ward, and important early Christian sites. The tour focuses on Strangford Lough, rich in marine biology and no less important to ornithologists.

Tour 23
Fermanagh is a very distinctive Ulster county, more water than land it seems, and the land is sparsely populated. The combination of water, woodland and ancient buildings is nowhere so varied as in Fermanagh. The tranquil waters of Lough Erne offer a fisherman's paradise. The route begins in the historic town of Enniskillen and includes the haunting beauty of the monastic round tower at Devenish and the neoclassical splendour of Castle Coole. Belleek pottery and Marble Arch caves provide additional interest.

Tour 24
Armagh, the ecclesiastical capital of Ireland, is the starting point for a tour that climbs from the gentle pastures and orchards of County Armagh to the rugged mountains of County Tyrone. This is a journey through Ulster's history, from the heroic era of the Red Branch Knights and the coming of Saint Patrick to the Irish emigrants' new world of America. Country houses, glens and forests, peatlands and parkland come together to form a picture of mid-Ulster.

Tour 25
County Down's distinctive landscape is that of the drumlins, small rounded hills that roll and roll, sheltering quiet green valleys and offering sudden views of sea or lough. The route leaves Newry and goes by way of the charming village of Hillsborough, and then winds through hills again until they give way to the Mountains of Mourne. The Kingdom of Mourne has its own identity, from the small fishing harbours of the rocky coast, through farmland crisscrossed by stone walls to the heights of the mountains. The end of the journey takes in beautiful Carlingford Lough, abundant in forests, castles and pleasant resorts.

The magnificent Palm House of Belfast's famous Botanic Garden, near the city centre (Tour 22)

Seascapes & Mountain Passes

History is in evidence all around Londonderry (or Derry), not least in the famous Walls of Derry, which form the most complete network of walls, gates and bastions in the British Isles. This town on the River Foyle is also a lively centre for the performing arts, and has craft shops, an art gallery and a museum.

2/3 DAYS • 172 MILES • 276KM

ITINERARY	
LONDONDERRY	▶ **Grianán of Aileach (7m-11km)**
GRIANÁN OF AILEACH	▶ **Letterkenny (18m-29km)**
LETTERKENNY	▶ **Rathmelton (8m-13km)**
RATHMELTON	▶ **Rathmullan (7m-11km)**
RATHMULLAN	▶ **Milford (31m-50km)**
MILFORD	▶ **Carrigart (10m-16km)**
ATLANTIC DRIVE	▶ **(10m-16km)**
CARRIGART	▶ **Creeslough (7m-11km)**
CREESLOUGH	▶ **Dunfanaghy (7m-11km)**
DUNFANAGHY	▶ **Errigal (16m-26km)**
ERRIGAL	▶ **Glenveagh (13m-21km)**
GLENVEAGH	▶ **Londonderry (38m-61km)**

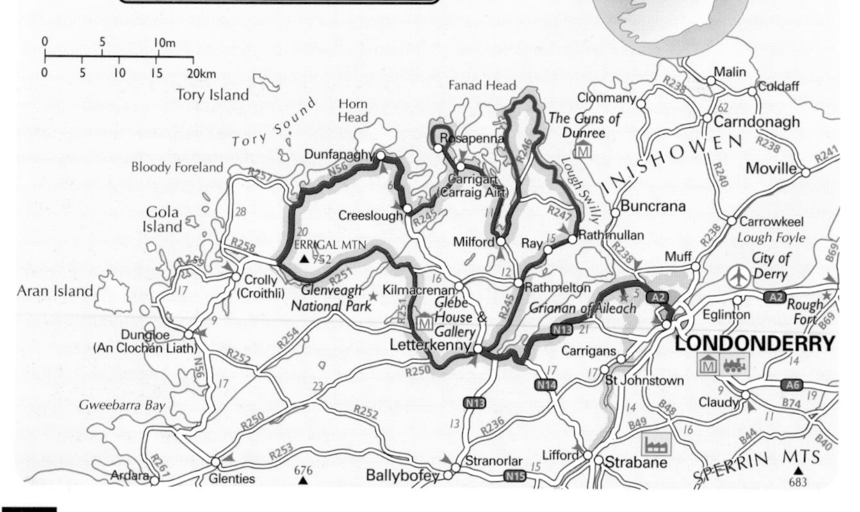

i Foyle Street, Londonderry

*Take the **A2** for Buncrana, then the **N13** Letterkenny road to the sign for Grianán of Aileach.*

1 The Grianán of Aileach, Co Donegal

This massive stone fort can be seen for miles around, and the climb to Grianán Mountain gives majestic views over Lough Foyle and Lough Swilly. It is easy to see why this commanding site should have been chosen for the royal residence of the O'Neills, Kings of Ulster. It was enthusiastically restored by Dr Bernard of Derry in 1870, and his work has left us with a complete picture of walls 17 feet (5.25m) high and 13 feet (4m) thick, with steps rising to four levels. The fine modern church at Burt has architectural echoes of Grianán.

*Return to the **N13** and turn left to follow it to Letterkenny.*

2 Letterkenny, Co Donegal

An administrative and commercial centre in the northwest, Letterkenny sits at the southwest end of Lough Swilly on a fertile plain. In the 19th century it was spoken of as 'fast becoming a place of importance and wealth' and had a steamer communication with Glasgow. It gained the richly Gothic St Eunan's Cathedral at the end of the last century.

i Derry Road

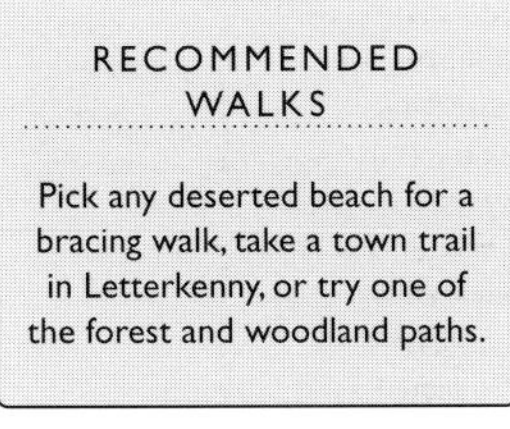

RECOMMENDED WALKS

Pick any deserted beach for a bracing walk, take a town trail in Letterkenny, or try one of the forest and woodland paths.

*Take the **R245** for 8 miles (13km) to Rathmelton.*

3 Rathmelton, Co Donegal

The long curve of the River Leannan, steep hills, tree-lined streets and handsome warehouses on the riverfront all combine to make Rathmelton a place of great charm. It was a Planters' town ('planters' were Presbyterian Scots and Anglican English settlers loyal to the English crown who were encouraged to settle in Ireland and replace the rebellious Catholic Irish landowners). Prosperity gained by the easy navigation from the river mouth brought fine Georgian houses, as well as corn mills, a brewery, bleach greens and linenworks in the early 19th century. The first Presbyterian church in America was organised in 1706 by Reverend Francis Makemie, who emigrated from Rathmelton. Anglers come here to fish, and 'The Pool', near by, is a well-known salmon beat.

Killydonnell Friary, founded by the Franciscans in the 16th century, is 2½ miles (4km) to the south in the grounds of Fort Stewart. There are excellent views of the surrounding countryside from Cam Hill.

The purpose of Grianán of Aileach may be revealed by its name – 'stone palace of the sun'

*Take the **R247** for 7 miles (11km) to Rathmullan.*

4 Rathmullan, Co Donegal

Rathmullan is a pretty village, fringed with trees, on a beautiful beach on Lough Swilly, looking over to the hills of the Inishowen peninsula, with the ruin of a 16th-century priory at the water's edge. Quite large fishing ships come into its pier, without upsetting the tranquillity. Despite its present peacefulness, Rathmullan has witnessed two major historical events. In 1587, Red Hugh O'Donnell was treacherously lured on board a disguised merchant ship and carried as prisoner to Dublin Castle; and that evocative moment in Irish history, the Flight of the Earls, took place from here in 1607. The O'Neill, Earl of Tyrone, and the O'Donnell, Earl of Tyrconnell, with about a hundred lesser chieftains, finally gave up their resistance to English law and authority in Ulster, and left for exile in Europe, leaving their estates to be forfeited and colonised by English and Scottish settlers. A Heritage Centre in Rathmullan tells the story.

Rathmullan is at the start of the Fanad Drive, with its beaches, streams, lakes and mountain ridges.

▶ *Follow the signposts for the Fanad Drive by Portsalon and Kerrykeel to Milford.*

5 Milford, Co Donegal
Milford offers a leafy contrast to the grand headlands and magnificent bays of Donegal. It stands at the end of the narrow, islanded inlet of Mulroy Bay, and among its wooded hills are two lovely glens with waterfalls, named Golan Loop and Grey Mare's Tail.

▶ *Take the **R245** to Carrigart.*

6 Carrigart, Co Donegal
This busy little town is tucked in an inlet of Mulroy Bay. To the north is Rosapenna, which boasts a championship golf course that is as scenic as it is challenging.

Nature challenged man and won in the 18th century, when a massive sandstorm engulfed houses and gradually overtook Rosapenna House, finally forcing the occupant, the Reverend Porter, from the top floor in 1808. From Rosapenna beach you can see the Muslac caves, cut by the sea into quartzite folds. The Downings is a small resort, particularly popular with families with small children, and has an important tweed factory and shop.

▶ *Follow the signs for the Atlantic Drive.*

7 The Atlantic Drive, Co Donegal
It is held that the feast of scenery along the road around the Rosguill Peninsula, called the Atlantic Drive, is Donegal's best.The spectacular circuit passes both Sheep Haven and Mulroy bays; Horn Head and Melmore Head are in focus, with Muckish and Errigal mountains more distant to the south. The road passes little shingly bays, and hillsides dotted with white cottages, then opens out to the incomparable sight of Tranarossan Strand. Here the Youth Hostel is in a slightly idiosyncratic building designed by the English architect Edwin Lutyens.

▶ *Return to Carrigart and follow the **R245** to Creeslough.*

8 Creeslough, Co Donegal
On a height overlooking Sheep Haven Bay is the little village of Creeslough. Doe Castle stands on a low, narrow promontory, bounded by the sea on three sides and a rock-cut ditch on the fourth. It is fortified with corbelled bartizans or turrets, firing platforms and musket loops, a round tower and a great square keep. It has had a colourful and turbulent history. It became the stronghold of the MacSweeneys, who were 'gallowglasses' (foreign warriors), a professional fighting force invited by the O'Donnells from Scotland. It was a refuge for Spanish Armada sailors, was taken by the Cromwellians and was used as a garrison for William of Orange. Finally it came into the hands of an English family, the Harts. The initials of General George Vaughan Hart are over the door.

▶ *Follow the signs for Dunglow, then take the **N56** for 7 miles (11km) to Dunfanaghy.*

RECOMMENDED WALKS

At Ards Forest Park, near Creeslough, Lough Lilly is rich with flowering water-lillies in high summer and an enclosed park contains deer. At this most northerly forest park, the trees go right down to the sea, and there are places to bathe as well as walk.

FOR CHILDREN

Marbel Hill, 4 miles (6km) to the east of Dunfanaghy, is a safe and beautiful strand, where windsurfing and canoeing have been tailored for children, with special lessons and the right size of wetsuits and equipment. Over-10-year-olds, even those with no experience, can join a canoe expedition. Basic instruction is given, and the expeditions, under qualified supervision, offer an ideal introduction to the joys of canoeing in magnificent surroundings.

9 Dunfanaghy, Co Donegal
This is a neat, bustling little place, a good point from which to explore Horn Head. Thought by many to be the finest of all Irish headlands, this wall of quartzite rises from the sea, its ledges alive with gulls, puffins,

SCENIC ROUTES

In this rugged part of Donegal it would be easier to mention those roads that are not scenic. Try the circuit around Bloody Foreland and its sheltered beaches, small fishing inlets, stone-walled fields and white cottages. Look for islands – Gola to the west, Inishbofin, Inishdooey, Inishbeg and Tory to the north – and learn that Bloody Foreland, the northwest tip of Ireland, gets its name, not from a grisly past, but from the granite boulders that glow red in the rays of the setting sun.

guillemots and razorbills. You can appreciate the full majesty of Horn from Traghlisk Point to the east.

To the northwest is Tory Island, still inhabited by people who make their living from the sea. The art world has considerable respect for the naïve paintings of the Tory Island artists. To the southwest is Falcarragh, the best point from which to climb the flat-topped mountain, Muckish.

▶ *Continue on the* **N56** *to Falcarragh, then to Gortahork. Turn left for Dunglow on the* **N56**.

Dunfanaghy and its superb beach lie sheltered behind Horn Head

SPECIAL TO...

Irish is the first language of many people in Donegal. The Gaeltacht is the name given to the areas where the language is widely spoken and Ireland's cultural traditions are vigorously promoted. The area around Falcarragh, Gortahork and Gweedore has a strong Irish-speaking population, and is the home of an Irish-speaking college, theatre and broadcasting station. Children from all over Ireland come to the Gaeltacht to stay in the cottages and houses of the farmers and fishermen to improve their schoolroom Irish.

10 Errigal Mountain, Co Donegal

Errigal Mountain is a distinctive peak, and once recognised you will see it from many parts of Donegal. Its cone-shaped summit rises 2,466 feet (752m) with silver-grey scree spilling around the slopes. Avoid the scree and, if you can, climb to the top for a panorama that can stretch from Scotland to Knocklayd in County Antrim, wide over the Donegal coastline and south to Sligo's Benbulben – on a clear day, of course. Below lies Dunlewy Lough, and the Poisoned Glen, a sinister name for so pretty a place, but probably deriving from the toxic Irish spurge which used to grow there.

▶ *Take a sharp left, and follow the signs for Glenveagh for 13 miles (21km) on the* ***R251****.*

11 Glenveagh, Co Donegal
Glenveagh is a beautiful place, and unusually for Donegal, the beauty here owes something to human hands. Henry McIlhenny, an American who acquired Glenveagh after it had been owned by several other Americans, developed a garden landscape of outstanding planting that never jars with the superb natural setting of water, mountain and bogland. He then gave the property to the nation to become a National Park. His 'garden rooms' are sensitively enclosed, and a walk through the garden follows the route he enjoyed showing to his visitors. The castle is redolent of the house parties for which Glenveagh became famous, when film stars mixed with aristocracy. It bears witness throughout to Mr McIlhenny's fascination with deer.

Glenveagh's origins lie in its use as a hunting lodge, and Ireland's largest herd of red deer still roams the hills in a very important wilderness area.

Close by at Church Hill is the Regency Glebe House, which has been exquisitely furnished and decorated by Derek Hill, the painter. The art gallery shows selections from the Derek Hill collection and beautiful gardens run down to the lakeside. The Columcille Heritage Centre at nearby Gartan celebrates the life and influence of the saint who is also known as St Columba.

Glenveagh Castle and its lovely gardens are at the heart of a spectacular national park

FOR HISTORY BUFFS

Eviction and emigration are recurrent nightmares that stalked the troubled history of land tenure in Ireland. At Derryveagh, one of the most notorious mass evictions took place and was the cause of contemporary outrage. In 1861, John George Adair, landlord of Glenveagh, evicted 244 people from their homes to face the workhouse or emigration after a bitter feud with his tenants and the murder of his land steward. The eviction cottage is marked by a plaque put up by An Taisce, the National Trust, at a spot 1 mile (1.5km) from the Glebe Gallery.

BACK TO NATURE

The peat bog, a familiar feature of the Irish landscape, is a natural habitat not to be taken for granted and is now increasingly protected. A lowland blanket bog lies at Lough Barra in a broad valley below Slieve Snaght, and contains pools and rivers. It is an important site for Greenland white-fronted geese, a protected species. There is a raised peat bog in the glacial valley of Glenveagh National Park. Here, a rich variety of ferns and mosses grow in the woodland, while red grouse and red deer can be seen on the moorland.

▶ *From Glenveagh, turn right on to the* ***R251*** *for Glebe Gallery, then follow this road before returning left on to the* ***R250*** *for Letterkenny. Take the* ***N13*** *back to Londonderry.*

The Causeway Coast

2/3 DAYS • 163 MILES • 263KM

Larne is a busy port, the terminus for the shortest sea-crossing between Ireland and Britain. To the north is Carnfunnock Park, which has a maze in the shape of Northern Ireland. Larne marks the start of the scenic Antrim Coast Road, which was constructed in the 1830s to link the remote Glens of Antrim to the rest of Ulster.

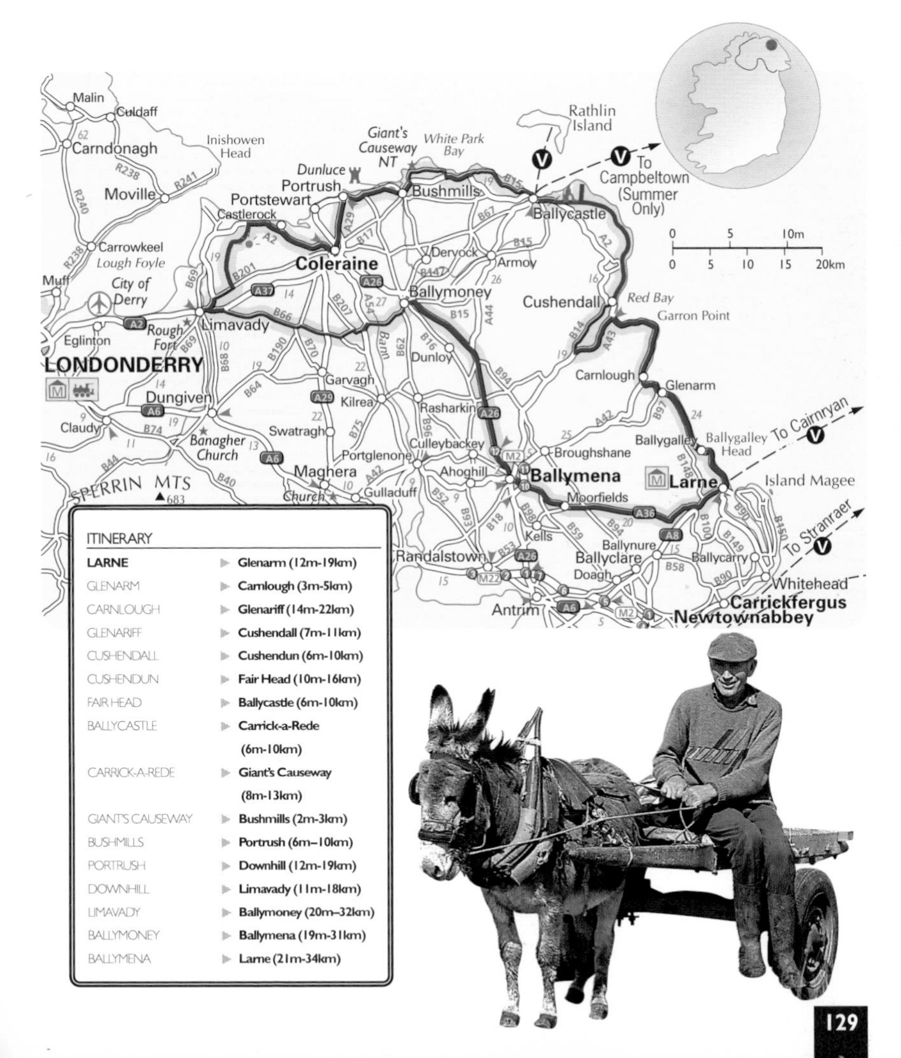

ITINERARY	
LARNE	▶ **Glenarm (12m-19km)**
GLENARM	▶ **Carnlough (3m-5km)**
CARNLOUGH	▶ **Glenariff (14m-22km)**
GLENARIFF	▶ **Cushendall (7m-11km)**
CUSHENDALL	▶ **Cushendun (6m-10km)**
CUSHENDUN	▶ **Fair Head (10m-16km)**
FAIR HEAD	▶ **Ballycastle (6m-10km)**
BALLYCASTLE	▶ **Carrick-a-Rede (6m-10km)**
CARRICK-A-REDE	▶ **Giant's Causeway (8m-13km)**
GIANT'S CAUSEWAY	▶ **Bushmills (2m-3km)**
BUSHMILLS	▶ **Portrush (6m–10km)**
PORTRUSH	▶ **Downhill (12m-19km)**
DOWNHILL	▶ **Limavady (11m-18km)**
LIMAVADY	▶ **Ballymoney (20m-32km)**
BALLYMONEY	▶ **Ballymena (19m-31km)**
BALLYMENA	▶ **Larne (21m-34km)**

i *Narrow Gauge Road, Larne*

▶ *Take the **A2** coastal road north for 12 miles (19km) to Glenarm.*

1 Glenarm, Co Antrim

The Antrim Coast Road is so attractive that it is difficult to resist its magnetic lure, but leave it for a moment to sample the charm of Glenarm, a village that clings to the glen rather than to the coast. The neo-Tudor Glenarm Castle is the seat of the Earls of Antrim; its barbican and battlemented, buttressed walls of 1825 rise above the river just as it approaches the sea. The village has twisting streets (Thackeray apparently enjoyed their names), pavements patterned in limestone and basalt, a market house with an Italianate campanile and good, modest Georgian houses and shops.

The forest, through the gateway at the top of the village, gives the first opportunity to walk up an Antrim glen. This one is narrow, leafy and dense with pathways and waterfalls.

▶ *Take the **A2** to Carnlough.*

2 Carnlough, Co Antrim

Carnlough, at the foot of Glencloy, the least dramatic of the glens, has a good safe beach. A railway used to carry lime from the kilns above the village to the harbour, over the bridge that spans the coast road. The bridge, the clock tower and the former town hall are made from great chunks of limestone. Frances Anne Vane Tempest Stewart, Countess of Antrim and Marchioness of Londonderry, was responsible for many major works, including Garron Tower, built in 1848, once a family home, now a boarding school. She is remembered in the town's main hotel, the Londonderry Arms, which was built in 1854 and has the feel of a coaching inn.

▶ *Take the **A2**, following signposts for Cushendall for 9 miles (14km) to Waterfoot. Turn left on to the **A43** for 5 miles (8km) to Glenariff Forest Park.*

3 Glenariff, Co Antrim

The road obligingly provides a perfect route along this magnificent glen. The bay at its foot is 1 mile (1.5km) long and the chiselled sides draw in the fertile valley symmetrically to the head of the glen. There, the Forest Park allows easy exploration of the deep, wooded gorge with its cascades, 'Ess-na-crub' (Fall of the Hoof), 'Ess-na-laragh' (Fall of the Mare) and Tears of the Mountain.

Waterfoot, the little village at the foot of the glen, hosts The Glens of Antrim Feis (pronounced 'fesh') in July, a major festival of traditional music and dancing.

All along the Antrim Coast Road, wonderful views unfold

Between Red Bay and the pier are three caves. Nanny's Cave was inhabited by Ann Murray until her death, aged 100, in 1847. She supported herself by knitting and by the sale of poteen (an illicit distillation, pronounced potcheen), or 'the natural' as she called it.

► *Turn right to follow the* ***B14*** *for 7 miles (11km) to Cushendall.*

4 Cushendall, Co Antrim

'The Capital of the Glens', Cushendall sits on a pleasant, sandy bay below Glenballyemon, Glenaan and Glencorp and in the curve of the River Dall. The rugged peak of Lurigethan broods over the village, while the softer Tieveragh Hill is supposed to be the capital of the fairies. Cushendall owes much to an East Indian nabob, Francis Turnley, who built the Curfew Tower in the centre as a 'place for the confinement of idlers and rioters'.

In a tranquil valley by the sea just north of the village is the 13th-century church of Layde. MacDonnells of Antrim are buried here, as are Englishmen stationed in these lonely posts as coastguards, and one memorial stone mourns an emigré killed in the American Civil War in 1865 when he was only 18.

► *Follow the* ***B92*** *for 6 miles (10km) to Cushendun.*

5 Cushendun, Co Antrim

The very decided character of Cushendun is a surprise. This is a black-and-white village, with an orderly square and terraces of houses that were designed to look Cornish. Lord Cushendun married a Cornish wife, Maud, and commissioned the distinguished architect Clough Williams-Ellis to create a streetscape with style.

A little salmon fishery stands at the mouth of the River Dun, the 'dark brown water'. To the south is Cave House, locked in cliffs and approachable only through a long, natural cave. Castle Carra is to the north, the place where the clan quarrel between the O'Neills and the MacDonnells caused the treacherous murduring of the great Shane O'Neill during a banquet in 1567.

► *At the north end of the village turn on to the road signposted 'scenic route' for Ballycastle by Torr Head. After 9 miles (14km) turn right to Murlough Bay.*

Cushendun is famous for its unusual architecture

6 Fair Head and Murlough Bay, Co Antrim

Paths from the cluster of houses known as Coolanlough cross the barren headland broken by three dark lakes – Lough Doo, Lough Fadden and Lough na Cranagh, which has a crannóg or lake dwelling. Fair Head itself is exposed and barren, a place inhabited by wild goats and choughs (red-legged crows). The careful walker can descend the cliff using the Grey Man's Path, which follows a dramatic plunging fissure.

By contrast, Murlough Bay is green and fertile, generous in contours and abundantly wooded. Tradition has it that the Children of Lir were transformed into swans to spend 300 years here. At the top of the road is a monument to the Republican leader Sir Roger Casement, and a row of lime kilns, which would have burned the stone for use in fertiliser, whitewash or mortar.

▶ *After 1 mile (2km) turn right for Ballycastle, then right again on to the* ***A2*** *to Ballycastle.*

BACK TO NATURE

For bird-lovers, a trip on the boat to Rathlin Island is not to be missed. Up to 20,000 guillemots, razorbills, fulmars, kittiwakes and puffins can be seen on the sheer rock stacks close to the West Lighthouse. Shearwaters can sometimes be seen offshore. Early summer is the best time for viewing.

7 **Ballycastle,** Co Antrim

Ballycastle is in two parts – the winding main street which carries you up to the heart of the town, and Ballycastle by the sea, with its fine beach and lawn tennis courts.

At the foot of the Margy River is Bonamargy Friary, founded by the Franciscans as late as 1500. The notorious Sorley Boy MacDonald is buried here. Elizabeth I found that he eluded all her attempts at capture, but in 1575, when he had sent his children to Rathlin Island for safety, he had to stand on the mainland helpless while they were murdered.

Ballycastle's museum illustrates the folk and social history of the Glens of Antrim.

At the harbour is a memorial to Gugliemo Marconi, who carried out the first practical test on radio signals between White Lodge, on the clifftop at Ballycastle, and Rathlin Island in 1898. You can travel by boat to Rathlin and savour the life of the 30 or so families who live and farm here. The island is a mecca for divers and birdwatchers. Robert the Bruce hid in a cave on Rathlin after his defeat in 1306. Watching a spider repeatedly trying to climb a thread to the roof, he was encouraged to 'try, and try again'. He returned to Scotland to fight on, and was successful at the Battle of Bannockburn.

[i] *Sheskburn House, Mary Street*

SPECIAL TO...

The Oul' Lammas Fair in Ballycastle, held every August Bank Holiday, is a real horse fair with a lot more besides. The streets of Ballycastle are crammed with stalls, including traditional games of chance, and the town is alive with music and fun. Horse-trading lives up to its reputation, and you are likely to hear the refrain:

Did you take your Mary Ann
For some dulse and yellow man.
At the oul' Lammas Fair in
Ballycastle-O.

Dulse is edible dried sea weed and yellow man a chewy sweet confection.

▶ *From the shore follow the* ***B15*** *coastal route west to Ballintoy, then turn right, following the signpost to Carrick-a-Rede and Larry Bane.*

8 **Carrick-a-Rede,** Co Antrim

A swinging rope bridge spans the deep chasm between the mainland and the rocky island of Carrick-a-Rede, and if you have a very strong heart and a good head, you can cross it. The bridge is put up each year by salmon fishermen, who use Carrick-a-Rede, 'the Rock in the Road', as a good place to net the fish in their path to the Bush and Bann rivers. The rope bridge is approached from Larry Bane, a limestone head which had once been quarried. Some of the quarry workings remain, and the quarry access to the magnificent seascape provides some guaranteed birdwatching. It is possible to sit in your car and spot kittiwakes, cormorants, guillemots, fulmars and razorbills, though you might have to use binoculars to catch sight of the puffins on Sheep Island further out to sea.

Just to the west is Ballintoy, a very pretty little limestone harbour, at the foot of a corkscrew road. A little further west is the breathtaking sandy sweep of White Park Bay, accessible only by foot, and worth every step. Among the few houses that fringe the west end of the beach, tucked into the cliff, is Ireland's smallest church, dedicated to St Gobhan, patron saint of builders.

▶ *Take the* ***B15****, which changes to the* ***A2****, to Portrush, then take the* ***B146*** *for the Giant's Causeway, 8 miles (13km).*

9 **Giant's Causeway,** Co Antrim

Sixty million years ago, or thereabouts, intensely hot volcanic lava erupted through narrow vents and, in cooling rapidly over the white chalk, formed into about 37,000 extraordinary geometric columns and shapes – mostly hexagonal, but also with four, five, seven or eight sides. That is one story. The other is that the giant, Finn MacCool, fashioned it so that he could cross dry-shod to Scotland.

Generations of fanciful guides have embroidered stories and created names for the remarkable formations – the Giant's Organ, the Giant's Harp, the Wishing Chair, and Lord Antrim's Parlour. The Visitor Centre tells the full story of the fact and fiction, the folklore and traditions, and provides a bus service down the steep road to the Causeway.

One story absolutely based on fact is of the *Girona*, a fleeing Spanish Armada galleon, wrecked in a storm on the night of 26 October 1588. A diving team retrieved a treasure hoard from the wreck in 1967, now on display in the Ulster Museum in Belfast. The wreck still lies under cliffs in Port na Spaniagh, one of a magnificent march of bays and headlands on the Causeway.

The most famous sight in Ireland, the Giant's Causeway never fails to amaze and delight

The 'water of life', patiently maturing in oak barrels at the Bushmills Distillery

Near the Visitor Centre is the Causeway School Museum, a reconstructed 1920s schoolroom, complete with learning aids and toys of the era.

i *Visitor Centre*

RECOMMENDED WALKS

There can be few more spectacular walks than the 10-mile (16km) coastal path between the Giant's Causeway and White Park Bay. Magnificent amphitheatres of rocky cliffs, dramatic clefted inlets, basalt sea stacks, an abundance of wild flowers and the company of seabirds add to the pleasure of this walk. A guide will help idenitfy the evocative names for each bay and the historic features, including the remains of tiny Dunseverick Castle.

▶ *Take the **A2** to Bushmills.*

10 **Bushmills,** Co Antrim

This neat village is the home of the world's oldest legal distillery, which was granted its licence in 1608. The water from St Columb's rill, or stream, is said to give the whiskey its special quality, and visitors can discover something of its flavour on tours of the distillery.

The River Bush is rich in trout and salmon, and its fast-flowing waters not only supported the mills that gave the town its name, but generated electricity for the world's first hydroelectric tramway, which carried passengers to the Giant's Causeway between 1893 and 1949.

▶ *Follow the **A2** west to Portrush.*

11 **Portrush,** Co Antrim

Portrush is a typical seaside resort, which flourished with the rise of the railways. It has three good bays, with broad stretches of sand, ranges of dunes, rock pools, white cliffs and a busy harbour.

Nearby Dunluce is one of the most romantic of castles, where a sprawling ruin clings perilously to the clifftop, presenting a splendid profile. The castle was a MacDonnell stronghold until half the kitchen fell into the sea on a stormy night in 1639. The Dunluce Centre is a high-tech entertainment complex.

i *Dunluce Centre*

▶ *Take the **A29** for Coleraine, then follow the **A2** for Castlerock, then on to Downhill, a distance of 12 miles (19km).*

FOR CHILDREN

Portrush has all the fun of a traditional seaside holiday town for children, from donkey rides to candy floss. It also has a countryside centre, with animals to pet, and there are regular firework displays on Ranmore Head. Should it rain, Portrush also has indoor activities, including Waterworld, with swimming and other facilities, the Dunluce Centre and an indoor funfair.

FOR HISTORY BUFFS

On the A2 just before Downhill, the Hezlett House, built in 1691, is a long thatched cottage. Restored and open to the public, it is important because of its construction. It was made with 'crucks' – frames of curved timber – which act as upright posts, and sloping rafters set straight on to a foundation of rock. This was a quick way of building in the 17th century. Sometimes Planters brought the frames with them, ready for assembly.

12 **Downhill,** Co Londonderry

The feast of magnificent coastal scenery is given a different face at Downhill. Here Frederick Hervey, who was Earl of Bristol and Bishop of Derry, decided to adorn nature with man's art, by creating a landscape with eyecatching buildings, artificial ponds and cascades, in keeping with the taste of the time. He was a great 18th-century eccentric, collector and traveller, who gave his name to the Bristol hotels throughout Europe. Although nature has won back much of the Earl Bishop's ambitious scheme, the spirit of the place is strongly felt, and Mussenden Temple, a perfect classical rotunda, sits on a wonderful headland.

Near by is 20th-century

man's idea of seaside recreation, at Benone Tourist Complex, beside the 7 mile (11km) Benone Strand, one of the cleanest beaches in Europe, backed by a duneland park.

SCENIC ROUTES

The Bishop's Road runs over Eagle Hill and Binevanagh Mountain, rising steeply from Downhill. The Earl Bishop had it built to provide local employment in the 18th century. From Gortmore viewpoint the panorama sweeps from Donegal to Fair Head, above the fertile shores of Lough Foyle and beyond to Scotland. The AA has placed a chart showing directions and distances of the views, and another plaque recalls that this was the site chosen in 1824 by surveyors for the most accurate measurement ever then achieved between two places.

► *From the **A2** turn left on Bishop's Road for Gortmore, then after 8 miles (13km) turn right on to the **B201**, then left on to the **A2** for Limavady.*

13 Limavady, Co Londonderry

The Roe Valley was the territory of the O'Cahans, and O'Cahan's Rock is one of the landmarks of the nearby Roe Valley Country Park. One story says that it was here a dog made a mighty leap with a message to help relieve a besieged castle, giving this pleasant market town its name, 'The Leap of the Dog'.

The Londonderry Air was first written down here by Jane Ross, when she heard it being played by a street fiddler. Limavady was the birthplace of William Massey (1856–1925), Prime Minister of New Zealand from 1912 to 1925.

i *Connell Street*

► *Take the **A37** for Coleraine, then turn right on to the **B66**; follow signs for the **B66** to Ballymoney.*

14 Ballymoney, Co Antrim

A bustling town, Ballymoney remembers its farming past at Leslie Hill Heritage Farm Park, where visitors can travel through the park by horse and trap. Drumaheglis Marina gives access to the River Bann, elsewhere a fairly secluded river, and offers waterbus cruises.

Three miles (5km) north-east, in Conagher, off the road to Dervock, is the birthplace of the 25th President of the US, William McKinley.

► *Take the **A26** to Ballymena.*

15 Ballymena, Co Antrim

Ballymena, the county town of Antrim, boasts as one of its sons Timothy Eaton, who founded Eaton's Stores in Canada. To the east the hump of Slemish Mountain rises abruptly from the ground. It was here that St Patrick worked when he was first brought to Ireland in slavery. In the south suburbs is the 40-foot (12m) high Harryville motte and bailey – one of the finest surviving Anglo-Norman earthworks in Ulster.

Just to the west is 17th-century Galgorm Castle, a Plantation castle built by Sir Faithful Fortescue in 1618. Beyond is the charming village of Gracehill, founded by the Moravians in the 18th century.

► *Take the **A36** for 21 miles (34km) and return to Larne.*

Farming the old-fashioned way at the Leslie Hill Historic Farm in northern County Antrim

Strangford Lough

From the centre of Belfast, the rolling hills which cradle the city catch the eye at the end of many streets. Belfast is an industrial city with a strong ship-building tradition and the skyline is dominated by two huge cranes in the dockyard. Near by the Waterfront Concert Hall is a splendid venue for international events. The city is rich in Victorian and Edwardian architecture, from the magnificent City Hall to the atmospheric Crown Liquor Saloon. A peaceful haven is the Botanic Gardens, which also contains the superb Ulster Museum.

2 DAYS • 87 MILES • 138KM

ITINERARY

BELFAST	▶ **Cultra (7m-11km)**
CULTRA	▶ **Newtownards (7m-11km)**
NEWTOWNARDS	▶ **Greyabbey (7m-11km)**
GREYABBEY	▶ **Portavogie (9m-14km)**
PORTAVOGIE	▶ **Kearney (6m-10km)**
KEARNEY	▶ **Portaferry (8m-13km)**
PORTAFERRY	▶ **Strangford (ferry)**
STRANGFORD	▶ **Downpatrick (9m-14km)**
DOWNPATRICK	▶ **Killyleagh (5m-8km)**
KILLYLEAGH	▶ **Nendrum (14m-22km)**
NENDRUM	▶ **Belfast (15m-24km)**

St Anne's Court, North Street, Belfast

▶ *Take the **A2**, following signposts for Bangor, and after 7 miles (11km) turn left for the Ulster Folk and Transport Museum.*

1 Cultra, Co Down
The Ulster Folk and Transport Museum, in the grounds of Cultra Manor (also open), tells the story of the province's past through buildings that have been saved and meticulously reconstructed at this site.

Visitors are free to wander through former Ulster homes, which include a thatched cottage, a rectory and a terraced house, and watch demonstrations of traditional crafts. A church, schoolhouse, water-powered mills and many other buildings give a vivid picture of the past.

In the transport section, the collection spans the history of transport, from creels used by a donkey carrying turf, through the grand ocean-going liners built in Belfast, to ultra-modern aircraft from the Belfast firm Short Brothers and Harland.

This is undoubtedly one of the best museums in Ireland.

▶ *Turn left and follow the **A2** for 4 miles (6km). Turn right following the signpost for Newtownards, 3 miles (5km) further.*

2 Newtownards, Co Down
This thriving town lies among some of the richest arable land in Ulster. St Finnian founded Movilla Abbey in AD540, and the Dominican priory was established by the Normans in the 13th century. The hollow, octagonal, 17th-century market cross also served as the town watch and gaol. The impressive town hall was built around 1770, by the Londonderry family who also built Scrabo Tower, on the hill overlooking the town.

This dominant landmark, standing 135 feet (41m) high, was erected in memory of the third Marquess of Londonderry. The surrounding country park has woodland walks, sandstone quarries and panoramic views.

Bustling shopping streets surround Donegall Square in the heart of Belfast

SPECIAL TO...

The area around Newtownards is home to some of the world's most famous roses. The Dickson family first opened a nursery here in 1836 and have been international prize-winning rose breeders since 1887, bringing much-loved favourites like 'Grandpa Dickson' and 'Iceberg' to a worldwide market. The dynastic chain has continued unbroken, and Dickson's are still perfecting new varieties at their nurseries at Newtownards.

31, Regent Street

▶ *Take the **A20**, following signs for Portaferry, to Greyabbey.*

3 Greyabbey, Co Down
The village derives its name from the 12th-century Cistercian abbey founded by Affreca, wife of the Norman lord John de Courcy.

North of the village is Mount Stewart, a magnificent garden where, enjoying the mild climate of the peninsula, many exotic plants flourish in formal terraces and parterres or in natural settings. Lady Londonderry, the renowned hostess and leader of London society, created it after World War I, and this unique garden is considered one of the finest in these islands. Each garden is given a name – 'Tir n'an Og' (the Land of Eternal Youth), the Mairi Garden, Peace Garden, the Dodo Terrace and the Italian Garden. The lake is particularly beautiful. The house, the early home of Lord Castlereagh, contains the 22 chairs used at the Congress of Vienna and a masterpiece by the painter Stubbs among its treasures. Designed as a banqueting house, the Temple of the Winds is an exquisite piece of 18th-century landscape architecture.

The shoreline is an excellent place for viewing birds, including thousands of Brent geese that winter on the lough.

► *Follow the **A20** for 4 miles (6km) to Kircubbin. Take a left turn on to the **B173** for 3 miles (5km), then turn left for Portavogie.*

The Mount Stewart estate is among the finest National Trust properties in Ireland

4 Portavogie, Co Down
Up to 40 boats fill the attractive harbour of Portavogie when the fleet is in. Shellfish are plentiful and hotels serve a good variety of fresh fish. Seals regularly follow the boats into the harbour to scavenge for food while the catch is being unloaded, and auctioned in the harbour.

► *Take the **A2** south for 2 miles (3km). At Cloughey turn left for and follow signposts to Kearney. After 1 mile (1.5km) turn left for Kearney and follow signposts at two left turns for Kearney, about 3 miles (5km).*

5 Kearney, Co Down
Kearney is a tiny village of whitewashed houses in the care of the National Trust. Once a fishing village, it now offers fine walks along a rocky shoreline that looks across the Irish Sea to the Isle of Man, Scotland and the north of England. Close by

is the sandy beach of Knockinelder, and south is Millin Bay cairn, a neolithic burial site with ancient decorated stones.

At Temple Cowey and St Cowey's Wells, on a remote and peaceful shore, are a penance stone and holy well at a site founded in the 7th century, and later used for worship in penal times. Mass is still said here from time to time.

▶ *Turn left and left again to follow the road around the tip of the peninsula by Barr Hall and Quintin Bay to Portaferry.*

6 Portaferry, Co Down

One of Ulster's most beautifully sited villages, Portaferry's attractive waterfront of colourful terraced cottages, pubs and shops is framed by green meadows and wooded slopes. No fewer than five defensive tower houses guard the narrow neck of the lough. The Marine Biology Station, part of Queen's University, Belfast, is situated opposite the ferry jetty. Close to the tower house is the Northern Ireland Aquarium, Exploris, set beside a pleasant park, which explains the unique nature of the marine life of Strangford Lough. Over 2,000 species of marine animal thrive in the waters of Strangford, including large colonies of corals and sponges in the fast-flowing tides of the Narrows, and sea anemones, sea cucumbers and brittle stars in the quieter waters. The lough is home to large fish, including tope and skate. A regular, 5-minute car-ferry service to Strangford, gives stunning views of the lough.

SCENIC ROUTES

The roads around Strangford are a delight for drivers, as they are generally quiet, with accessible picnic sites. Many small roads hug the water's edge, as does the road just north of Portaferry. The views across the lough are breathtaking, as the scenery changes from noble parkland with ancient towers, to a tree-lined bay filled with yachts at mooring, then pleasant farmland dotted with cottages. Sunsets on Strangford can be spectacular, and often a change of light will reveal the profile of the Mourne Mountains in the distant southwest.

i *Castle Street*

▶ *Take the car ferry to Strangford. Boats leave at half-hourly intervals.*

7 Strangford, Co Down

Strangford is a small village with two bays, pretty houses and a castle. Close by is Castle Ward, set in fine parkland with excellent views over the lough. The 18th-century house is exactly divided into Gothic and classical architectural styles, the result of disputed tastes between Lord and Lady Bangor. Restored estate buildings demonstrate the elaborate organisation which once supported a country house. A small theatre is used for many events, including a midsummer opera festival.

One mile (1.5km) south, on the A2 to Ardglass, a lay-by at Cloughy Rocks is a great place for viewing seals when the tide is right. Further south is Kilclief Castle and Killard Point, at the narrowest point of the neck to the lough. This lovely grassland area with low cliffs and a small beach is rich in wild flowers.

FOR CHILDREN

Castle Ward, west of Strangford, has a Victorian playroom with toys, rocking horse, books and dressing-up clothes, which can all be enjoyed. Children can expriment with hoops, or stilts, or tops and whips. The Strangford Lough Barn on the estate provides another 'hands-on' display about the wildlife of the area and also presents regular video shows.

▶ *Take the **A25** to Downpatrick.*

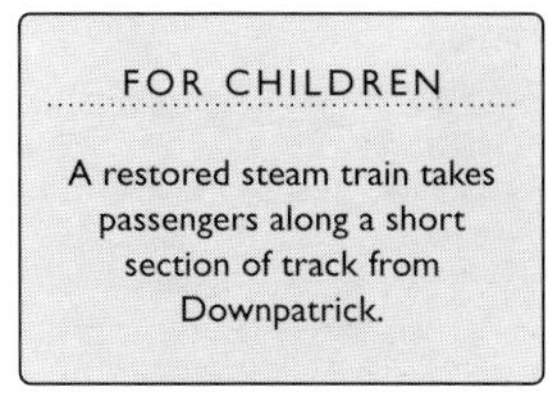
FOR CHILDREN

A restored steam train takes passengers along a short section of track from Downpatrick.

8 Downpatrick, Co Down

Down Cathedral stands on the hill above the town, while English Street, Irish Street and Scotch Street jostle together below. There has been a church on the site of the cathedral since AD520, but the present building dates largely from the 18th century. Ireland's patron saint is reputed to be buried in the churchyard with the bones of St Brigid and St Columba. The Norman John de Courcy ordered their reinterment:

In Down three saints one grave do fill
Brigid, Patrick and Columcille.

The supposed grave is marked by a granite stone erected in 1900. Down County Museum relates the

RECOMMENDED WALKS

St Patrick's Way passes many of the sites associated with St Patrick around Downpatrick. The saint is said to have landed at the mouth of the River Slaney in AD432, and to have come back there to die. At Saul, a small church with a distinctive round tower in traditional style marks the spot where he preached his first sermon. The Way is a network of marked paths, lanes and quiet roads, and is designed to be as long or as short as the walker wishes, from 1 to 7 miles (1.5km to 11km).

The graveyard of Downpatrick's cathedral is said to contain the burial place of St Patrick

story of St Patrick.

Quoile Pondage is an area of meandering freshwater wetland between wooded shores, with fine walks. Just north is 12th-century Inch Abbey, and to the southwest is the popular Downpatrick race course.

i *Market Street*

▶ *Follow the **A22** to Killyleagh.*

9 Killyleagh, Co Down

A fairy-tale castle with towers and battlements overlooks this quiet loughside village. The Hamilton family has lived there for 300 years, and although the original castle was built by the Normans, its present appearance owes more to the 19th century. Sir Hans Sloane, the physician and naturalist whose collection formed the nucleus of the British Museum, was born in Killyleagh in 1660 and educated in the castle. It is said that the famous Emigrant's Lament – 'I'm sitting on the stile, Mary', written by Lady Dufferin, a guest at the castle during the Famine – was inspired by the stile at Killowen Old Churchyard.

▶ *Follow the **A22** for 5 miles (8km) to Balloo crossroads. Turn right at the sign for Killinchy, and continue for 4 miles (6km), turning right three times for Comber. After 2½ miles (4km) turn right, following the sign for Nendrum Monastic Site.*

FOR HISTORY BUFFS

Driving through the centre of Comber, you cannot fail to see the statue of Major General Rollo Gillespie. Born in this square in 1766, he became a cavalryman at 17, eloped, fought a duel, was acquitted of murder, shipwrecked off Jamaica and attacked by pirates, of whom he killed six. He then settled down to an army life, and the list of his battles in Java, Bengal and elsewhere is recorded at the foot of the column, together with his famous last words – 'One shot more for the honour of Down' – uttered after he had been shot through the heart attacking the fort of Kalunga.

10 Nendrum Monastic Site, Co Down

A place of great tranquillity, Nendrum monastic site was established on one of the many islands that are sprinkled along Strangford's calm middle waters, and is now reached by a causeway. The site is one of the most complete examples of a very early monastery in Ireland, and the ruins, in three concentric rings, include the stump of a round tower, monks' cells and a church with a stone sundial.

BACK TO NATURE

A short distance from Nendrum is Castle Espie Wetlands and Wildlife Centre. When disused clay pits began to fill with water, a sensitive owner quickly realised that this was an important habitat for wildfowl. The careful management that followed has made Castle Espie a haven for birds and an attractive place to visit. Birds which use Strangford Lough can be seen here, as well as endangered species from exotic places. In particular, look for Brent geese, wigeon, sanderling, knot and grey plovers. There is also an art gallery, and the tea-room has views over the lough.

▶ *Return across the causeway and after 3 miles (5km) turn right for 3 miles (5km) to join the **A22** to Comber, then to Belfast.*

Fermanagh Lakeland

At Enniskillen, 'the Island Town', water greets you at every turn – from Lower and Upper Lough Erne and the River Erne, which flows through the town. Places of interest include the museums housed in the Watergate, a former castle, and the fine, neo-classical Castle Coole.

1/2 DAYS • 84 MILES • 133KM

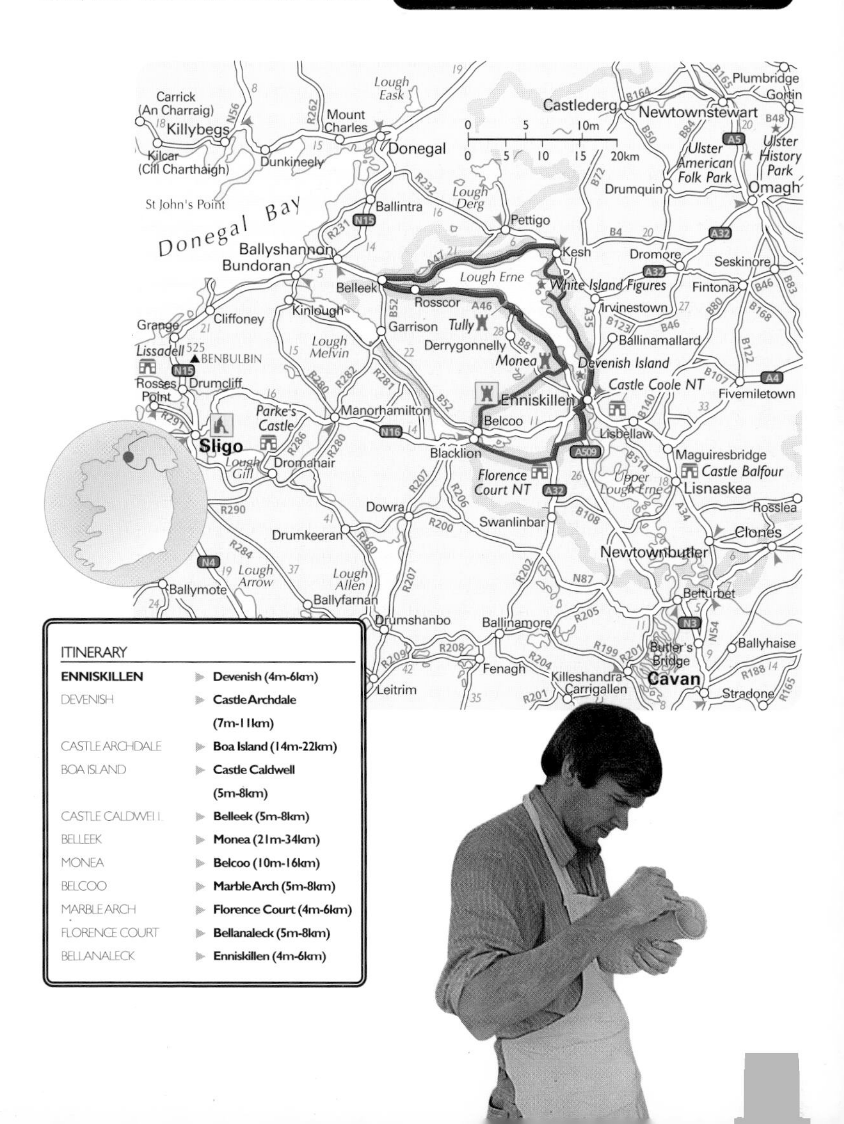

ITINERARY

ENNISKILLEN	▶ **Devenish (4m-6km)**
DEVENISH	▶ **Castle Archdale (7m-11km)**
CASTLE ARCHDALE	▶ **Boa Island (14m-22km)**
BOA ISLAND	▶ **Castle Caldwell (5m-8km)**
CASTLE CALDWELL	▶ **Belleek (5m-8km)**
BELLEEK	▶ **Monea (21m-34km)**
MONEA	▶ **Belcoo (10m-16km)**
BELCOO	▶ **Marble Arch (5m-8km)**
MARBLE ARCH	▶ **Florence Court (4m-6km)**
FLORENCE COURT	▶ **Bellanaleck (5m-8km)**
BELLANALECK	▶ **Enniskillen (4m-6km)**

i Fermanagh Information Centre, Wellington Road, Enniskillen

FOR CHILDREN

Much of Fermanagh is ideal for cycling, with gentle hills and quiet roads. Bicycles are available for hire in Enniskillen.

RECOMMENDED WALKS

There are 114 miles (183km) of the Ulster Way, the province's network of paths, in County Fermanagh. A helpful booklet is available from tourist information centres.

▶ *Take the **A32** towards Omagh for 2 miles (3km) until you reach the signpost for the ferries to Devenish.*

1 Devenish, Co Fermanagh
Take a ferry from Trory to get to Devenish Island. Across the silvery water is one of the most important monastic sites in Ulster, founded by St Molaise in the 6th century, although the remarkable group of buildings dates mostly from the 12th century. The round tower was repaired in the 19th century, and is regarded as one of the finest in Ireland, beautifully proportioned, with finely cut stone and precision of line. The towers, famous symbols of Christianity in Ireland, acted as signposts, bell towers and places of refuge and retreat in attack, and a safe storage place for treasures during Viking raids. The great treasure of Devenish, the book shrine of Molaise, which is a masterpiece of early Christian art, is kept at the National Museum in Dublin.

On a hill, with uninterrupted views over both loughs, Devenish was such a favoured place for parleys in disputes between Ulster and Connacht that it was sometimes called 'Devenish of the Assemblies'.

▶ *Take the **B82** for 7 miles (11km) for Kesh and Castle Archdale.*

2 Castle Archdale, Co Fermanagh
With a marina, caravan sites, youth hostel and recreational activities, Castle Archdale is one of the busiest places around Lough Erne, but it is still very easy to find a quiet place in this country park. In the old estate of the Archdale family is an arboretum, butterfly park and farm with rare breeds. The ruins of the old castle, burnt in the Williamite wars of 1689, can be seen in the forest, and the stable block of the 18th-century house is an important part of the park. The focus of Castle Archdale is the marina, where concrete jetties and slipways, built for flying boats taking off for the Battle of the Atlantic in 1941, have been turned to more peaceful use. You can hire a boat with a 'gillie' (a man to help you with the fishing). It is possible to reach White Island from here to see the enigmatic carved

Round towers are an evocative symbol of ecclesiastical sites. This one is on Devenish Island

stones that for centuries have puzzled experts and fascinated visitors. Set in the little 12th-century church, they seem to represent biblical figures, with the exception of 'Sheil-na-gig', a female fertility figure, a strange meeting of Celtic pagan art and Christianity.

► *Turn left on to the **B82**. After 2 miles (3km), turn left for Kesh via the scenic route for 4 miles (6km). At Kesh turn left for Belleek, on to the **A35**, then after 1 mile (1.5km) turn on to the **A47** and drive for 8 miles (13km) to Boa Island (pronounced Bo).*

BACK TO NATURE

If you are extremely fortunate, you may hear the distinctive call of the corncrake or land rail. Fermanagh is one of the last refuges of this bird, whose population has diminished rapidly in Britain and the rest of Europe, as it has become increasingly disturbed by mechanical methods of hay-making. Some experts feel that the complete extinction of this attractive bird is inevitable, but it can still be found here. You are, however, more likely to hear its grating 'crex-crex' call than see this secretive bird.

3 Boa Island, Co Fermanagh

Two bridges connect Boa Island to the mainland. Just before the bridge at the west end is a track on the left to Caldragh graveyard, where there are two pagan idols in stone. One is called a Janus figure because it is double-faced; the other, a small, hunched figure, was moved here from Lusty Beg Island. Boa Island, with its echoes of pre-Christian Ireland, is said to be called after Badhbh, the Irish goddess of war.

► *Continue on the **A47** for 5 miles (8km) to Castle Caldwell.*

The carved stone Janus Figure on Boa Island is a mysterious relic of pre-Christian times

4 Castle Caldwell, Co Fermanagh

The Fiddler's Stone at the entrance to Castle Caldwell, is in memory of the fiddler Dennis McCabe, who fell out of Sir James Caldwell's family barge on 13 August, 1770, and was drowned. The obituary ends:

On firm land only exercise your skill
That you may play and safely drink your fill.

The castle, now in ruins, had the reputation of enjoying one of the most beautiful situations of all Irish houses. The fine views are still the same, across water rich in wildlife, with bird hides that allow an opportunity to catch sight of many ducks, geese and grebes.

FOR CHILDREN

Older children can enjoy a wide variety of water sports. Windsurfing, canoeing, swimming, sailing and water-skiing are all available at the Lough Melvin Holiday Centre at Garrison, south of Belleek.

► *Continue on the **A47** to Belleek.*

5 Belleek, Co Fermanagh

This border village is famed for its fine parian china, best known for its delicate basketwork, shamrock decoration and lustre-finish. The range of goods produced by the Belleek Pottery has expanded to include designer items alongside the classic patterns, and visitors can tour the 1857 factory, see the best examples of the china and watch exquisite craftsmanship – the result of skills handed down from generation to generation. To this, Belleek adds the lure of a restaurant where the food is served on Belleek tableware.

RECOMMENDED WALKS

A very stiff ascent forms part of the Ulster Way off the A46 at Magho, and gives superb views over Tyrone, Donegal, Sligo and Leitrim. The climb of 365 steps is rewarded by a fresh, stone-arched well.

Visitors can witness the art of the craftspeople at Belleek

SCENIC ROUTES

The Marlbank Loop runs in a semi-circle round the heights of the Cuilcagh plateau, giving majestic mountain and valley views. Half-way round, a stream, the Sruth Croppa, disappers into the Cat's Hole, part of a maze of caves below. On the scenic diversion from the A46 on the south side of Lower Lough Erne, the road gains height to afford a fine panorama over the water. This beautiful area is dominated by the cliffs of Magho, which rise to over 1,000ft (300m), and the splendid backdrop of Lough Navar.

SPECIAL TO...

Fermanagh offers a variety of quality fishing, unrivalled anywhere in Europe. Its clean lakes and rivers are burdened with fish in a county where coarse fishing competition catches are measured in tons rather than pounds. Game fishing is plentiful, too, with trout, salmon and the unique gillaroo of Lough Melvin. It is essential to check at the Fermanagh Tourist Information Centre about permits and licences.

▶ *Take the **A46** for Enniskillen. After 13 miles (21km) turn right on the Slavin scenic route for 2 miles (3km). Rejoin the **A46** and after 6 miles (10km) turn right, and follow signs to Monea.*

6 Monea, Co Fermanagh
Monea (pronounced Mon-ay) is the ruin of a Plantation castle, remote among marshy ground on a rocky outcrop. Built by 'undertakers', or Planters, arriving from the lowlands of Scotland in the early 17th century, it has a Scottish look about it, particularly in the corbelling. The castle was captured by the Irish in 1641 and finally abandoned in 1750. There are still remnants of the bawn wall that surrounded the castle, and an ancient crannóg, or artificial island dwelling, can be picked out in the marsh in front of Monea. In the parish church is a 15th-century window, removed from Devenish.

▶ *Turn left leaving Monea, then left for Enniskillen. Turn right, following signs to Boho for 5 miles (8km), then right again for Belcoo.*

7 Belcoo, Co Fermanagh
Belcoo sits neatly between the two Lough Macneans, surrounded by mountains and adjacent to its neighbouring County Leitrim village, Blacklion. The two loughs are large and very beautiful.

To the south of Lower Lough Macnean is the limestone cliff of Hanging Rock, and by the road is the Salt Man, a great lump of limestone, which, it is said, fell off the cliff and killed a man pulling a load of salt.

Just north of Belcoo is the Holywell, traditionally visited by pilgrims in search of the curative powers of St Patrick's Well.

▶ *From Belcoo, cross the border into the Republic and Blacklion for a very short distance, then cross back into Northern Ireland, taking the road along the south shore of Lower Lough Macnean. Turn right along Marlbank Scenic Loop and drive for 3 miles (5km) to Marble Arch.*

> **FOR HISTORY BUFFS**
>
> The narrow strip of land occupied by Belcoo was part of Black Pig's Dyke, a great prehistoric earthwork that formed part of the early boundary of Ulster. The section at the top of Lough Macnean was known as 'The Pig's Race'. The Black Pig's Dyke ran with 'The Dane's Cast' and 'The Worm Ditch', from the Atlantic to the Irish Sea. The Black Pig is a familier emblem in Ulster folklore. There are many 'races' and paths over which the pig is reputed to have rampaged.

8 **Marble Arch,** Co Fermanagh

One of the highlights of a visit to Fermanagh, the mysterious beauty of the Marble Arch Caves is enhanced by a ride on a quiet, flat-bottomed boat through still, dark waters. Over 300 million years of history is here among a strange landscape of chasms and valleys, amid stalactites and stalagmites. The deep gorge of Marble Arch is dramatically beautiful, and it is worth taking time to walk further into the Cladagh Glen. Common wild flowers are seen in glorious abundance and variety, as well as some Irish rarities.

▶ *Turn left, then right and drive for 4 miles (6km) to Florence Court.*

9 **Florence Court,** Co Fermanagh

Florence Court was the home of the Enniskillen family, who moved from a castle in the county town to this wild and beautiful setting in the 18th century. The house was named after a new English wife.

The present building, which dates from the middle of the 18th century, is very Irish in character with exuberant rococo plasterwork of the highest order, fine Irish furniture, pleasure grounds and interesting estate buildings. In the gardens is the original Florence Court yew, the originator of all Irish yews.

> **RECOMMENDED WALKS**
>
> For clearly marked trails of varying lengths, difficulty and interest, try the walks in Florence Court Forest Park, through parkland, woods and open moorland.

▶ *From Florence Court, turn right. After a mile (1.5km) turn left on to the* A32*, then after 2 miles (3km) turn right for Bellanaleck.*

10 **Bellanaleck,** Co Fermanagh

A base for cruising, with a popular marina, Bellanaleck gives a glimpse of the winding, mazy ways of Upper Lough Erne, as its waters thread through 57 islands between Enniskillen and Galloon Bridge to the southeast. Here are hidden remote treasures such as Castle Balfour and the estate at Crom, rich in history and rare in wildlife.

▶ *Return to Enniskillen via the* A509.

Expansive parkland surrounds lovely Florence Court

The Heart of Ulster

2 DAYS • 123 MILES • 198KM

The ecclesiastical capital of Ireland, Armagh is a gracious and historic city richly endowed with the culture and architecture of centuries of Christianity. Two cathedrals dedicated to Saint Patrick rise above winding streets which follow the contours of ancient earth mounds. Just outside the city is the ancient site of Emain Macha.

ITINERARY

ARMAGH	▶ **Loughgall (6m-10km)**
LOUGHGALL	▶ **Moy (15m-24km)**
MOY	▶ **Dungannon (5m-8km)**
DUNGANNON	▶ **Cookstown (11m-18km)**
COOKSTOWN	▶ **Gortin (24m-39km)**
GORTIN	▶ **Omagh (9m-14km)**
OMAGH	▶ **Fintona (11m-18km)**
FINTONA	▶ **Fivemiletown (10m-16km)**
FIVEMILETOWN	▶ **Armagh (32m-51km)**

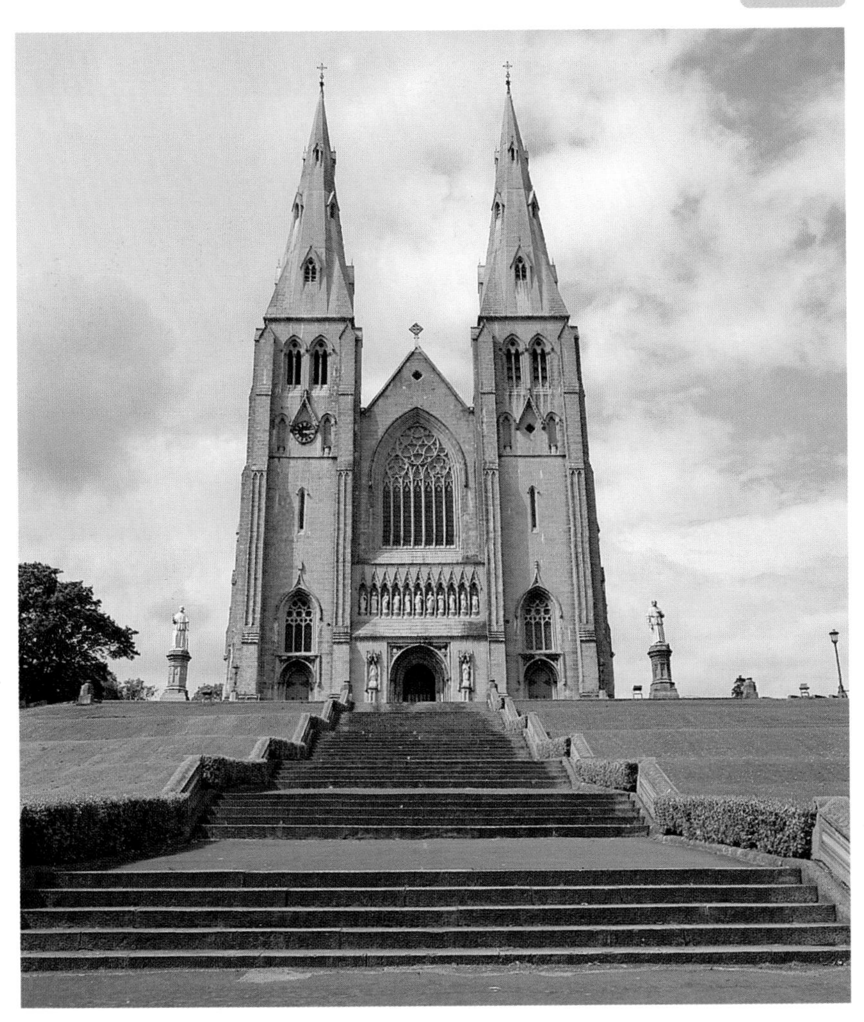

The impressive Roman Catholic Cathedral of St Patrick in Armagh was completed in 1873

[i] *40, English Street, Armagh*

FOR CHILDREN

Not far from Loughgall is Benburb, a hidden valley with adventurous walks, a castle on a clifftop and a restored linen mill. The Heritage Centre has a model and talks about the Battle of Benburb in 1646, when Irish forces under Owen Roe O'Neill defeated General Monroe's Scottish and English armies.

▶ *Take the **B77** to Loughgall.*

0 Loughgall, Co Armagh
This is one of the pretty flower-filled villages, surrounded by orchards, in the heart of Armagh, which is known as the Orchard County. The Orange Order was founded near here after a battle in 1795.

Close by is 17th-century Ardress House, which was given an elegant new look in the 18th century with exquisite plasterwork by stuccodore Michael Stapleton, and some remarkably fine Irish furniture. Ardress still has the feel of a gentleman farmer's residence, and the restored farmyard is full of fowl, animals and traditional farming equipment. A woodland playground is popular with the children and there is a pretty garden and a woodland walk.

▶ *Follow the **B77** for 3 miles (5km), then turn on to the **B131**. After 2 miles (3km) turn left on to the **B28**, following the signs for Moy. After a mile (1.5km) pass Ardress House, and immediately after, branch right on to an unclassified road. Turn right again and follow signs for the **M1** for 3*

The wide main street of Moy, on the Tyrone-Armagh boundary

BACK TO NATURE

The Peatlands Park, at the Loughgall junction of the M1, is the first of its kind in the British Isles, designed to protect bogland and to tell the story of peatlands in an enterprising way. The park is a mosaic of cutaway bogland, with small virgin bogs, low wooded hills and small lakes. The bog is seen as a living archive covering 10,000 years. An outdoor turbary (turf-cutting) area gives an insight into the process of cutting turf, and a most attractive feature is the narrow-gauge railway, originally set up for carrying turf and now a popular way of carrying visitors out on to the bog, thus saving it from the wear and tear of human erosion.

*miles (5km). At the roundabout, take the **B131**, which becomes the **B34**, towards Dungannon for 3 miles (5km), then turn left on to the **B106** for a further 3 miles (5km) to Moy.*

2 Moy, Co Tyrone
More commonly called 'the Moy', this is on the Tyrone side of the Blackwater river. Charlemont lies opposite on the banks of the river in County Armagh. Once one of the most important strongholds of the English, only the impressive wrought-iron gates of Roxborough House and earthworks that were artillery bastions remain. The Moy had one of the most famous horse fairs in Ireland in the 19th century, held in a fine square, where a plaque recalls a son of the village, John King, Australian soldier and explorer.

The Argory close by, situated above the river in lovely grounds, is a pleasant 19th-century house, still lit by gas and full of fascinating objects.

RECOMMENDED WALKS

An attractive stretch of the Ulster Way takes the walker along the banks of the Blackwater from Caledon in County Tyrone through Amagh to Lough Neagh.

▶ *Take the **A29** to Dungannon.*

3 Dungannon, Co Tyrone
A flourishing town, this was once the chief seat of the O'Neills, kings of Ulster for 500 years. Now it is more famous for fine cut glass, and the Tyrone Crystal factory is a popular attraction. At Park Lane, a fishery offers catches of trout by the pound, as well as an equestrian centre and walks.

Off the main Dungannon-Ballygawley road, at Dergenagh, is the ancestral home of Ulysses S Grant, President of the US from 1869 to 1877, restored to its appearance of 1880, and set on a farmstead worked by traditional methods of the time.

▶ *Continue on the **A29** for 11 miles (18km) to Cookstown.*

4 Cookstown, Co Tyrone
The broad main street runs through a typical mid-Ulster farming town, but the area around Cookstown has plenty to interest the visitor.

Drum Manor Forest Park to the west is small but very attractive, with a butterfly garden, a demonstration shrub garden, a forest garden containing small plots of many tree species, and an arboretum. There is a heronry, and waterfowl inhabit the fish ponds.

In the same area is Wellbrook Beetling Mill, a

water-powered mill used for beetling or polishing, the final process in the manufacture of linen, dating from 1765. Not so long ago there would have been many such mills operating on the Ballinderry river.

The Beaghmore stone circles to the northwest of Cookstown are mysterious in their origin and purpose. Perhaps they were formed in the Stone Age or Early Bronze Age for ceremonial purposes, with lines pointing to the midsummer sunrise.

[i] *Molesworth Street*

▶ *Take the* ***A505*** *for Omagh. After 13 miles (21km) turn right on to the* ***B46*** *to Gortin for 11 miles (18km).*

FOR HISTORY BUFFS

Northeast of Cookstown is Springhill, a lovely 17th-century house with 18th- and 19th-century additions, built at a time when strength and fortification were giving way to comfort and convenience. The Lenox-Conynghams, who built Springhall and lived there for nearly 300 years, were a family of soldiers; their story, and the house, provides a fascinating view of the history of Ireland and of events further afield. The charming house has a fine oak staircase, a good library, lovely old gardens and an interesting costume museum.

SCENIC ROUTES

Linking the Cookstown-Gortin road with the Gortin-Omagh road is Gortin Lake scenic route. The blend of loughs, evergreen and deciduous forests, heather-topped moors and the village below create a fine panorama. Features with evocative names like Curraghchosaly (Moor with the Rocky Face), the meandering Owenkillew (River of the Curlew) and Mullaghbolig (Humped Top) add richness to the picture.

A splendid way to travel, and to enjoy the sights and smells of the lovely Gortin Lake scenery

The Ulster American Museum has brought the New World back to the Old Country

5 Gortin, Co Tyrone
This beautiful, sparsely populated area offers a gateway to the Sperrin Mountains. Those who want to venture further and even pan for the gold occasionally found in these hills should go north and call at the Sperrin Heritage Centre. Gortin has a fine forest park with a herd of Japanese sika deer, and the area is rich in good walks. On the Gortin side of the entrance to the forest park look out for a stone seat beside a cool stream, which has the inscription 'Rest and be thankful'.

The Ulster History Park is here, too, tracing the story of settlements in Ireland from the Stone Age to the Normans. Full-scale models of houses and monuments vividly re-create life in a mesolithic or neolithic home, and other exhibits include a round tower, monastic dwellings, a crannóg, or artifical island built as a defended lake dwelling, and a motte-and-bailey Norman structure.

Four miles (6km) from Gortin on the B48 look out for the place known locally as the Magnetic Hill, which gives the illusion that your car is travelling uphill, when it is really going downhill.

RECOMMENDED WALKS

From Gortin a number of walks radiate over ideal walking country, with panoramic views. Children enjoy the Burn Walk, which follows a stream all the way to the heart of Gortin village.

▶ *Take the **B48** to Omagh.*

6 Omagh, Co Tyrone
Omagh sits high on a hill, spires and the outline of the court house giving the town a distinctive profile.

The outstanding attraction of the area is the Ulster-American Folk Park, on the A5 to Newtownstewart. It is designed very much in the American style, with costumed interpreters baking bread or spinning by a turf fire. In the Dockside Gallery you are invited to sail away to the New World. The park illustrates the two cultures in Ulster's tradition of emigration, from the reconstructed street of shops and the thatched cottages, representing the Old World (Ulster), to the American street and the log cabins, representing the New World. One of the most telling exhibits is the re-creation of the brig *Union*, an emigrant ship. Here, visitors can experience the dreadful conditions, smells and sounds of a transatlantic passage. There is an extensive programme of special events throughout the year.

i *1, Market Street*

▶ *Take the **A5** signed for Belfast. After 7 miles (11km) turn right on to the **B46** for Seskinore and Fintona.*

7 Fintona, Co Tyrone

Fintona is a very quiet little village, once celebrated for its horse-drawn tram. The Forest of Seskinore is extremely productive, growing high-quality crops of hard and soft woods. It harbours a rich variety of wildlife and game. Pheasant, grouse, partridges, wild ducks and geese are reared here, as well as ornamental species such as golden pheasant and peacocks. Seskinore was once dependent on using horse power to extract timber. Today's Forest Service has brought back Irish draught horses and trained them to this work once again.

▶ *Take the **B122** to Fivemiletown and the Clogher Valley.*

8 The Clogher Valley, Co Tyrone

Augher, Clogher and Fivemiletown are the villages of the Clogher Valley, and the names roll off the local tongue, being the stations of the old Clogher Valley railway, much loved by Ulster people.

Visitors to the tiny village of Clogher will be surprised to learn that it has a cathedral, its importance dating from the 5th century, when St Patrick made McCartan first Bishop of Clogher. The folly on a hill to the south of Clogher was a mausoleum erected by a newly rich landlord, Brackenridge, so that 'he could look down on the neighbours who had looked down on him'.

Fivemiletown has a small museum and recreational facilities around the lake. The valley has three forests with different attractions – Fardross, Knockmany and Favour Royal.

▶ *Take the **A4** for Augher for 8 miles (13km), then the **A28**, passing through Aughnacloy and Caledon to Armagh.*

SPECIAL TO...

If you are very lucky you may catch a game of Ireland's most unusual sport, road bowls or 'bullets', now found only in Armagh or Cork. Players hurl a 28oz (794g) metal ball (it is said that the game started with cannon-balls) on a set course along winding roads. The aim is to get the ball to the end of the road in the least number of throws, Spectators beware! Watching crowds tend to be quickly dispersed by hurtling missiles, but organised championships are held in Armagh annually in August.

The lanes of rural Ireland are dotted with wayside shrines and curiosities

TOUR
25

Mourne Country

A town of great historic importance in the Gap of the North between Slieve Gullion and the Carlingford Mountains, Newry is close to the Mourne Mountains and Carlingford Lough. Its town hall, which actually spans the Clanrye River, has been converted into an arts centre.

2 DAYS • 95 MILES • 153KM

ITINERARY

NEWRY	▶ **Rathfriland (10m-16km)**
RATHFRILAND	▶ **Banbridge (10m–16km)**
BANBRIDGE	▶ **Hillsborough (11m-18km)**
HILLSBOROUGH	▶ **Castlewellan (11m-18km)**
CASTLEWELLAN	▶ **Dundrum (6m-10km)**
DUNDRUM	▶ **Newcastle (4m-6km)**
NEWCASTLE	▶ **Annalong (8m-13km)**
ANNALONG	▶ **Silent Valley (6m-10km)**
SILENT VALLEY	▶ **Spelga Dam (7m-11km)**
SPELGA DAM	▶ **Rostrevor (11m-18km)**
ROSTREVOR	▶ **Warrenpoint (4m-6km)**
WARRENPOINT	▶ **Newry (7m-11km)**

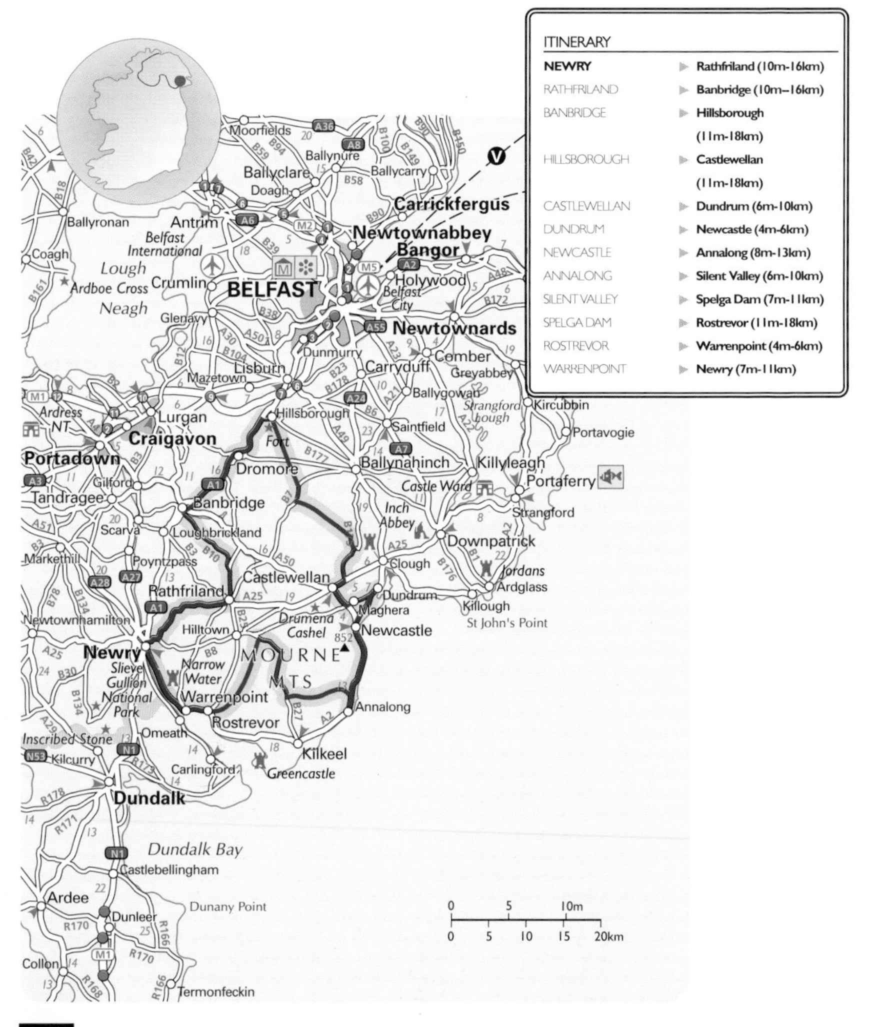

Town Hall, Bank Parade, Newry

▶ *Take the **A25** following signposts for Rathfriland.*

1 Rathfriland, Co Down
A quiet village atop a steep hill, Rathfriland commands views over a tranquil valley, where shady roads wind among small farms. This is the country of Patrick Brontë, father of the famous writers Charlotte, Emily and Anne, and it is said that his stories of County Down were a memorable part of their childhood. Little Drumballyroney school, where he taught, marks the beginning of the 10-mile (16km) signposted Brontë Homeland route. In 1835, Catherine O'Hare was born in Rathfriland. She became the first woman to cross the Rocky Mountains.

▶ *Take the **B25** northwards from Rathfriland, turning left on to the **B10** for Banbridge.*

2 Banbridge, Co Down
The steep hill in the centre of Banbridge was cut through in 1834 to spare the horses on the busy Belfast–Dublin road, and now the wide thoroughfare is divided into three with an elegant underpass. At the foot of the hill, close to the River Bann, is an elaborate monument guarded by polar bears. It commemorates Captain Crozier (1796–1848), who was second-in-command of the expedition which found the North-West Passage.

Gateway Centre, Newry Road

▶ *Take the **A1** for Belfast. After 11 miles (18km) turn right for Hillsborough.*

3 Hillsborough, Co Down
Take time to explore this pretty and elegant Georgian village, full of interesting shops, pubs and historic buildings. Hillsborough Castle is the residence for members of the royal family when they visit Northern Ireland, and the permanent residence of the Secretary of State. It stands in a square, not typical of an Ulster village, lined with graceful Georgian terraces. In the centre is the 18th-century market house, aligned with a fine gateway and tree-lined avenue to a fort. There was a defended settlement here in early Christian times, but the present building was rebuilt as a picturesque toy-like fort in the 18th century by the Hill family, who carefully planned the village through successive generations. The Georgian parish church adds to the harmony of Hillsborough, and the forest park has a lake with pleasant walks.

▶ *Take the road for Newry, but before joining the **A1** turn left for Dromara. After 1 mile (1.5km) turn left again and drive for 8 miles (13km) to Dromara. In Dromara, turn left following signposts for Dundrum. After 8 miles (13km) turn right and follow the **B175** for 5 miles (8km) to the junction with the **A25**. Turn right for Castlewellan.*

Castlewellan Lake, overlooked by a Victorian castle, is at the heart of the superb forest park

4 Castlewellan, Co Down
Another County Down village of steep hills, broad views and quiet tree-lined squares of pleasant terraces, Castlewellan's centre is marked by a solid market house, now a library, and its boundaries enhanced by two handsome churches.

Close to the village, the forest park covers 1,500 acres (600 hectares) of hilly ground, including a small mountain, Slievenaslat, and surrounds a beautiful lake. A 19th-century castle, in Scottish baronial style, stands at its heart. It is now a conference centre. The arboretum is particularly fine, and a popular cypress, Castlewellan Gold, which was developed here, has spread the name of the forest throughout the world. Fishing, pony trekking and camping can be enjoyed here, and in the handsome Grange, a fine range of courtyards, a Craft Centre has been set up.

FOR HISTORY BUFFS

At Drumena, 2 miles (3km) from Castlewellan, there is a good example of an elaborate stone construction, a cashel from the early Christian period with very thick walls. This cashel, overlooking Lough Island Reavy, also has a souterrain or underground passage, used for storage or as refuge in time of danger.

▶ *Take the **A50** for Newcastle. After 2 miles (3km) turn left on to the **B180**, and after 3 miles (5km) turn left again for Dundrum.*

FOR CHILDREN

At Seaforde, a pretty village 3 miles (5km) north of Dundrum, is a butterfly house. It is an extraordinary experience to find that these beautiful creatures are attracted to visitors and will settle on arms and shoulders.

5 Dundrum, Co Down
You can just see the top of the keep of the Norman castle among the trees above Dundrum. John de Courcy chose a superb rocky site commanding strategic views over sea and countryside to build his castle in the 13th century, although the name 'the Fort of the Ridge' goes back to an early Christian defence. The sand dunes below

Left: a mixture of pastureland and wild moorland in the lovely Mountains of Mourne

Above: a delightful rocky cascade in the ever-popular Tollymore Forest Park near Newcastle

have yielded evidence of Stone-Age and Bronze-Age settlements, while at Sliddery, just south of the village, an 8-foot (2.5m) dolmen was erected probably 4,000 years ago.

▶ *Take the **A2** to Newcastle.*

BACK TO NATURE

Murlough National Nature Reserve at Dundrum is as beautiful as it is interesting. The dune system here has been carefully managed and it merges into heathland, the whole area bounded by estuary and sea. The range of habitats nurture a wide variety of plants, insects and birds, and wardens lead guided walks through restricted areas. From the magnificent beach, sea birds and seals can be seen, while the inner bay estuary has a good variety of birds such as redshank, greenshank, Brent geese and godwits in the winter. Migrant birds often shelter among the marram grass and sea buckthorn in the dunes.

FOR CHILDREN

Experience warm seawater in the open air at the Tropicana in Newcastle, where water fun is provided with games and slides.

6 Newcastle, Co Down

When Percy French wrote of the place where 'The Mountains of Mourne sweep down to the sea', he must have had this part of County Down's coast in mind. Newcastle itself is in the shelter of the highest of the peaks, Slieve Donard, but to the south of the town there is barely room for the road to scrape through between the mountains and the sea.

The town is a traditional seaside resort, with a promenade, parks, swimming pools and holiday recreation facilities. A magnificent beach sweeps from Dundrum to the harbour, and borders the championship golf course, Royal County Down. The staff of the Mourne Countryside Centre, who provide general information about the mountains, also organise a series of walks for the inexperienced visitor.

Two miles (3km) to the west is Tollymore, a magnificently situated and very popular forest park on the slopes of

Slievenabrock and Luke's Mountain, in the valley of the Shimna river, with attractive walks enlivened by the picturesque cascades, bridges and numerous follies built by the Roden family.

i *Central Promenade*

RECOMMENDED WALKS

There are many excellent walks in the Mournes. Generally they will not be sign-posted, but walks leaflets are available locally. From Bloody Bridge, a short distance south of Newcastle on the A2, a path climbs the mountain along the Bloody River, so called because of the massacre in the 1641 rebellion. This is part of the Brandy Pad, a track that winds its way through the mountains by Hare's Gap to Hilltown, and which was used by smugglers distributing wines, spirits, tobacco, silks and spice, a thriving 18th-century trade.

▶ *Take the* ***A2*** *following signs for Kilkeel to Annalong.*

7 **Annalong,** Co Down

Two rocky clefts shelter the small fishing fleet that uses Annalong harbour, with lobster pots and fishing nets lining the stone pier. A fine corn mill right on the edge of the harbour can produce flour and oatmeal, and the Marine Park is a pleasant focal point on the shore with a play area, boat park and herb garden. A fish smokery and granite-cutting yards add activity to the narrow, winding streets and low cottages.

▶ *Return to the* ***A2*** *towards Newcastle, then turn left following signs for Silent Valley for 6 miles (10km).*

8 **The Silent Valley,** Co Down

Impressive gates admit the visitor to the vast area of the Silent Valley, which contains two reservoirs and dams which provide water for the Greater Belfast area. The Water Commissioners of the early part of this century planned the landscaping of the reservoirs, and the area has a peculiarly municipal feel with flowering shrubs and formal flowerbeds. The splendid mountain panoramas predominate, and today's guardians, the Department of the Environment, have provided walks, a visitors' centre and a shuttle bus (you cannot take a car up to the Silent Valley).

SPECIAL TO...

The drystone walls, or more properly, stone ditches, of the Mournes are an especially attractive feature, enclosing tiny fields and creating intrguing patterns below the high peaks. Some are single width, seemingly higglegy-piggledy and gaping with holes – no mortar here – others are comapct, thick and splendidly flat on top. The Mourne Wall is quite different. Solid and massive, it provided employment between 1904 and 1922. The Wall starts and ends at the Silent Valley. Travelling 22 miles (35km), it spans the summits of 15 mountains, and encloses the entire Mourne water catchment area.

▶ *Turn right and right again for Spelga Dam. After 1½ miles*

The shoreline at Newcastle, a coastal resort and centre for the Mourne Mountains

(2km) turn right on to the **B27** *for Hilltown. After 5 miles (8km) turn left, still following the* **B27**.

9 Spelga Dam, Co Down
Just above Spelga is the highest point a road reaches in Northern Ireland. To the east is a good place for access into the inner Mournes, the ring of mountains – Doan, Meelbeg, Bearnagh, Donard, Lamagan and Binnian – that shields the beautiful, deep blue Lough Shannagh, and the source of the River Bann. To the north is the pretty Fofanny dam, and the Trassey river, where a path gives an approach to the north Mournes.

SCENIC ROUTES

On the road from Silent Valley, past Spelga to Rostrevor, look for the red metal gates with round knobs on the posts, which mark the water pipelines. Each mountain has its own characteristics, scattered with firs and pines and rocky outcrops, or smothered with naturalised rhododendrons. As the road dips into dark forest, there is a perfect picnic site at the Yellow River, with imaginative tables in wood and stone in an idyllic setting beside a fast-running stream.

▶ *Continue west on the* **B27** *and after 3 miles (5km) turn left and continue for 8 miles (13km) to Rostrevor.*

10 Rostrevor, Co Down
Rostrevor is a picturesque place with a flourishing arts festival every year. Exotic plants and lush vegetation prove its claim to be the most sheltered spot in Northern Ireland, tucked between Slieve Martin and the temperate waters of Carlingford Lough. As the Mournes descend to Rostrevor the forest pines and conifers give way to native oakwood, which forms a National Nature Reserve. Climb to Cloughmore, the 'Big Stone' reputedly thrown by Finn MacCool from Slieve Foye across the lough.

A real Irish giant is buried in Kilbroney churchyard. He was the tallest man in his day at over 8 feet (2.5m) tall, and died in Marseilles in 1861. Two ancient crosses stand in this churchyard, but a Celtic bronze hand-bell, which was found in a ruined church wall, is preserved in St Mary's Church. A granite obelisk commemorates Major General Robert Ross, who captured Washington DC in 1814, and ate the dinner prepared for the fleeing President Madison. He died three weeks later in Baltimore.

Rostrevor Forest Park and Kibroney Park have amenities, a playground, picnic sites and a forest drive.

▶ *Take the* **A2** *for 4 miles (6km) to Warrenpoint.*

11 Warrenpoint, Co Down
Warrenpoint is a resort with a growing port where Carlingford Lough narrows to become an enclosed fiord-like waterway. The Vikings gave Carlingford

The restored 19th-century corn mill at Annalong overlooks the pretty little harbour

its name, and this steep-sided inlet must have seemed familiar to them. Carlingford gave good access for their plundering of the rich pickings of Armagh. They may have been the 'foreigners of Narrow Water' recorded in AD841.

The English garrison built a stronghold at Narrow Water in 1560 for £361, and the three-storey tower house with battlements, murder hole and bawn wall is a stone's throw from County Louth in Leinster. Close by, in the Burren Heritage Centre, once an old National School, are models and information about other historic sites in the area, as well as changing exhibitions.

Warrenpoint is a traditional seaside resort, with park and bandstand, marina, beach, sports and boat trips to Omeath.

i *Town Hall, Church Street*

▶ *Take the* **A2** *for 7 miles (11km) to Newry.*

PRACTICAL INFORMATION

ACCIDENTS

In the event of an accident, the vehicle should be moved off the carriageway wherever possible. (See also **Warning Triangle/ Hazard Warning Lights** page 159.)

You must also stop immediately and exchange particulars with the other party. If this is not possible you must report the accident to a member of the Garda Siochana or at the nearest Garda station.

If damage or injury is caused to any other person or vehicle you must stop, give your own and the vehicle owner's name and address and the registration number of the vehicle to anyone having reasonable grounds for requiring the information. If for some reason you do not give your name and address at the time of the accident, you must report the accident to the police as soon as reasonably practicable, and in any case within 24 hours.

BREAKDOWNS

If the car is rented, contact the rental company. If it is your own car, and you are a member of the Automobile Association or one of the AIT (*Alliance International de Tourisme*) driving clubs you can call on the AA rescue service run by the Automobile Association of Ireland in the Republic and the Automobile Association in Northern Ireland. The RAC operates a similar service for its members, but only in Northern Ireland.

In the event of a breakdown, the vehicle should be moved off the carriageway wherever possible. (See also **Warning Triangle /Hazard Warning Lights** page 159.)

MOTORING IN IRELAND

CARAVANS

Brakes

Check that the caravan braking mechanism is correctly adjusted. If it has a breakaway safety mechanism, the cable between the car and caravan must be firmly anchored so that the trailer brakes act immediately if the two part company.

Caravan and luggage trailers

Take a list of contents, especially if any valuable or unusual equipment is being carried, as this may be required on arrival. A towed vehicle should be readily identifiable by a plate in an accessible position showing the name of the make of the vehicle and the production and serial number.

Lights

Make sure that all the lights are working – rear lights, stop lights, numberplate lights, rear fog guard lamps and flashers (check that the flasher rate is correct: 60-120 times a minute).

Speed limits – see general notes on speed limits.

Tyres

Both tyres on the caravan should be of the same size and type. Inspect them carefully: if you think they are likely to be more than three-quarters worn before you get back, replace them before you leave. If you notice uneven wear, scuffed treads, or damaged walls, get expert advice on whether the tyres are suitable for further use.
Find out the recommended tyre pressures from the caravan manufacturer.

CAR HIRE AND FLY/DRIVE

Renting a car in the Republic is expensive compared with Northern Ireland. Though rates vary, smaller local firms often offer cheaper deals than the larger international companies. However, larger companies will often allow you to pick up your car in one town and return it in another. If you are going to hire a car, you can often get a good deal if you arrange a fly/drive package tour.

Drivers must hold, and have held for one year, a valid national licence or an International Driving Permit. The minimum age for hiring a car ranges from 18 to 25, depending on the model of car. With some companies, there is a maximum age limit of 70.

CHILDREN

The following restrictions apply to children travelling in private motor vehicles:

Children under 3 years: front seat – appropriate child restraint must be worn, rear seats – appropriate child restraint must be worn if available.

Child aged 3 to 11 and under 1.5 metres tall: front seat – appropriate child restraint must be worn if available, if not adult seat belt must be worn. Rear seat – appropriate child restraint must be worn if available, if not adult seat belt must be worn if available.

Child aged 12 or 13 or younger child 1.5 metres or more in height: front and rear – adult seat belt must be worn if available.

Note: under no circumstances should a rear-facing restraint be used in a seat with an airbag.

CRASH (SAFETY) HELMETS

Visiting motorcyclists and their passengers must wear crash or safety helmets.

DOCUMENTS

You must have a valid driver's licence (with an English translation if you wish to rent a car). If you are bringing a vehicle you need its registration book with a letter of authorisation from the owner if they are not accompanying the vehicle.

DRINKING AND DRIVING

The laws regarding drinking and driving are strict and the penalties severe. The best advice is if you drink don't drive.

DRIVING CONDITIONS

Traffic drives on the left (it goes clockwise at roundabouts [traffic circles]). Signposts give distances in miles. (See also **Warning Triangle /Hazard Warning Lights** page 160.)

FUEL

Fuel stations in villages in the Republic usually stay open till around 8.00pm and open after mass on Sundays. In Northern Ireland, where fuel is cheaper, 24 hour stations are fairly common and many stations are open on Sundays.

INSURANCE

Fully comprehensive insurance, which covers you for some of the expenses incurred after a breakdown or an accident, is advisable. Ensure that you are covered for both the Republic and Northern Ireland if you intend to cross the border.

LIGHTS

You must ensure your front and rear side lights and rear registration plate lights are lit at night. You must use headlights when visibility is seriously reduced and at night on all unlit roads and those where the street lights are more than 600 feet (185m) apart.

ROADS

In the Republic roads vary tremendously and the road classification gives no reliable indication of the width, or surface quality – some primary roads are little better than country lanes.

There are a few stretches of motorway in the Dublin and Belfast areas, but not elsewhere. Potential hazards include loose chippings, livestock and the relaxed attitude of Dublin drivers to red traffic lights.

In Northern Ireland the major roads are fast and well maintained and seldom congested, though checkpoints are a potential cause of delay.

ROUTE DIRECTIONS

Throughout the book the following abbreviations are used for roads:

M – Motorways
Republic of Ireland only
N – National primary/seconday roads
R – Regional roads
Northern Ireland only
A – Main roads
B – local roads

SEAT BELTS

The wearing of seat belts is compulsory for drivers and their front seat passenger. Passengers travelling in the rear seats of the vehicle must wear a seat belt if one is fitted.

SPEED LIMITS

Republic of Ireland
Speed limits are 30mph (48kph) in built-up areas and 55mph (88kph) elsewhere, unless other-wise indicated and 70mph (113kph) on motorways; for non-articulated vehicles with one trailer, the maximum is 40mph (64kph).

Northern Ireland
Speed limits are 30mph (48kph) in built-up areas, 60mph (96kph) in country areas and 70mph (113kph) on dual carriageways and motorways, unless otherwise indicated; for trailers the maximum is usually 40mph (64kph).

WARNING TRIANGLE/ HAZARD WARNING LIGHTS

If the vehicle is fitted with hazard warning lights, they should be used in the event of a breakdown or accident.

If available, a red triangle should be placed on the road at least 165 feet (50m) before the obstruction and on the same side of the road.

ACCOMMODATION

Wherever possible the hotels are on the tour route and have been chosen to offer a variety of hotel styles.

The AA Hotel Booking Service is a service exclusively for AA personal members. It is a free, fast and easy way to find a place for a short break, or holiday; tel: 0870 5 05 05 05.

Full listings of the Irish hotels and B&Bs available through the service can be found and booked at the AA's Internet site:

www.the AA.co.UK/hotels

Prices

The hotels lsited below are grouped into three price categories based on a nightly rate for a double room with breakfast:

Expensive **£££** – over £100
Moderate **££** – between £60 and £100
Budget **£** – up to £60

TOUR 1

ENNIS, Co Clare
Auburn Lodge ££
Galway Road, on the outskirts of Galway, on the N18
(tel: 065 21247, fax: 065 21202)
Magowna £
Inch, Kilmaley
(tel: 065 6839009, fax: 065 6839258). Closed 24–26 Dec
Queen's £
Abbey Street
(tel: 065 28963, fax: 065 28628). Closed 25 Dec

LAHINCH, Co Clare
Aberdeen Arms ££
Off Main St
(tel: 065 81100, fax: 065 81228)

BALLVAUGHAN, Co Clare
Gregans Castle ££
(tel: 065 7077005, fax: 065 7077111). Closed 18–31 Mar

To find your way around, you can try to decipher the signs or ask a local for directions. Neither method guarantees success

LISDOONVARNA, Co Clare
Sheedy's Spa View Hotel & Orchid Restaurant £
(tel: 065 74026, fax: 065 74555)
Closed Nov–Mar

BUNRATTY, Co Clare
Fitzpatrick Bunratty £££
(tel: 061 361177, fax: 061 471252). Restricted service at Christmas

TOUR 2
LIMERICK, Co Limerick
Jurys Inn £
Lower Mallow Street
(tel: 061 207000, fax: 061 400966). Closed 24–26 Dec
South Court ££
Raheen
(tel: 061 487487, fax: 061 487499)

ADARE, Co Limerick
Dunraven Arms ££
Edge of village
(tel: 061 396633, fax: 061 396541)

TOUR 3
LIMERICK, Co Limerick
Royal George £
O,Connell Street
(tel: 061 414566, fax: 061 317171).Closed 25 Dec; restricted service 24 Dec
Woodfield House ££
Ennis Road, on the outskirts of the city.
(tel: 061 453022, fax: 061 326755). Closed 24–25 Dec

TIPPERARY, Co Tipperary
Royal £
Bridge Street
(tel: 062 33244, fax: 062 33596)

CASHEL, Co Tipperary
Cashel Palace £££
In the centre of town
(tel: 062 62707, fax: 062 61521)

ROSCREA, Co Tipperary
Grant's ££
Castle Street, off the main Dublin/Limerick road, N7. Opposite Roscrea Castle.
(tel: 0505 23300, fax: 0505 23209)

NENAGH, County Tipperary
Nenagh Abbey Court ££
Dublin Road, close to O'Connors Shopping Centre on Dublin side of Nenagh
(tel: 067 41111, fax: 067 41022). Closed 25 Dec

TOUR 4
TRALEE, Co Kerry
Abbey Gate ££
Maine Street
(tel: 066 29888, fax: 066 29821)
Closed 25 Dec
Brandon ££
Town centre
(tel: 066 7123333, fax: 066 7125019).

DINGLE, County Kerry
Dingle Skellig £
On the outskirts of town overlooking the bay.
(tel: 066 51144, fax: 066 51501)
Closed Jan–mid-Feb

TOUR 5
KILLARNEY, Co Kerry
International ££
Kenmare Place
(tel: 064 31816,
fax: 064 31837)
Closed 23–27 Dec
Killarney Court ££
Tralee Road
(tel: 064 37070,
fax: 064 37060). Closed 25 Dec

Lake ££
Muckross Road. the Kenmore road out of Killarney.
(tel: 064 31035, fax: 064 31902)
Closed 3 Dec–11 Feb

White Gates ££
Muckross Road
(tel: 064 31164, fax: 064 34850)
Closed 21–29 Dec

WATERVILLE, Co Kerry
Butler Arms £££
In the centre of the village
(tel: 066 74144, fax: 066 74520)
Closed Jan–April & Oct–Dec

KENMARE, Co Kerry
Dromquinna Manor ££
Blackwater Bridge, beside the Kenmare River
(tel: 064 41657, fax: 064 41791)

TOUR 6
KENMARE, Co Kerry
Park £££
On the R569, overlooking the Kenmare River estuary
(tel: 064 41200)

Riversdale House ££
(tel: 064 41299, fax: 064 41075)
On the shores of Kenmare Bay.
Closed Nov–Mar

Sheen Falls Lodge £££
Take the N71 to Glengariff, over the suspension bridge, then take the first turn left
(tel: 064 41600, fax: 064 41386)
Closed end Nov–mid-Dec & 2 Jan–early Feb

TOUR 7
CORK, Co Cork
Hotel Ibis £
Lee Tunnel Roundabout, Dunkettle
(tel: 021 354354, fax: 021 354202)

Imperial Hotel ££
South Mall (Hanover International)
(tel: 021 274040, fax: 021 275375). Closed 24 Dec–2 Jan

Vienna Woods £
Glanmire
(tel: 021 821146, fax: 021 821120)

BLARNEY, Co Cork
Blarney Park ££
Off the village green.
(tel: 021 385281, fax: 021 385106)

Christy's ££
Part of the Blarney Woollen Mills Complex
(tel: 021 385011, fax: 021 38350). Closed 24–26 Dec; restricted service Good Fri

MALLOW, Co Cork
Springfort Hall ££
(tel: 022 21278, fax: 022 21557)
Closed over Christmas and New Year period

CAHIR, Co Tipperary
Cahir House ££
The Square
(tel: 52 42727, fax: 52 42727)
Closed 25 Dec; restricted service 24–26 Dec & Good Fri

LISMORE, Co Waterford
Ballyrafter House ££
Opposite Lismore Castle
(tel: 058 54002, fax: 058 53050).
Closed Nov–Feb

YOUGHAL, Co Cork
Devonshire Arms ££
Pearse Square
(tel: 024 92827, fax: 024 92900).
Closed Christmas.

TOUR 8
CORK, Co Cork
Ambassador ££
Military Hill, St Lukes
(tel: 021 551996, fax: 021 551997). Closed 24–26 Dec

Arbutus Lodge ££
Middle Glanmire Road, Montenotte
(tel: 021 501237)

Jurys ££
Western Road
(tel: 021 276622, fax: 021 274477). Closed 25–27 Dec

Travelodge £
Blackash
(tel: 01 21310722, fax: 01 21310707)

KINSALE, Co Cork
Actons £££
Pier Road
(tel: 021 772135, fax: 021 772231)

Trident £££
Worlds End, just beyond the pier, on the waterfront
(tel: 021 772301, fax: 021 774173). Closed Christmas.

ROSSCARBERY, Co Cork
Celtic Ross ££
On N71, overlooking a lagoon at the edge of the village
(tel: 023 48722, fax: 023 48723)

GOUGANE BARRA, Co Cork
Gougane Barra ££
Off N22
(tel: 026 47069, fax: 026 47226)
Closed early Oct–mid-Apr

MACROOM, Co Cork
Castle ££
Main Street, on N22
(tel: 026 41074, fax: 026 41505)
Closed 25–27 Dec

TOUR 9
BANTRY, Co Cork
Bantry House ££
Cork Road, overlooking Bantry Bay
(tel: 027 50047). Closed Nov–late Dec & Feb

Westlodge £££
On the outskirts of town overlooking the bay
(tel: 027 50360, fax: 027 50438)
Closed 23–27 Dec

TOUR 10
WATERFORD Co Waterford
Ivory's ££
Tramore Road (tel: 051 358888, fax: 051 358899)

Tower £££
The Mall
(tel: 051 875801, fax: 051 870129). Closed 25–26 Dec

TRAMORE, Co Waterford
Majestic ££
(tel: 051 381761, fax: 051 381766)

DUNGARVAN, Co Waterford
Lawlors ££
(tel: 058 41122, fax: 058 41000)
Closed 25 Dec

LISMORE, Co Waterford
Ballyrafter House ££
(tel: 058 54002, fax: 058 53050)
Closed Nov–Feb

CAHIR, Co Tipperary
Cahir House ££
(tel: 52 42727, fax: 52 42727)
Closed 25 Dec; restricted

service 24–26 Dec & Good Fri

CLONMEL, Co Tipperary
Minella ££
(tel: 052 22388, fax: 052 24381) Closed 24–26 Dec

TOUR 11
ATHLONE, Co Westmeath
Hodson Bay £££
Hodson Bay
(tel: 0902 92444, fax: 0902 92688)

BIRR, Co Offaly
County Arms ££
Just before the church
(tel: 0509 20791, fax: 0509 21234). Restricted service 25 Dec

BALLINASLOE, Co Galway
Hayden's £
(tel: 0905 42347, fax: 0905 42347). Closed 24–26 December.

TOUR 12
DROGHEDA, Co Louth
Boyne Valley Hotel & Country Club ££
Stamenn, Dublin Road
(tel: 041 9837737, fax: 041 9839188)

SLANE, Co Meath
Conyngham Arms ££
(tel: 041 9824155, fax: 041 9824205)

NAVAN, Co Meath
Ardboyne ££
Dublin Road
(tel: 046 23119, fax: 046 22355). Closed 24–26 Dec

TOUR 13
DUBLIN, Co Dublin
Bewley's £
Newlands Cross Newlands Cross, Naas Road
(tel: 01 464 0140, fax: 01 464 0900). Closed 24–26 Dec
Charleville £
268–272 North Circular Road, near Phoenix Park
(tel: 01 8386633). Closed 19–26 Dec
Longfield's £££
Fitzwilliam Street
(tel: 01 6761367, fax: 01 6761542). Restricted service 23 Dec–27 Jan
Shelbourne £££
St Stephen's Green
(tel: 01 6766471)

DUN LAOGHAIRE, Co Dublin
Royal Marine £££
Marine Road
(tel: 01 2801911, fax: 01 2801089). Closed 24–27 Dec

KILLINEY, Co Dublin
Fitzpatrick Castle ££
(tel: 01 2840700, fax: 01 2850207)

BRAY, Co Wicklow
Royal £££
Main Street
(tel: 01 2862935, fax: 01 2867373)

ENNISKERRY, Co Wicklow
Enniscree Lodge Hotel & Restaurant ££
Glencree Valley
(tel: 01 2863542, fax: 01 2866037)

GLENDALOUGH, Co Wicklow
Glendalough ££
(tel: 0404 45135, fax: 0404 45142). Closed Dec & Jan

BLESSINGTON, Co Wicklow
Downshire House ££
On N81
(tel: 045 865199, fax: 045 865335). Closed 22 Dec–6 Jan

TOUR 14
KILKENNY, Co Kilkenny
Kilkenny ££
College Road
(tel: 056 62000, fax: 056 65984)
Langton House £££
69 John Street
(tel: 056 65133, fax: 056 63693). Closed 25 Dec
Newpark ££
On the outskirts of the town
(tel: 056 22122, fax: 056 61111)

THOMASTOWN, Co Kilkenny
Mount Juliet £££
(tel: 056 73000, fax: 056 73019)

NEW ROSS, Co Wexford
Brandon House ££
Wexford Road, a mile outside New Ross on the N25.
(tel: 051 421703, fax: 051 421567)

CARLOW, Co Carlow
Dolmen ££
Kilkenny Road
(tel: 0503 42002)

CASHEL, Co Tipperary
Cashel Palace £££
One mile west of Recess
(tel: 062 62707, fax: 062 61521).

TOUR 15
WEXFORD, Co Wexford
Ferrycarrig £££
Ferrycarrig. On N11 by Slaney Estuary, beside Ferrycraig Castle
(tel: 053 20999, fax: 053 20982)
Talbot ££
Trinity Street
(tel: 053 22566, fax: 053 23377)
Whitford House ££
New Line Roa
(tel: 053 43444, fax: 053 46399) Restricted Service 24 Dec–Jan

COURTOWN HARBOUR, Co Wexford
Courtown ££
(tel: 055 25210, fax: 055 25304) Closed Nov–16 March.

GOREY, Co Wexford
Marlfield House £££
(tel: 055 21124, fax: 055 21572) Closed mid-Dec–Jan

ENNISCORTHY, Co Wexford
Riverside Park ££
The Promenade
(tel: 054 37800, fax: 054 37900)

WATERFORD, Co Waterford
Dooley's ££
30 The Quay
(tel: 051 873531, fax: 051 870262). Closed 25–27 Dec

ROSSLARE, Co Wexford
Kelly's Resort £
(tel: 053 32114, fax: 053 32222) Closed mid-Dec–late-Feb

TOUR 16
SLIGO, Co Sligo
Sligo Park ££
Pearse Road
(tel: 071 60291, fax: 071 69556) Restricted service 24–26 Dec

Silver Swan ££
Situated in the town centre.
(tel: 071 43231, fax: 071 42232)
Closed 25–26 Dec
Tower ££
Quay Street
(tel: 071 44000, fax: 071 46888)
Closed 21–30 Dec

TOUR 17
BOYLE, Co Roscommon
Royal ££
Next to the bridge in the town centre
(tel: 079 62016, fax: 079 62016).
Closed 25–26 Dec

TOUR 18
WESTPORT, Co Mayo
Old Railway ££
The Mall
(tel: 098 25166, fax: 098 25090)
Westport £
The Demesne, Newport Road
(tel: 098 25122, fax: 098 26739)

KNOCK, Co Mayo
Belmont ££
On the N17
(tel: 094 88122, fax: 094 88532).
Closed 25–26 Dec

CASTLEBAR, Co Mayo
Breaffy House £
(tel: 094 22033, fax: 094 22276)
Closed 23–26 Dec

TOUR 19
GALWAY, Co Galway
Lochlurgain ££
22 Monksfield, Upper Salthill
(tel: 091 529595, fax: 091 522399). Closed 2 Nov–13 Mar.
Victoria Place £
Eyre Square
(tel: 091 567433, fax: 091 565880)

ROUNDSTONE, Co Galway
Eldons ££
Off N59 through Toombedla then left to village
(tel: 095 35933, fax: 095 35871)

CLIFDEN, Co Galway
Abbeyglen Castle ££
Sky Road
(tel: 095 21201, fax: 095 21797).
Closed 11 Jan–1 Feb
Alcock & Brown £
(tel: 095 21206, fax: 095 21842)
Closed 23–25 Dec

Rock Glen Country House £££
(tel: 095 21035 or 21393, fax: 095 21737). Closed late Nov–late Dec & early Jan–early Feb

OUGHTERARD, Co Galway
Ross Lake House £££
Rosscahill
(tel: 091 550109, fax: 091 550184). Closed Nov–mid-Mar

TOUR 20
LONDONDERRY, Co Londonderry
Beech Hill Country House ££
32 Ardmore Road
(tel: 01504 349279, fax: 01504 345366). Closed 24–25 Dec
Trinity ££
22–24 Strand Road
(tel: 01504 271271, fax: 01504 271277)

LETTERKENNY, Co Donegal
Clarence £
Near roundabout on the edge of town
(tel: 074 24369, fax: 074 25389)

RATHMULLAN, Co Donegal
Fort Royal ££
(tel: 074 58100, fax: 074 58103)
Closed Nov–Easter
Hunter's £
One mile from the village off N11
(tel: 074 58178, fax: 074 58115).
Closed Christmas.

DUNFANAGHY, Co Donegal
Arnold's ££
(tel: 074 36208, fax: 074 36352)
Closed Nov–mid-Mar

TOUR 21
CARNLOUGH, Co Antrim
Londonderry Arms ££
20 Harbour Road
(tel: 01574 885255, fax: 01574 885263)

CUSHENDALL, Co Antrim
Thornlea £
6 Coast Road, in the centre of the village
(tel: 012667 71223, fax: 012667 71362)

PORTRUSH, Co Antrim
Causeway Coast ££
36 Ballyreagh Road, opposite Ballyreagh Golf Course
(tel: 01265 822435, fax: 01265 824495). Closed 25 Dec

LIMAVADY, Co Londonderry
Radisson Roe Park Hotel & Golf Resort £££
One mile outside the town
(tel: 015047 22222, fax: 01547 22313)

BALLYMENA, Co Antrim
Adair Arms ££
1 Ballymoney Road
(tel: 01266 653674, fax: 01266 40436). Closed 25 Dec
Galgorm Manor £££
One mile outside Ballymena on A42, between Galgorm and Cullybacky
(tel: 01266 881001, fax: 01266 880080). Restricted service 25–26 Dec

TOUR 22
BELFAST
Crescent Townhouse ££
13 Lower Crescent
(tel: 01232 323349, fax: 01232 320646). Closed 25–27 Dec
Europa ££
Great Victoria Street
(tel: 01232 327000, fax: 01232 327800. Closed Christmas.
Holiday Inn Garden Court ££
15 Brunswick Street
(tel: 01232 333555, fax: 01232 232999)
Malone ££
60 Eglantine Avenue
(tel: 01232 382409, fax: 01232 382706)
Renshaws ££
75 University Street
(tel: 01232 333366, fax: 01232 333399)
Stormont ££
587 Upper Newtownards Road
(tel: 01232 658621, fax: 01232 480240). Closed 25 Dec

PORTAFERRY, Co Down
Portaferry ££
10 The Strand
(tel: 012477 28231, fax: 012477 28999). Closed 24–25 Dec

Beautiful Glendalough remains a wonderfully atmospheric place in spite of its enormous popularity with visitors

TOUR 23
ENNISKILLEN, Co Fermanagh
Killyhevlin ££
Off the A4
(tel: 01365 323481, fax: 01365 324726)
Railway £
(tel: 01365 322084, fax: 01365 327480)

TOUR 24
DUNGANNON, Co Tyrone
Cohannon Inn £
212 Ballynakilly Road
(tel: 01868 724488, fax: 01868 752217)

OMAGH, Co Tyrone
Royal Arms ££
51 High Street (tel: 01662 243262, fax: 01662 245011)

TOUR 25
HILLSBOROUGH, Co Down
White Gables ££
14 Dromore Road
(tel: 01846 682755, fax: 01846 689532). Closed 24–25 Dec; restricted service on Sun

NEWCASTLE, Co Down
Enniskeen House ££
98 Bryansford Road
(tel: 013967 22392,
fax: 013967 24084). Closed 12 Nov– 14 Mar
Slieve Donard ££
Downs Road
(tel: 013967 23681, fax: 013967 24830)

ANNALONG, Co Down
Glasdrumman Lodge £££
85 Mill Road
(tel: 013967 68451)

TOUR INFORMATION
The addresses, telephone numbers and opening times of the attractions mentioned in the tours, including the telephone numbers of the Tourist Information Offices are listed below tour by tour.

TOUR 1

[i] Arthur's Row, Ennis. Tel: 065 28366.

[i] Cliffs of Moher. Tel: 065 81171.

[i] Folk Park, Bunratty. Tel: 066 947 5267.

Ennis
Ennis Friary
Ennis, Co Clare. Tel: 065 29100.
Open late May-late Sep, daily 9.30–6.30; last admission 5.45.

De Valera Library and Museum
Harmony Row, Ennis, Co Clare. Tel: 065 21616.
Open Mon, Wed, Thu 10–5.30, Tue & Fri 10–8, Sat 10–2.

3 Cliffs of Moher
O'Brien's Tower
Liscannor, Co Clare. Tel: 065 81565.
Open daily 9.30–5; Jun–Aug 9.30-8.

5 Lisdoonvarna
Spa Centre
Kilfenora Road, Lisdoonvarna, Co Clare. Tel: 065 7074373.
Open Jun–Oct daily 10–6

6 Kilfenora
The Burren Centre
Kilfenora, Co Clare. Tel: 065 88030.
Open Jun–Oct, daily 9.30–6.

7 Kinvarra
Dunguaire Castle
Kinvarra, Co Clare. Tel: 091 637108.
Open May–Oct, daily 9.30–5.

Thoor Ballylee
Gort, Co Galway. Tel: 091 631436.
Open Apr–Sep, daily 10–6.

8 Quin
Knappogue Castle
Quin, Co Clare. Tel: 061 368103.
Open Apr–Oct, daily 9.30–5.

Craggaunowen Project
Kilmurry, Sixmilebridge, Co Clare. Tel: 061 367178
Open Apr–Oct, daily 9–6; last admission 5pm.

9 Bunratty
Bunratty Castle
Bunratty, Co Clare. Tel: 061 360788.
Open daily, 9.30–5.30.

Bunratty Castle Banquets
Bunratty, Co Clare. Tel: 061 360788.
Open all year, at 5.30pm and 8.45pm, subject to demand.

Cratloe Woods House
Shannon Dual Carriageway, Cratloe, Co Clare. Tel: 061 327028.
Open Jun–Sep Mon–Sat 2–6.

Dromore Nature Reserve
Ruan, Ennis, Co Clare. Tel: 065 6837166.
Open mid-Jun–mid-Sep, daily 10–6; last admission 5.15.

For Children
Ailwee Cave
Ballyvaughan. Tel: 065 77036.
Open early Mar–mid-Dec, daily 10–6.30.

TOUR 2

[i] Arthur's Quay, Limerick. Tel: 061 317522.

[i] St John's Church, Listowel. Tel: 068 22590.

[i] Heritage Centre, Adare. Tel: 061 396255.

Limerick
Limerick Museum
Castle Lane, Nicholas Street, Limerick, Co Limerick. Tel: 061 417826.
Open Tue-Sat, 10–1, 2.15–5.

The Hunt Museum
The Custom House, Rutland Street, Limerick, Co Limerick. Tel: 061 312833.
Open Mon-Sat 10–5, Sun 2–5.

2 Foynes
Flying Boat Museum
Foynes, Co Limerick. Tel: 069 65416.
Open Apr–Oct, daily 10–6; last admission 5pm.

3 Glin
Glin Castle and Gardens
Glin, Co Limerick. Tel: 068 34173.
Open May–Jun daily 10–12, 2–4; last tour half hour before closing.

9 Rathkeale
Castle Matrix
Rathkeale, Co Limerick. Tel: 069 64284.
Open Apr–Sep, daily ex Fri, (visitors are requested to telephone in advance of visit).

10 Adare
Heritage Centre
Adare, Co Limerick. Tel: 061 396666.
Open Mar–Dec daily ex Sat 9–6.

For history buffs
King John's Castle
Limerick, Co Limerick. Tel: 061 360788.
Open daily 9.30–5.30; last admission 4.30pm.

Special to...
Irish Palatine Association
Rathkeale, Co Limerick. Tel: 069 64397.
Open Apr–Oct, Mon–Sat 10–5, Sun 2–6.

TOUR 3

[i] Arthur's Quay, Limerick. Tel: 061 317522.

[i] James Street, Tipperary. Tel: 062 51457.

[i] Main Street, Cashel. Tel: 062 61333.

[i] Connolly Street, Nenagh. Tel: 067 31610.

[i] Killaloe Heritage Centre, Killaloe. Tel: 061 376866.

1 Tipperary
Tipperary Heritage Unit
The Bridewell, St Michaels Street, Tipperary, Co Tipperary. Tel 062 52725.
Open Mon–Thu, 9–4.30, Fri 9–6.

2 Cashel
Rock of Cashel
Cashel, Co Tipperary. Tel: 062 61437.
Open daily, 9.30–5.30 (phone to check availability of guides.

Bru Boru Heritage Centre
Cashel, Co Tipperary. Tel: 062 61122.
Open: centre May–Sep, 9–6. Theatre Jun–Sep, 9pm.

3 Thurles
Famine Museum
St Mary's Church, Thurles, Co Tipperary. Tel: 0504 21133.
Open Jun–Aug, Sun and bank hol, 2–6.

4 Roscrea
Roscrea Heritage Centre and Damer House
Roscrea Castle, Roscrea, Co Tipperary. Tel: 0505 21850.
Open Jun–Sep, 9.30–6.30; last admission 5.45.

5 Nenagh
Nenagh District Heritage Centre
Nenagh, Co Tipperary. Tel: 067 32633.
Open Mon–Fri 9.30–5.

6 Portumna
Portumna Castle
Portumna, Co Galway. Tel: 0509 41658.
Open May–Oct, Tue–Sun, 10–5; last admission 4.15.

7 Mountshannon
Lough Derg Holy Island
Mountshannon, Co Clare.
Open daily. Tel: 086 8749710 for boat trip.

8 Killaloe
Heritage Centre
Killaloe, Co Clare. Tel: 061 376866.
Open Apr–Sep, daily 10–6.

Special to...
Bolton Library
Cashel, Co Tipperary. Tel: 062 61944.
Open Jun–Aug Tue–Sat 11–4.

[i] Tourist Information Office
12 Number on tour

TOUR 4

[i] Ashe Hall, Denny Street, Tralee, Co Kerry. Tel: 066 21288.

[i] The Pier, Dingle, Co Kerry. Tel: 066 51188.

[i] Village Centre, Ventry. Tel: 066 51188.

Tralee

Kerry the Kingdom
Tralee, Co Kerry. Tel: 066 27777.
Open mid-Mar–Dec, daily 10–6.

Siamsa Tire
Town Park, Tralee, Co Kerry. Tel: 066 7123055.
Summer 8.30pm.

For children

Tralee–Blennerville train
Tralee, Co Kerry. Tel: 066 7128888.
Open May–Oct, daily, except second Mon & Tue of each month, trains leave every hour, on the hour 11–5. (10.30–4.30 Jul–Aug).

Blennerville Windmill
Tralee, Co Kerry. Tel: 066 7127777 or 7121064.
Open Mar–Oct daily; Nov–Feb by appointment.

Aquadome
Tralee, Co Kerry. Tel: 066 7128899
Open all year daily.

4 Dingle

Dolphin Boat Trips
Dingle Boatmen's Association, Dingle Pier, Dingle, Co Kerry. Tel: 066 51967.
Sailings depart daily, weather permitting..

Older even than Stonehenge, Newgrange is at the heart of an area containing at least 40 prehistoric sites

6 Dunbeg
Dunbeg Fort
Fahan, Ventry, Co Kerry.
Tel: 066 59070.
Open throughout the year. Telephone for details.

8 Slea Head
Blasket Centre
Dun Chaoin, Dingle Peninsula, Co Kerry.
Tel: 066 9156444
Open Apr–Oct, daily 10–6; last admission 5.15.

10 Ballyferriter
Butterfly Farm
Ballyferriter, Co Kerry.
Tel: 066 9156116.
Telephone for details.

TOUR 5

i Beech Road, Killarney.
Tel: 064 31633.

i Kenmare Heritage Centre, Kenmare. Tel: 064 41233.

2 Glenbeigh
Kerry Bog Village Museum
Glenbeigh, Co Kerry.
Open Mar–Nov daily 8.30–7; Nov–Mar on request.

3 Cahersiveen
Valentia Island Ferry
Cahersiveen, Co Kerry.
Tel: 066 9476141.
Open Jan–Sep, Mon–Sat 7.30am–10.30pm; Sun 8.30am–10pm.
The Barracks Heritage Centre
Bridge Street, Cahersiveen, Co Kerry. Tel: 066 72777.
Open all year, Tue–Fri 11–5.

5 Sneem
Derrynane House
Caherdaniel, Co Kerry.
Tel: 066 9475113.
Open May–Jan, Mon–Sat 9–6, Sun 11–7; last admission 45 minutes before closing.

8 Ladies View
Killarney National Park Centre
Muckross House, Muckross, Co Kerry.
Tel: 064 31440.
Open mid-Mar–Oct, daily 9–6.

Muckross House and Gardens
Killarney, Co Kerry. Tel: 064 31440.
Open mid-Mar–Oct, daily 9–6. Gardens open all year.

Recommended Walks
Ross Castle
Ross Road, Killarney, Co Kerry. Tel: 064 35851.
Open May–Oct, daily 10–6; last admission 5.15.

Back to nature
Skellig Experience Heritage Centre
Skellig, Co Kerry. Tel:066 76306.
Open Mar–Oct, daily 10–6.

TOUR 6

i Kenmare Heritage Centre, Kenmare. Tel: 064 41233.

i Eccles Car Park Glengarriff. Tel: 027 63084.

For history buffs
Kenmare Heritage and Lace Design Centre
Kenmare. Tel: 064 41233.
Telephone for details.

1 Glengarriff
Garinish Island
Reached by boat from Blue Pool, Glengarriff, Co Cork. Tel: 027 63333.
Open Mar–Oct, Mon–Sat 10–5.30, Sun 11–6.

3 Castletownbear
Dursey Island Cable Car
Castletownbear, Co Cork.
Tel: 027 73017.
Cable Car operates all year, weather permitting, Mon–Sat 9–11, 2.30–5, 7–8, Sun 9–10.15, 12–1, 7–8.

TOUR 7

i Tourist House, Grand Parade, Cork City. Tel: 021 273251.

i Blarney. Tel: 021 381624.

i Lismore. Tel: 058 54975.

i Heritage Centre, Market Square, Youghal. Tel: 024 92390

Cork
Cork City Gaol
Sundays Well, Cork, Co Cork. Tel: 021 305022.
Open Mar–Oct, daily 9.30–6; last admission 5.

Crawford Art Gallery
Emmet Place, Cork, Co Cork. Tel: 021 273377.

See also Tour 8

1 Blarney
Blarney Castle
Barney, Co Cork. Tel: 021 385252.
Open all year, Mon–Sat 9–6.30, Sun 9.30–5.30.

2 Kanturk
Rural Farm Museum
Mealehara, Co Cork.
Tel: 029 51319.
Open all year daily.

4 Mitchelstown Cave
Burncourt, Cahir, Co Tipperary. Tel: 052 67246.
Open all year, daily 10–6.

5 Cahir
Cahir Castle
Cahir, Co Tipperary.
Tel: 052 41011.
Open all year, daily 9.30–5.30.

7 Lismore
Lismore Castle Gardens
Lismore, Co Waterford.
Tel: 058 54896.
Open mid-Apr–Sep, daily 1.45–4.45.

Lismore Heritage Centre
The Courthouse, Lismore, Co Waterford. Tel 058 54975.
Open Apr–Oct, Mon–Sat 9.30–5.30, Sun 12–5.30.

8 Youghal
Heritage Centre
Market Square, Youghal, Co Cork. Tel: 024 92390 or 92447.
Open all year, ex 2 weeks at Christmas/New Year, Mon–Sat 10–5.30.

For History Buffs
Queenstown Story
Cobh Heritage Centre, Cobh, Co Cork. Tel: 021 813591.
Open Feb–Dec, daily 10–6; last admission 5.

For children
Fota Island Wildlife Park
Carrigtwohill, Co Cork.
Tel: 021 812678.
Open Apr–Oct, Mon–Sat 10–6, Sun 11–6; last admission 5.

TOUR 8

i Grand Parade, Cork.
Tel: 021 273251.

i Pier Road, Kinsale.
Tel: 021 772234.

i 25 Ashe Street, Clonakilty. Tel: 023 33226.

Cork
Cork Public Museum
Fitzgerald Park, Cork, Co Cork. Tel: 021 270679.
Open Mon–Fri, 11–1, 2.15–5, Sun 3–5(to 6pm Jun–Aug).

1 Kinsale
Charles Fort
Summercove, Kinsale, Co Cork. Tel: 021 772263.
Open all year, ex mid-Mar–mid-Apr, daily 10–6; last admission 5.15.

2 Clonakilty
Timoleague Castle Gardens
Clonakilty, Co Cork.
Tel: 023 46116.
Open Jun–Aug, Mon–Sat 11–5.30, Sun 2–5.30; other times by arrangement.

West Cork Regional Museum
The Old Methodist School, Western Road, Clonakilty, Co Cork. Tel: 023 33115.
Open daily 11–5.30; out of season phone Michael O'Connel on 023 33225 to check opening times.

Michael Collins Memorial Centre
Woodfield, Co Cork.
Tel: 023 33226.
Open all year, daily.

6 Gougane Barra Forest Park
Coilte Teoranta, Inchigeelagh, Macroom, Co Cork. Tel 026 49028.
Open all year daily, except during tree harvesting times.

[i] Tourist Information Office
12 Number on tour

8 Macroom
Macroom Museum
Castle Street, Macroom, Co Cork. Tel: 026 41848.
Open daily 10–4.

For children
Cork Harbour Cruises
Kennedy Pier, Cobh, Co Cork. Tel: 021 811485.
Cruises Jun–Sep at 12, 2 & 3.

TOUR 9

[i] The Old Courthouse, The Square, Bantry. Tel:027 50229.

[i] Town Hall, Skibbereen. Tel: 028 21766.

Bantry
Bantry House and Gardens
Bantry, Co Cork. Tel: 027 50047.
Open 17 Mar–Oct, daily 9–6.

2 Skibbereen
Sherkin Island Ferry
Baltimore. Tel: 028 20125.
All year daily, outward 9–8.30, return 9.45–8.45. Sightseeing and fishing tours also available.

Cape Clear Heritage Centre
Cape Clear Island, Co Cork. Tel: 028 39119.
Telephone for opening times.

3 Schull
Schull Planetarium
Schull Community College, Schull, Co Cork. Tel: 028 28552.
Telephone for opening times.

Cape Clear Ferry
Pier Road, Schull, Co Cork. Tel: 028 28278.
All year daily (weather permitting).

4 Mizen Head
Mizen Vision Visitor Centre
Mizen, Goleen, Co Cork. Tel: 028 35591.
Open daily 10.30–5.

TOUR 10

[i] 41, The Quay, Waterford. Tel: 051 875788.

[i] Railway Street, Tramore, Co Waterford. Tel: 051 381572.

[i] Grattan Square, Dungarvan, Co Waterford. Tel: 058 41741.

[i] Courthouse, Lismore. Tel: 058 54975.

[i] Castle Street, Cahir. Tel 052 41453.

[i] Main Street, Town Hall, Cashel. Tel: 06261333.

[i] Community Office, Sarsfield Street, Clonmel. Tel: 052 22960.

[i] Heritage Centre, Main Street, Carrick-on Suir. Tel: 051 640200.

Waterford
Waterford Crystal
Waterford, Co Waterford. Tel: 051 373311.
Open Apr–Oct, daily 8.30–6; Nov–Mar, Mon–Fri, 9–3.15.

Reginald's Tower
The Quay, Waterford, Co Waterford. Tel: 051 858958.
Open Jun-Aug, daily 10–8; May & Sep, Mon–Fri, 10–5, Sat & Sun 2–5.

3 Tramore
Stradbally Hall, Demesne and Steam Museum
Stradbally, Co Waterford. Tel: 0502 25160.
Telephone for opening times; railway runs bank hols and in summer on request.

4 Dungarvan
Dungarvan Museum
Market House, Lower Main Street, Dungarvan, Co Waterford. Tel: 058 41231.
Open all year, Mon-Fri, afternoons only.

5 Cappoquin
Cappoquin House and Gardens
Cappoquin, Co Waterford. Tel: 058 54004.
Open Apr–Jul, Mon-Sat, 9–1.

6 Lismore
Lismore Castle Gardens
Lismore, Co Waterford. Tel: 058 54424.
Open May–Sep, 1.45–4.45.

7 Cahir
Cahir Castle
Cahir, Co Tipperary. Tel: 052 41011.
Open mid-Mar–mid-Oct daily 9.30–5.30 (to 7.30pm mid-Jun–mid-Sep); mid-Oct–mid-Mar, 9.30–4.30. Last admission 45 minutes before closing.

Swiss Cottage
Kilcommon, Co Tipperary. Tel: 052 41144 or 41011.
Open May–Nov daily 10–6.

8 Rock of Cashel
Cashel, Co Tipperary. Tel 062 61437.
Open daily 9.30–5.30. Telephone in advance to check availability of guides.

9 Clonmel
Clonmel Museum of Transport
Richmond Mill, Market Place, Clonmel, Co Tipperary. Tel: 052 29727.
Open all year, Mon–Sat 10–6; Jun–Sep 2.30–6.

Tipperary County Museum
Parnell Street, Clonmel, Co Tipperary. Tel: 052 25399.
Open all year, Tue–Sat 10–1, 2–5.

10 Carrick-on-Suir
Tipperary Crystal
Ballynoran, Carrick-on-Suir, Co Tipperary. Tel: 061 379066.
Open Mon–Fri 9–6, Sat 9.30–5. Last admission 4.30.

TOUR 11

[i] Dublin Road, Mullingar. Tel: 044 48650.

[i] Castle Street, Birr. Tel: 0509 20110.

[i] Clonmacnoise. Tel: 0905 74134.

[i] Keller Travel, Main Street, Ballinasloe, Co Galway. Tel: 0905 42131.

Athlone
Athlone Castle and Visitor Centre
St Peters Square, Athlone, Co Westmeath. Tel: 0902 94630.
Open May–mid-Oct, daily 10–4.30.

Athlone Crystal
Pearse Street, Athlone, Co Westmeath. Tel: 0902 92867.
Open all year, Mon–Sat 10–6.

1 Mullingar
Tullynally Castle and Gardens
Castlepollard, Co Westmeath. Tel:044 61159.
Gardens open May–Sep, daily 2–6; Castle mid-Jun–Jul & early Sep, 2–6.

2 Tullamore
Locke's Distillery Museum
Kilbeggan, Co Offaly. Tel: 0506 32134.
Open Nov–Mar, 10–4, Apr–Oct 9–6.

3 Birr
Castle Demesne and Ireland's Historic Science Centre
Rosse Row, Birr, Co Offaly. Tel: 0509 20336.
Open daily 9–6.

4 Clonmacnoise
Shannonbridge, Co Offaly. Tel: 0905 74195.
Open mid-May–Dec daily 9–7.

For Children
Clonmacnoise and West Offaly Railway Bog Tour
Shannonbridge, Co Offaly. Tel: 0905 74114 or 74172.
Open Apr–late Oct, daily 10–5.

TOUR 12

[i] Drogheda. Tel: 041 37070.

[i] Bru na Boinn, Tullyallen, Drogheda. Tel: 041 80305.

[i] Main Street, Slane. Tel: 041 84055.

[i] Headfort Place, Kells. Tel: 046 49336.

[i] Railway Street, Navan. Tel: 04673426.

[i] Hill of Tara, Tara. Tel: 046 26222.